MW01265623

Relationship Wrecked

by Ulanda Brinson

Copyright © 2017 by Ulanda Brinson

Published by Kingdom United Publishing

Chicago, IL

Printed in the United States of America

ISBN: 978-0-692-90307-0

All rights reserved. No part of this publication may be reproduced, store in a retrieval system, distributed, or transmitted in any form or by any means—electronic, mechanical, photocopy, recording, or otherwise—without the prior written permission of the publisher author, except in the case of brief quotations embodied in critical reviews and certain other noncommercial uses permitted by copyright law.

This book is dedicated to my grandfathers, Apostle Dr. Sylvester Brinson Jr. and Mr. Reynold Wesley Groves, who have left this earth, but not our hearts.

Hello Reader,

Life happens, and sometimes what we experience in love and in life can leave us and our relationships "Wrecked."

I wanted to be the first to welcome you on this journey to a new-found sense of you, a closer look at purpose and a clearer picture of how the other side thinks and processes.

This self-help guide was created to help avoid, reset, undo, and/or navigate through the wreckage men and women may be encountering in relationships. From relating to one's self, to friendship, dating, marriage, parenting, step-parenting, or even dealing with an "Ex", this book has something for everyone. It encourages, motivates, enlightens and it has many principles that, when applied, could help in bringing people and families closer to a place of unity and understanding.

I wrote this book in a conversational style of writing and designed it to be relatable to both males and females, no matter where they are in life relationally. So, whether you are single and satisfied, single and looking, or married, this book is full of helpful tips that could impact your life and your relationships.

I pray that this book serves as a light on the path to a bright future. May God be ever with you and guide you. I salute and pray for you on your journey and I hope you enjoy the ride.

- *Ulanda*

Table of Contents

Boundaries

"And God called the dry land Earth; and the gathering together of the waters called he Seas: and God saw that it was good."
(Genesis 1:10 KJV)

Give it a name and put it in its place.

When it comes to relationships, it is easy to assume positions that you are not ready for in name, title, and deed, when one continuously operates without clear and understood boundary lines. It leaves a lot of room for assumption and personal interpretation when both parties do not identify and agree upon what the relationship is and is going to be.

For example:

A guy is walking around when he sees this attractive girl. He knows that he may never get this opportunity again, so he walks up and introduces himself. Although she is caught off guard and begins to blush, she engages in small talk. After talking for a bit, they both realize they have to run so they decide to exchange numbers.

One night, they start talking on the phone and the conversation goes on for hours and, as the weeks pass, they start spending more and more time together hanging out and having fun.

Let's stop the story here.

This is a scenario that happens over and over in everyday life but let's go over some points that can better bring to light why some stories end with confusion and a broken heart.

- **When the guy approached the girl, he saw <u>the opportunity to potentially approach.</u>**

  When he decided to get her attention, he wanted to get a closer look at what he saw from a distance.

  His approach is to gain information. He is not yet at the stage of finding out **"if"** something could be built with her. His goal was: Not missing out on what could be an opportunity.

- **When the girl was approached, she saw it as <u>being approached by potential.</u>**

  When the guy made the conscious effort to get her attention, it said to her, "He is interested in building something with you." A woman never sees herself as an opportunity; she sees herself as the choice.

When looking for a potential mate or embarking on a potential relationship, it is wise to remember that a male's perception may often be different from a female's.

- **A conversation is not just conversation.**

  When he spends time on the phone talking to her for hours, it is still a collection of data. Normally, you will notice that he is the one doing the most listening while she talks. He is getting a feel for who she is and what she is about.

When she spends time talking on the phone, she is making conversational investments. Through conversation, she is allowing him to see parts of her that would not be seen initially. Although she also is collecting data of who he is and what he is about, she also gives him information to see if he capable of handling the essence of who she is.

- **Spending time and hanging out are two different things.**

To a guy, they may be hanging out and having fun, but, to a girl she is spending time. Women do not view time as something to play around with. There is no "extra" to waste.

Once a woman has given her time, she has given an investment. Whether it be friendship or otherwise, if she says yes to "hanging out," it means she has set aside her time, attention, and agenda to prepare for them. <u>Conversations and Time</u> are gifts that she is not giving to just anybody and are not things to be taken for granted.

Every process is important and important to keep in mind.

<u>Men think either logically OR emotionally.</u>

When they meet someone new, it is only logical to get as much information as they can before 1. Making a decision or 2. Involving emotion. It is not that they are trying to be insensitive to the needs of a woman. It takes time for them to process **the information that is given** and **the information that is being received**. They don't just take into account her words but also her actions and reactions as well.

Ladies, its best to keep in mind that every man has their own time frame in processing and **should not be forced in their decision**.

You never want anyone to be forced into wanting to be with you. Remember that you are not only valuable, but you are also a choice. Allow him to make his choice. Men eventually reach a conclusion and they, with word and action, will tell you **if and when** they are ready to be (or should be) anything other than an associate or friend. Until he states otherwise and is worthy for otherwise, invest in being an associate. If the friendship builds (and deserves to be built), then you can invest in being a friend.

<u>Women think Logic AND Emotion.</u>

Although, logic from a males' perspective may say, **"Approach to Gain Info to Proceed"**, the female perspective may say **"He Approached because he has gotten the Info and wants to Proceed."**

It's not that she is wired to be preemptive, she was created to be presented by GOD to a man that is ready and prepared to receive her.

Our minds still process 1-2-3

> 1. Adam was working.
> 2. God said, "it is not good for man to be alone."
> 3. God presents Eve.

When "Adam" arrives, our process still causes us to look for him to be 1. in his prepared place 2. functioning in his personal responsibilities and 3. ready to receive us.

Communication is good and often necessary in establishing boundaries.

It is important that you are clear with where you are. Even though people have been hanging out and having a good time, they both may not be on the same page with where "this" is going. While a guy may be thinking "This girl is cool to hang out with," the girl may be thinking that the time being spent is building a dating relationship.

If the boundaries of a relationship are not discussed and understood, then someone could continue to invest in building a relationship that doesn't exist.

Just like the girl in the story, many people, especially women, are eventually brought to the realization of what was really going on and end up feeling hurt and cheated for investing time and themselves in something they thought was building up to something. Often, the other party ends up left in confusion because, to them, it was always two friends hanging out and then the other person got all "crazy".

When a relationship is formed without clear and expressed boundaries, it leaves room for personal interpretation. It is like trying to build a house with imaginary bricks. By the time you find out that the bricks are not real, you realize that you have wasted time and effort and have accomplished nothing.

If a relationship is a mutual goal, then there are questions that you, in wisdom, may want to ask yourself.

It is imperative that you ask, "Am I ready?" BEFORE committing to a position. It is important that you take time to think about it before you give an answer. Be sure to be honest. Trying to motivate yourself to do something with denial is never good.

Here are a few questions that may help in laying a foundation before agreeing and committing to building a dating relationship. Feel free to have a writing pad or journal to write your thoughts and answers. Each person has their own way of processing, so take as much time with each question as you need.

- *Am I ready to date? Why?*
- *Is he/she ready to date me? Why?*
- *What are the responsibilities that come with dating him/her?*
- *What is his/her responsibilities when dating me?*
- *Are we ready to handle the responsibilities?*
- *What are the benefits for me in dating this person?*
- *What are the benefits for him/her in dating me?*
- *What are the negatives about dating him/her?*
- *What are the negatives about dating me?*
- *What are my goals in dating him/her?*
- *What are their goals in dating me?*

- *What do I expect to give in this relationship?*
- *What do I expect for them to give me in this relationship?*
- *What are the boundaries in this relationship? Do we both agree?*

You must have boundaries. Without them, you begin to spill over into other areas and you end up putting in more work without being paid the proper benefits and/or giving out free benefits to someone who is not working.

Pick a "SHIP"

This is the part I like to call: "Pick a Ship."

Relation-SHIP's were designed to take you places. It is always best to identify and KNOW what ship you are getting on, what is expected of you as a crew member, what kind of "cargo" you are carrying, and the destination.

There are different types of "SHIPS". Each one carries different cargo and goes in different directions.

The Working Relation "SHIP"

A Working RelationSHIP is a ship where the people who come aboard all have a common goal of working. This relationSHIP is like a barge. It travels short distances and the people in this ship did not board for the long haul. Every person who boards this ship is putting in work and is a part of the team that works together to get a job done.

There will be some people on this boat you will like and there will be some that you won't but **feelings are not the priority on this boat, achievement is**. When traveling on this boat the focus is to accomplish the goals as quickly and wisely as possible as a team.

Many people go on to build friendSHIPs but not everyone is meant to travel on that boat with you. The Working RelationSHIP makes short trips and its best to identify who is capable of making a longer trip with you before inviting them to the next SHIP.

Take the time to ask yourself the questions:

1. **Why should they make a longer trip with me?**

   There will be people that you meet that GOD will use you to minister to, speak life into, and even befriend but not everyone that you encounter is meant to continue to be a part of your destiny.

   Keep in mind that everyone on each ship is required to put in the necessary work. If you ask yourself the question above and the only answer is "because they are nice", it may just be for them to stay on the Working RelationSHIP. People *SHOULD* be nice to each other at work. Just because they are friendly doesn't necessarily mean they could or should make the journey with you. Examine both you and them closely before you send out friendship invitations, especially if they are of the opposite sex.

2. **How will it affect my work and those that I work with?**

   You don't want a reputation built on assumption or to be known as someone who shows favoritism. We tend to gravitate to those we can talk or relate to. This is not bad thing, but if we do not monitor how much time we spend at work talking to and/or interacting with certain close individuals or group of individuals, we can inadvertently alienate other co-workers.

In working relationships, we must keep in mind that we are a part of a team and that each team member is important. When we focus more on a certain group or individual, it can open doors that cause the "team" to divide and people start to choose sides.

3. **Does their baggage belong on the next ship and how will it affect me?**

Examine what they will bring to the table as a friend that they do not bring in the Working RelationSHIP and if it's wise to bring them and their baggage along.

If a person is into certain lifestyles that you know you struggle with, it may be best to give them love by sharing life words instead of friendship. It is not that you are judging or condemning them; it is so that you guard your mind and heart so that you do not fall back into temptation.

Negative practices are highly contagious and infectious. What you do and who you are today will affect your tomorrow. It's better to be the nice guy who speaks kindly to everyone at work, remains task focused and gets the job done.

4. **How will this affect the other passengers in my SHIPS?**

If they are of the opposite sex, and you or they are married, it may be wisest to keep it **completely work related**. No side texts, phone calls or visits. No extra conversations that do not strictly deal with work. No after-hours "work conversations". STRICTLY WORK. Even if it's a text about a joke, it is unwise, even if you mean well. Anything other than keeping it strictly work related can cause major problems and doors to open that never even needed to exist.

The Working RelationSHIP is also not the place to discuss the other "SHIPS". It is very unwise to discuss personal, private and relational things in the work place or with co-workers, especially when it comes to what happens or doesn't happen in the Dating, Courting and Marriage RelationSHIPs.

Do not allow people in the workplace to have knowledge of what goes on in your home and relationships, especially when it comes to discussing it with co-workers of the opposite sex. Although you may be "expressing yourself", you are also giving information you may not know you are giving. Unlocked doors and keys to locked doors within yourself, your situation, and relationship, can be given even in simple conversation. Be wise and, often, be silent. Your business is not work business.

Friend "SHIP"

A FriendSHIP is a SHIP that carries people and cargo containing everything that goes with being FRIENDS. All parties involved are working towards the common goal of friendship. They do the necessary work it takes to keep this SHIP functional and know that it takes all hands on deck to get them where they need to be. They are vested in this ship and its cargo.

When embarking on this ship you must **be careful of the stowaways**. These are individuals who are not really there to put in the work that it takes to be on the FriendSHIP. Stowaways are only there for the free ride and to get what they want from you and out of you.

Each person in the FriendSHIP should be able to speak life into you and concerning you. This is a give and receive RelationSHIP. There are NO TAKERS HERE. There should be a balance; imbalance could cause injuries and cause the SHIP to turn over.

Look for people who build others, not monuments for themselves through pride, hatred, negativity and drama. Connect yourself with likeminded people and those who represent what you want to become. Your friends should be ones who motivate you to be better, but still love, support, and cherish who you are.

When choosing a passenger for the FriendSHIP, always remember: **1. You are fertile ground** and **2. Everyone has a seed.**   Allow only to be planted in you **what you intend to grow**.

The Dating Relation "SHIP"

A Dating RelationSHIP is the ferry that you take to see what boat you want to be on. This ship doesn't carry cargo. It is only meant to carry you over to the Courting RelationSHIP.

Unfortunately, many people get stuck on this ferry, going back and forth from FriendSHIP to Dating RelationSHIP and then back to the FriendSHIP then back to the Dating RelationSHIP and never end up anywhere.

The Dating RelationSHIP is designed to take you on a ride with your "tour guide." The "tour guide", or person you are dating, will be telling you of what you can expect when you reach the next ship. Be sure to pay attention on this ride. Your "tour guide" is going to try to wow you but never forget that this ferry ride is his/her **interview process**. They are trying to be your "co-captain" on the next SHIP. If the information, destination and presentation do not add up, GET OFF THE BOAT! Don't worry, you will be fine if you jump off the boat. The waters are shallow enough that you will make it back "home" in no time.

If all goes well and you decide that you want to go on to the Courting RelationSHIP, please remember that you and your future "co-captain" packed light to travel over on the ferry ride. The rest of your luggage(s) will be delivered later.

As time goes on, you will become more and more comfortable. Certain formalities that you saw on this ferry as a "tour guide" and "passenger" will end up lost or left behind when you get promoted to "Co-Captain" on the next SHIP.

The Courting Relation "SHIP"

The Courting RelationSHIP is a ship that you board when you and your "co-captain" have decided it's time to journey in the next direction. No one knows how long this journey will take, so don't get on this ride with an "estimated time of arrival."

Understand that this ship goes over calm AND rough seas. There will be storms and both must work together if the SHIP is going to make it to the next destination.

This SHIP should be headed towards the ferry called Engagement that leads the SHIP called Marriage. If either party is not capable or has no intention of making the full journey, then it's best to dock the ship and return home.

Before purchasing the ticket on the Courting Relationship, all passengers must know: **This ride is exclusive.** No Stowaways. No extra passengers.

At this point, this is a journey for three: God, you and him/her. There has to be a mutual understanding that you two are on this ride alone with GOD, and that from this point on, as long as you both continue to travel together, boat by boat, it must stay that way.

On this SHIP, you will begin to see baggage that you have never seen before. Be careful that you do not preemptively pack or bring luggage that only belongs in the Marriage RelationSHIP. It is too heavy and wasn't made for this boat. It will cause damages to this RelationSHIP, cause you to sink, and you may never make it to your destination.

Allow GOD to show you what to pack and carry on this trip. Yes, you will have fun. The itinerary was designed to be that way, BUT there are way more things you must do. Don't be so blinded by love that you miss reality. Watch and pray. Pray for each other, with each other, and allow GOD to be your foundation.

Be careful of the late-night temptations.

The more time you spend with each other, the closer you will want to be with each other. Be mindful of your conversations. Keep it a conversation between three; you, him/her and GOD. Establish boundaries that will keep you, your emotions, and urges under submission. Let God be the first one you talk to in the morning and the last one you talk to at night.

The Engagement Relation "Ship"

The Engagement RelationSHIP is the boat that is designed to bring you over to the Marriage Relation "SHIP." This is the boat that begins the process of the two preparing to become one. It is wise to undergo counseling before even reaching for the sails. Pre-marital counseling is like getting the engine of the ship assessed to see if it's going to be able to make the trip.

Remember, **this is the boat that takes you to marriage; it is not the marriage boat itself.**

On this ride, you have the opportunity to ensure that this is the individual you want to sail the Seas of Life with forever.

As the Courting "Co-Captain", he/she did a great job and now he/she is up for promotion but this is still his/her probationary period.

It is very important that you pay attention on this boat.

Really look closely. Check for things that could poke holes and damage the Marriage RelationSHIP. Be sure that the RelationSHIP's foundation is secure, and that it can hold and withstand pressure before the SHIP taken out to sea.

If the relationSHIP is not sea worthy, it may be best to dock the ship.

Never feel like you are mandated to continue to take this ride. If you see that things are not healthy or right, this is the time to speak up. The worst thing you could do is to continue to the next ship well knowing that the cargo you are now carrying contains explosives that can blow it up.

If you decide that it is best to jump ship it is best to remember that the waters here are a little deep. This boat has taken you pretty far out and it will take you a little longer get back "home".

When jumping from this ship you may be hurt and get bruised but don't choose to die in these waters. Don't give up.

Keep pressing. In time the hurt will subside, the bruises will heal, and you will make it back.

If you decide that 1) this person is the one and 2) it is the season, then allow GOD to steer the SHIP all the way to marriage. Never feel that you can do this on your own. It took three to get to this place and it will take three to go on.

The Marriage Relation "SHIP"

Marriage is a SHIP set to sail forever. On this boat, you both should be finding ways to consolidate the luggage you brought on board with you in order to make room for the new things you will gain together. It is important to still carry the good things from the FriendSHIP and the Dating and Courting RelationSHIPs with you. Don't leave those behind.

This boat takes all hands on deck in order for the ship to sail. It is not a row boat, where one rows while the other takes in sun and relaxes. It's going to take each one doing their part especially in stormy seas.

The course that the Marriage RelationSHIP is on goes over rough and calm seas. There is no such things as a marriage that has only smooth sailing.

On your journey, there will be good times and not so good times. There will be storms. You may even encounter storms so severe that you think you would be better off overboard but don't jump ship! Let the Captain steer the ship to safety.

Now, the "Captain" hires many crew members to keep the Marriage RelationSHIP running in tip top shape. Each and every member has their place and has their job to do. They are here to help you. Everyone must work together daily if this SHIP is to sail.

Marriage, Cargo and Crew

The previous chapter used ships to represent what should be IN a relationship. In keeping with the theme of "Ships", this chapter will shed a bit of light on what and who belongs in the Marriage Relationship and the roles they play.

Captain: GOD

The Captain is equivalent to the Master of the ship. HE is responsible for everything concerning the ship, its crew, and its course.

Mates:

First Mate - Husband

A First Mate is second in charge to the Captain and sees to it that the Captain's orders are carried out.

As a husband, it is your job to ensure the safety of your crew by following the Captain's orders. You are the LEADER that is the representation of leadership. Although the Captain leads the ship, He has chosen you to be the face that the crew gets to see.

It is your job to represent the Captain and provide what is needed to the second mate (wife) and passengers (children).

Disclaimer: It is important that that you keep open communication with the Captain. HE is interested in and has accounted for EVERY need and concern that you have. Don't stress yourself out with things that only the Captain can handle. Do your part and leave HIS job to HIM.

A First Mate is a "watchstander" and is in charge of the ship's cargo and crew and is also responsible for the crew's welfare, training, safety and the security of the ship.

It is your job to communicate what orders the Captain has given so that the crew may have a clear understanding. When a crew understands the orders, they can better know what is needed of them and how to do their job and/or lend a hand.

Take necessary time to explain the orders and instruction. Keep in mind that your wife and your children speak different languages than you. It is always best to bring Love and Patience with you to translate what you are trying to say.

It is your job to watch over and take the correct actions to protect that and those for which you are responsible. As the Husband, it is your job to ensure the safety of this SHIP and all those aboard.

A First Mate is a strong leader who makes himself available to Captain and crew.

You are a leader under God and for the people. Your ear and attention is necessary.

The First Mate, though next in command, should seek wisdom and direction from the Captain when establishing order and dealing out correction. To mishandle and/or mistreat any member could result in confusion, dissention, members wanting to abandon ship, and disciplinary actions from the Captain. Keep in mind that you represent the Captain and HE is holding you responsible for not only what you do but also "how" you do. Although, outside of the Captain, all passengers on the ship are under your command, you must remember that this is HIS ship and they are HIS people.

Second Mate - Wife

A Second Mate or officer is the second highest ranked officer on the crew, right under the first mate.

The First Mate and the Second Mate often share responsibilities on the ship.

You both are in this together. As a wife, it is your responsibility to share in responsibilities. GOD created you as a HELP MATE, so help your mate.

Second Mates are responsible for maintaining bridge navigational and communications equipment.

As a wife, it is your job to do what it takes to maintain the wellbeing of your husband. You are in this together. What affects him will affect you. Protect him. Pray for him. Speak to the essence of him. Bring peace to him through life words and actions.

Second Mates also assist in communicating, enforcing and training on all company policies and procedures.

As a wife/mother, it is your job to teach your children. As a mother, it is quite possible that you will have the opportunity to spend the most time with your children; use this time wisely. They will only be little for so long. Your words, along with the words of your spouse, can go very far. It is your job as parents to teach and train your children in the way they should go. You can only know where they should go when you seek the Creator for the designs of those He has created.

Second Mates watch out for the vessel to avoid hazards.

You are not only a worker but a protector. You <u>MUST</u> have your husband's back by watching out and praying for him. A Second Mate is vigilant. There will be things that you see that he will not be able to see. Cover him, protect him, pray for him, and talk to him. Let him know what is going on. Never assume that he knows.

There are many things that he has to deal with by being the First Mate. He needs you to help him avoid the hazards that come to attack the ship as a whole. As a team, the First Mate and Second Mate work together to protect and cover their children. You cannot see everything and he cannot see everything, but together you can see more and will be able to pray together in the power of agreement.

Crew members:

Captain God always hires His staff and crew members to help you operate this boat. Every crew member is important for the operation and upkeep of this SHIP and all those on this journey.

Trust- Trust is a deck hand and is a very important crew member. His job is to maintain an open and clear path so that the passengers and crew can move freely. He understands that if he doesn't do his job, people can trip over Insecurity and cause Strife, Emotional Separation and Infidelity.

Love- Love is the Head chef. He prepares "heart healthy" meals and understands that every individual has specific needs. Some meals require more attention than others but it is HIS pleasure to serve.

Patience and Compassion- Both are right hand men who work along with Love. Many of the jobs set out to do with Love could not be as successful without these two. Love, Compassion, and Patience can speak every language and the Captain refers them to everybody HE meets because they do such a great job. Patience is specially assigned by the Captain to work along with Love, to serve what LOVE prepared, while Compassion sees and searches to understand what the crew needs and takes it to LOVE.

Prayer- He is like your own personal messenger who transports things like questions, concerns, answers, and messages between you and the Captain.

Holy Spirit- Helps you understand and carry out the instructions the Captain gives.

Truth- Truth is the Head Deck Hand that works closely with Love, Trust and Communication to keep the ship clean and protect people from falling over things like lust, insecurities, and distrust.

Forgiveness- Ships Physician. His job is to keep the ship healthy and free from diseases like unforgiveness and bitterness that can infect the heart, mind and spirit. He also works with Love, Compassion, and Understanding to keep the heart from getting hard and callused.

Understanding- Understanding is a Courier/Runner. He works with Love and Compassion to bring things to Forgiveness.

Romance- Works in maintenance. He does everything he can to keep the ship running. His main focus is to keep the fire in the engine room going because he knows that if the engine stops then the ship will come to a standstill.

Spontaneity- Spontaneity occasionally comes on board as a part of the refueling crew. He often works with Romance to bring him what he needs to keep the ship going.

Me: The Person BEFORE the Passenger

Before you can pick a ship where you relate to others, it is imperative that you **Relate to yourself.**

Who are you?

What do you like? Dislike?

What are your inner strengths? Weaknesses?

You cannot fully relate to anyone without first identifying who you are and what you bring to the table.

How you fit is secondary to realizing "what" you fit. You are a person. Simply complicated. You are made up of so many working parts and it is important to find out about that which is "you", the good and the not so good.

Understanding yourself, where you are in life, where you are headed to, what you were born to do, what you enjoy and what you struggle with are necessary things to know before adding anyone to yourself. If you don't know, you can go through life looking for something that you already have or something that you don't even need.

Having a clear understanding not only helps you see you, but it puts you in a better position to understand the purpose and the placement of others when it comes to you. If you struggle with validation and you don't know it, a person could use that knowledge to manipulate you by simply approaching in that in which you lack. Instead of seeing them for the truth, you can begin to see them as a friend and not a foe.

The lack of validation is not the only area that could attract. Whether it be in the areas of attention, loneliness, brokenness, or many others, it's always good to know 1. **where you stand** and 2. **where you struggle.**

When you identify where you stand, you know your convictions, your beliefs, the areas that are unwavering, what you uphold, hold firm to, where you are confident and assured, where you are bold, what you know for certain, where you are fearless, where you are valiant and what in your mind, heart, and spirit is absolute.

When you know where you struggle, you begin to know and understand what areas or behaviors you waver in. By definition, a struggle is when two or more opposing sides fight to win. The most common struggle is with our own desires. The inner battle, often beginning in the mind, is where the fight is between what we want to do verses what we should do. The struggle happens when we entertain them both but are not sure which one will win.

If you struggle with anger, depression, infidelity, lust, etc., then it may be wise to identify it and work on eliminating it before including anyone else by dating or marrying someone. Including someone else does not fix the problem; it enhances the opportunity for the problem to grow.

Remember that taking time out for you is not always a bad thing. You cannot relate to yourself if you do not spend time with yourself. Who you are in the noise may not be who you become in the silence.

Having a group of people around you or filling up time with obligations and/or responsibility does not make a person who they are; it is often an escape from who or what they are afraid to be or become. Many times, a publicly confident person is inwardly insecure. We, as mankind, have been taught to show the world a smile even when we are broken. We are taught "turn that frown upside down" instead of finding out or fixing what is causing the frown in the first place. (The mask behind the person with the mask.)

How you feel matters to how you process. Don't get stuck in just feeling. Identify what you feel, why you feel, and then what steps need to be taken to bring you past it.

Don't be afraid to be alone. Separation anxiety and the feeling of abandonment is not God's gift or plan for you. God promised to be with you always, so you are never truly alone. Anxiety is worry. Worry is neither for you nor helpful to you. You can be physically alone and not be lonely. Never forget that GOD is with you, He hears you and He loves you.

Take time to enjoy life.

If you are working most the time and giving others all the in between times, when do you have time to regroup, rest, and replenish?

A vacation here and there may be helpful to not only your body but to your overall well-being. Stress is a killer. It kills time, joy, peace, and the body.

Rest is important.

There will be times when you "can" and when you "can't". To everything there is a season, and sometimes, that season is rest.

In the beginning, God created and then HE rested. Let that be an example to you. Even God rested. There will always be people to see, things to do, those who need help and work to be done. Do what you can do but leave it ALL to God.

With all the hustle and bustles of life, **you must take time out for you**. It is important that you not only take time for yourself but that you do what is needed. Take time to invest in the "you" that God created and in the dreams that HE has given you. Discover what you like, what you don't like, where you want to go, reestablish your goals, etc.

Be sure to take time out to experience the life that you live; you only get one.

Don't despise your seasons.

To everything there is a season. Every season has the ability to be a blessing, be a lesson, be a time of resting, or be an opportunity. Even if the opportunity is to reflect, reset, release, restore, and to adjust, it is for your good. It's important to allow your seasons to run their course. Even the season of waiting can be beneficial.

Remember that every person has <u>SEEDS</u> and <u>SEASONS.</u>

Seed = Potential

You have potential. But it is important that you don't become comfortable and complacent with remaining just a "potential." Potential will require wisdom, action, and discipline in order to reach reality.

Discipline keeps your seed grounded so it is not tossed around in the wind and helps with creating a stable foundation so the seed can grow. Wisdom tells you where to plant, when to plant, and how to water. Action is not just movement but movements that establish and benefit growth.

Do you know your potential?

Take time to identify what seeds you possess. Whether it be a gift, or a talent, or a dream, it has the potential to be something. Sometimes potential is hidden in the things we enjoy.

Maybe that love for cooking could be a profession, a business or a way to bless others. Maybe that love for helping people is destined to be a passion that develops and redevelops a community. Maybe that natural born leadership was meant for more than seeing that people follow you. Maybe the knowledge and wisdom is meant to be imparted to others instead of keeping it yourself. Maybe your kind words and smile could change a life forever.

Whatever "it" is, you have it. Use it. God didn't just create you, HE created you to "BE".

As long as you are breathing, you have the ability to grow. You are never too old, too "broke," or too broken to grow from what God has given you. Everything GOD gives us has a purpose and has value, even life. Life may not be how you dreamed it, but you have the potential to dream again.

"I Have a Seed. Now What?"

There will be times that you will be in your "planting season." This is the season where all you see is potential, goals, and/or dreams.

"… 'Write the vision; make it plain on tablets, so he may run who reads it.'" Hab 2:2

Before you "run," write it down.

During this time, it is important to know what kind of "seed" you are carrying. Writing your vision, dream or goal puts it in front of you, reminding you that it exists and that it needs to exist. You won't know what to do if you don't know what you have.

For Example:

> Three people are given fruit seeds and are instructed to plant them. Each person is given different seed. One is given apple seeds, another is given grape seeds and the last is given orange seeds.
>
> Although each person has seeds that have the ability to produce fruit, each type of seed requires its own specific details, conditions, and places conducive for growth that is very different from the others.

Always remember that, just like in the example, each seed has its own way, place and time to be planted. If you have a dream, goal or vision, write it down, and then pray where, when, and how it should be planted. You cannot know how or where to plant without knowing your seed. For example, if your goals were to start a business, you would want to be in the right place to impact and increase. The first step is not building a business; the first step is acknowledging that there is a seed for one.

If your vision is to one day be a good husband or wife, then the first step is recognizing and understanding that one day you will become one. It is the seed, not the harvest. You don't just "become" a good husband or wife just because there is a seed. A seed that is not prepared for its harvest, cannot grow.

It takes planting, watering, and the **processes of time, understanding, and pruning**, to see the harvest of being a good mate. Understanding the seed of a potential, helps in knowing that it will also take watering, nurturing, and upkeep to get you there. If you want to be a good mate, friend, person, philanthropist, etc., write it down, and then gain the understanding, mindset, and qualities it will take to become it.

Remember that Seasons = Timing

It takes time to plant. It takes time to nurture. It takes time to harvest that which has been planted. And, in order to see successful growth, it requires knowing to when it's the right time to do all three.

Seed time. Harvest time. And the time in between...

"To everything there is a season..." Ecc. 3

Seed Time.

Just like apple seeds, pumpkin seeds, and many other fruit, it is important **when** you plant your seed. Some can be planted anytime, year-round, but there are some that require a specific season.

Not everything was meant for right now. Some dreams are for later. It is not that it doesn't belong to you; it just may be that it requires a little more time, experience and maturity before you are in the position to walk in it.

A driver's license is not unreachable. It is something that we will need and it will take us places, but it is not wisdom to give it and its freedoms and responsibilities to six-year old's. The reason isn't because a license is not meant for them; it is just not their season yet.

At six years of age, they are not fully in the position to understand, operate in or carry what comes with it. Even at age 16, there is still maturity that is yet to come.

If you must wait, don't complain. It's for your good. You are being prepared for it and it is being prepared for you.

If it is your time, do what you need to do when you need to do it. Don't wait until tomorrow to do what should be done today. Keep your focus. Take each day, each step, and each assignment as they come. Pay attention to what is in front of you.

Don't allow yourself to be so overwhelmed with tomorrow that you miss your opportunities of today. Fretting about tomorrow never helps. Each day has its own cares, live in your today.

Don't be discouraged by yesterday. What was done is done. All you can do is learn and grow from it and make a difference today, in the here and now. Never let the past be the direction you look to, to see the future. It is behind you.

Harvest Time

Harvest is when you see, gather, and experience what has grown from the seeds that have been planted. It is also when you begin to learn the "Why?" of the seed.

Keep in mind: <u>The harvest is always bigger than the seed that produced it.</u>

Every seed has the potential to bring a harvest and every harvest has the potential to bring a seed. We were made for perpetual growth. Don't think that what you have to offer is not enough. Whatever GOD has given you, even if it is just a kind heart, it has the potential to bring a harvest. Your seed could harvest life and revive fruit in others.

Whether it be your new business or degree or new endeavor, it has moved from potential to a harvest that holds potential. Whatever "it" is, it's valuable.

The time in between

Remember that EVERY SEED has its own amount of time it needs to grow and/or flourish. Each seed is different, so never gauge your growth on the growth time of others. Even if the seed seems to "look" the same, where it is growing, how its growing and the purpose in which it grows is different.

In the time in between you must:

1. **Water it-** Don't let it die. Nurture it. Feed it. Speak life to it.
2. **Wait -** Allow it the time it needs to grow
3. **Prepare –** Get ready to be ready. Prepare yourself. Prepare life to receive it when it comes. Strengthen yourself to be ready to carry it from harvest to the prepared table. Prepare your mind and mindsets to receive. Remove harmful thoughts, practices, conversations, people, and things that will harm or kill it once harvest comes. Learn and understand what it is you are about to receive and the purpose for it.

Never be discourage with your seed and its process by looking at the seeds and processes of others. Your process is yours and it is necessary.

Protecting Your "Seed"

Seeds, like babies, grow in you until it is released in the earth. Seeds can be physical, spiritual, financial, creative, in business, etc., and they need to be protected in order to ensure it lives, grows to maturity, and produce a harvest.

Just like giving birth, you must beware of what you allow in your birthing season. Birthing seasons are seasons when you are in the process of 1. Becoming, 2. Creating, and/or 3. Producing.

Beware of what you "eat."

Be careful of what you consume in your birthing season especially when you are pregnant with hope, potential, and the promise. Unhealthy consumption could harm and even kill "the baby".

Who are you around? What are you allowing to be spoken out of you and spoken into you? What are you practicing that does not reflect the promises that you are carrying? Who do you allow to feed you?

Be careful. Some people carry poison with the intent to sabotage. Some "cook" with things that shouldn't be consumed. You can't "eat" everywhere and you can't "eat" with everybody.

Sometimes you will have those who will instruct you on what to eat in order to see the baby sooner. Your process is your process and to shorten it could deform the baby.

Be careful of where you go and what you participate in. Some things will make you lose your baby.

Be careful of what you speak in your birthing season.

Sometimes it's best to keep silent until AFTER it's born. Mary said *"Yes,"* Sarah said *"Ha!"* and Zacharias said, *"I don't believe it, prove it!"*

All three were given the promise but each one said something different in their hearts. Zacharias was the one, out of the three, that GOD shut his mouth so that he may not speak to it or about it until its birth.

His first words were to name the child.

Sometimes it takes you to be quiet until you are aligned with what GOD says about it. And sometimes you won't understand the purpose of it until it's born. Don't speak prematurely or negatively.

When you don't know what to say about what GOD has promised you, go back to beginning and start with the heart, mind and spoken words of *"Let there be..."*

Beware of who you entertain.

Mary, once pregnant, left the city and surrounded herself with her cousin Elizabeth who was also pregnant with promise.

Sometimes you are going to have to leave where you are and be around other pregnant with promise people who have been walking in their pregnancy.

When Elizabeth saw Mary, her baby leaped. Pay attention to those who understand and can identify with the birth.

Though both Mary and Elizabeth carried different promises that would fulfill different purposes, they both understood that what GOD gave them was important and that it was an honor that GOD chose them.

You can't share your pregnancy and your process with everybody. They won't understand.

People are going to talk, both negative and positive; let them. You carry promise; they carry questions.

No matter what is said, stay focused. Don't allow the voices of men to be louder than the voice of GOD.

Beware of the "little foxes."

Beware of the little things that can harm you and your seed. Just because it's not "big", it does not mean that it is not dangerous.

"Take us the foxes, the little foxes, that spoil the vines: for our vines have tender grapes." Song of Solomon 2:15

Little foxes represent little things. Just like the foxes, it's the little things that have the potential to eat away at your destiny, bit by bit, little by little.

Sometimes it's the *"Aww, it's not that bad"* or *"It's not that big"* things that we need to stay away from. **Truth is:** It does exist, it is affecting you, and over time the vine and the tender grapes will die.

The little "foxes" also have the potential to ruin other vines. If you see it, catch it and stop it. It's not just the "tender grapes" that need it.

Who Touched Me?

Identifying who, what and when virtue is being taken from you in dating, relationships and friendships.

Sometimes we can be so used to pouring ourselves into people through time and conversation, we can end up missing the point of "that's enough". We can sometimes pour out so much, that, while others become full, we become empty.

Everyone has a measure that was meant for them and a measure that was meant for others. It is important to know the difference or you could lose virtue.

Virtue is like having a bank account. The funds in it have purpose. If you spend too much in one thing, it affects what was meant for another thing. Overspending can really have an effect on you and your ability to affect.

Are you pouring yourself into a pitcher, a cup or empty hands?

Pitcher

> Pitchers require a lot to be filled to capacity, but what is poured into it is meant for more than one serving.

There will be some things that you will pour into people that will be meant to serve them long term. Then, there are some things that will be poured so that they can serve others.

Be careful that you don't get so used to pouring into the pitcher that you don't know when it's full and you need to stop. And, also be careful in thinking that every empty pitcher needs to be full or that the pitcher wants to be filled by you.

Cup

When pouring into a cup, it is best to realize that the vessel you are pouring into is something to feed and sustain a person or group for now. "Cups" have a one serving capacity. These are people who will only require what you have to give them. Many "cups" are grateful to just be filled. "Cups" vary in size and capacity and once they are filled it is time to stop. Sometimes, you may desire to pour out more into them, but they may only be able to handle or may just be comfortable with just their cup's capacity.

Empty hands

Empty hands have no real capacity, but will cause you to keep pouring and pouring because they are never full. These are people who want what you have, but do not have the capacity to carry or hold it. These people will take and take from you, but will do nothing with the information or direction that is given or imparted.

Whether it's a pitcher, cup, or empty hands, it best to assess 1. what you have, 2. their assigned measure/what you are meant to give, and 3. their capacity. Not everyone who has a vessel is going to want to be filled. And, not every "filled cup" is going to tell you that they are full. Don't waste what GOD has given you, especially when there are so many who are thirsty for what you have.

Do you know when you are being "touched"?

"And Jesus said, 'Somebody has touched me; for I perceived that virtue has gone out of me'" Luke 8:46

1.You must identify and acknowledge that you have been touched.

   "Somebody has touched me..."

2.You must assess what has been taken.

   "...virtue has gone out of me."

Here, virtue means: 1) to be able, have power whether by virtue of one's own ability and resources, or of a state of mind, or through favorable circumstances, or by permission of law or custom

2) to be able to do something

3) to be capable, strong and powerful

Who or what have you been allowing to take your ability? Take your power? Stand in the way of possibilities?

Has it been you? Procrastination? Laziness? Friends? Boyfriend/girlfriend? Video games? Fear? Doubt? Gauging your life by the lives of others? The need to "fit in"?...

Anything that is blocking you from fulfilling purpose is touching you. It is taking virtue.

Virtue can be lost in various ways and each area has the potential to be "overspent," underappreciated, and undervalued.

When you don't know what you have, then you don't know what you have to lose.

- **Virtue can be lost through conversation.**

  Conversation is the sharing of heart and mind through words. It is also a door that lets people in and lets you out. This can be a good thing yet a damaging thing when there is no guard at the door. Unguarded doors can 1. let too many people in, 2. Let too much of you out and 3. Invite burglars that steal time, joy, peace, sound thinking, trust, and more.

  Drama, confusion and negative conversations also pull from virtue. It weighs heavy on the mind, emotion, and spirit.

- **Virtue can be lost through the physical, including touch.**

Virtue can be spent when you give too much of yourself to constant running, doing things and especially when it comes to other people.

When we do not take care of ourselves physically, it takes away from our physical virtue. When we do not rest or take time to reset, it also takes from our virtue, physically, emotionally and even spiritually.

Virtue can also be lost when you, single or married, allow others (people outside of your spouse) to physically touch you in ways and in places they have no business.

Certain touches can lead to the weakening of the will, unbalancing of emotion, and cause things like lust to rise. Be careful what you allow, and keep in mind that a little bit can go a long way.

- **Virtue can be lost in the mismanagement of time.**

You ever just looked at your calendar and wondered *"what happened to the time?"* And then, when you think about where it went, you realize how much time was wasted?

Self-doubt, social media, fear, people who don't want anything but to take up your time, and even yourself thinking *"I've got time"* are just a few of the things we allow to consume time and virtue.

Time is a gift. It's one of the most valuable things man will ever have on this earth, yet it is being spent instead of investing.

- **<u>Virtue can be lost through the things that we allow within.</u>**

Virtue can be lost by what we allow to get in us and become us in mind, body and spirit. When mindsets become DEFEAT before we even give dreams a chance, it takes away from the power to fulfill it.

When we allow unforgiveness to become a part of us, we lose virtue. When we allow ourselves to not only be bitter but to feed unforgiveness bitterness, or resentment, we continue to lose virtue.

When we decide it's better to hold on to hurt than to love, it takes away from our virtue. When we see ourselves as fat, unattractive, sick, a failure, used up, or "not enough," it can affect our virtue. Whenever we take in or choose to hold on to negative thoughts, practices, mindsets and words it eats away at our strength.

The Battle of the Mind

2 Corinthians 10:5

"I don't have to push you. All I need is for you to 'look' at me." -Distraction

Focus

The human condition is that we often go where we focus. The focus is the problem. Your greatest battles are not with the giants you face, but with the things that could cause you to lose focus.

Watch your imagination.

*"Casting down imaginations, and every high thing **that exalts itself** against the knowledge of God..." 2Cor 10:5*

"Just because a bird flies over your head doesn't mean you should allow it to make a nest in your hair" was just one of the many sayings that my father used to tell us growing up. As I grow older, I gain a better understanding of how important it is I remember that not every thought or word spoken to me deserves my attention and/or focus, especially if it is damaging, defeating or distracting.

Images are like brief snapshots, like advertisements to the movie you get to create.

"Imagination begins with an image that grows to become a nation of images"*, my* dad also used to tell us.

When it comes to imagination, it helps to remember that images can come from anywhere but it's your choice if they will grow. Just because you think it, doesn't mean that you have to entertain it.

Sometimes it begins with a simple thought of *"what if...?"*

> *"What if I don't go to work today?"*- **It starts off as a thought.**

> *"Yeah. What IF I don't go in today?"*- **It becomes a question.**

> *"Man, I could sleep in, relax, read a book, catch up on my shows..."*- **It becomes an answer.**

> *"Hmm...I could use a sick day, I do have some saved up."*- **It becomes a strategy.**

> *"Cough. Cough. Yea, I'm not coming in today."*- **It becomes an action.**

Many times, it starts just like this, and we end up thinking things that we don't need to.

First, we have a thought. It does not necessarily have to come from us, but it is a thought that leads us to produce a question. After we ask ourselves the question, we can begin to find ourselves imagining what we **would** do. Then, after we see it as pleasurable or having benefit, our minds begin to think of ways to make it happen.

At what point should we stop it?

As soon as we see that it conflicts with our purpose, promise, productivity, convictions, and destination. If it could distract, detour or derail you, then it's not something that you want to hold on to.

There is a fight of "within."

David was one of the greatest warriors in history. He killed lions, bears, a giant, and even defeated armies but his biggest battles were the ones that came from within. One of David's most difficult battles that he had to face was with what came out of him, his son Absalom.

Many times, our greatest struggles are the ones that happen with **what is in us** and **what comes out of us**.

Sometimes we have confidence for the giants, but, when it comes to facing Absalom, we are conflicted. The conflict is not in knowing that there is an enemy; it is because it comes from the "inner me."

We, at times, allow things that come FROM us to have opportunities to come FOR us. Even when it comes with the intent to kill and overtake us, we can still remain conflicted.

This is a good time to pause and think about:

1."*What enemies in the "inner me" have I allowed to live?*"

2. "What have I allowed to attack me (and others) just because it comes from me?"

From Head to Heart...

Unhealthy thoughts can cause infected hearts.

"Guard your heart more than anything else, because the source of your life flows from it." Prov. 4:23(GWT)

When you "self-reflect" be sure that you are using the proper "view." God's view of you will NEVER cause you to see defeat as your God-given destiny.

Many self-reflections happen when we reach birthdays or major life events. Whether it's an event that is because or regarding us, or if it is with those that we know or are around, it may cause us to sit and ponder our lives, our situations, or the lives that we have VS the life that we thought it should be.

For example:

An announcement of a marriage or a new engagement can:

1. cause a married person to think about their marriage, hopes, past, life before marriage, and their current and past situations.

and/or

2. cause a single person to reevaluate their own situations, devalue themselves, and

ponder/regret/hope for their own relationship or be reminded of their current relational status.

In both cases, news of the life event of another person caused a reaction, reflection, introspection.

Birthdays, especially major birthdays like 25, 30, 40, 45, 50, 55+, bring us to places mentally. We begin to look back and reflect on our lives. We look at how far we have come and how far we have to go. Many get stuck in "how far away they are from where they have to go" or "how far they are from where they wanted to be" and they begin to get depressed.

They begin thinking and/or wallowing in thoughts like: ***"This not where I said I would be at this time in my life!"*** or ***"What have I accomplished?!"*** But, who told you that life was supposed to be what you thought it would be when you were a kid? And, who says that life has to remain where it is at 30, 40, 50, etc.?

Don't get depressed. Do something.

You are alive. You have ability to change and be better as long as you have life. If you are unhappy then take the necessary steps to reach a "better you".

Don't get stuck on what has not happened yet or what you have not accomplished. Think about what you are going to do or do better with the life that you have.

Don't snub the life that you have just because it didn't go the way that you planned. Life may not be as your dreamed it, but you have the power to make a difference and even make some changes.

If you have always dreamed of writing a book, write it. Don't be so consumed with publishing that you don't take time to write the manuscript. Write first. Publish after.

If you dreamed of making a difference in the lives of others, try volunteering or coming up with ways to bless, reach or help others. There are a lot of shelters, food pantries and soup kitchens that are looking for volunteers.

If you feel like you are overweight and/or don't like your weight, work on it. Begin to do a little something every day. Eliminate or exchange certain things in your diet. Add more vegetables. Watch your salt intake. Drink more water. There are many exercise programs online that you can do at home for free. If you can afford a gym membership, get one and commit to going 2-3 times a week.

If you don't like how you dress, try changing your style. Ladies try new hair styles or colors. If you don't like it don't do that style or color again. Don't want to dye your hair or are afraid to commit to a color? Go ahead and try on some wigs. See what you like and don't like. If you have long hair and want it short, take the short hair on a test drive. If you have short hair and want it long, it's a quick fix.

Men, if you can, you can try a different hairstyle too. Now I'm not recommending wigs and hair pieces, but a change of mustache and beard does make a difference. Try new things. Try wearing a suit if you don't usually wear a suit. Try new styles in casual wear. Don't want to commit to spending money on clothes just yet? Go to the men's clothing store and try it on. Bring someone (your wife, your sister, someone that you know who is good in fashion) with you. Try on things that you don't usually wear and see how it looks on you. Don't know what you would like to try? Start off by going online or in a magazine and cut out things that you like and think would look good on you and try them on. Now, be sure to leave room for constructive and honest critique. Remember: You are just testing it out.

Don't like how you feel?

There will be times, man or woman, when you may need to talk. Then there are times when it could be that you need more alone time with God. And then, it could also be times that you need to see a doctor.

"Lack of luster" could be coming from the body, not the mind. Lack of rest and/or certain vitamins and minerals, raised or lowered blood sugar, high or low blood pressure, low iron, low testosterone or stress can cause the body to become "out of whack." You can begin to feel "off," "down," and "out of it" because the body is out of balance. Something that your body needs, may be missing. You may want to have your health specialist check it out.

*Disclaimer: Not all symptoms require medicine. Some may require rest, healthy diets, adding supplements and vitamins, and by releasing/lessening stress.

It may be time to seek counsel.

Whether it's for yourself, for your business, for your idea, for your money management, for health, for your marriage, etc., you may want to give counseling a try. You never know what strategies and help could come from it.

Counseling doesn't mean you did something wrong. It means you are taking steps to do something better. Better is good. Look at counseling as a learning experience. There will always be something that everyone on this earth doesn't know and has room to learn.

Protecting the Close Friendship

The title "Close Friend" can be defined in many ways, but the best way to describe a Close Friendship is "Brotherhood" or "Sisterhood." It is the place where two or more bond so well that they become like family.

Close friends meet in different ways and often unexpectedly. You may have met them in grade school and grew up together or met a few years ago, at an event and just something just "clicked." Somehow, over time, the friendship and the friend began to mean more and more to you until you really could not see life without having them be a part of it.

Friendships like these are things we tend to want to keep and to protect.

Although we hold these friendships dear, it is important and wise to take time throughout the course of our relationships/friendships to **1. Evaluate, 2. Examine**, and **3. BE.**

1.EVALUATE:

Is this relationship something that should be protected?

Proverbs 12:26 "The righteous choose their friends carefully, but the way of the wicked leads them astray."

If the connection with them damages your marriage, your character, your integrity, weakens your morals, and affects and infects you negatively, then it may be time to step back and step away. Don't allow your loyalty to kill you and/or your purpose.

Time after time, people have gone down with a knowingly sinking ship, when all that was needed was for them to "jump out" to safety. Your marriage, integrity and your destiny are never bargaining chips.

There will be times that are tough when it comes to friends, and I am not saying "jump out when things get tough", I am saying "Use wisdom and stay out if things (or they) are causing trouble"

Be wise and careful of keeping company with those who cannot control their tempers. Hotheads with bad tempers will not only get into trouble, but it can change you.

Proverbs 22:24-25 "Do not make friends with a hot-tempered person, do not associate with one easily angered, or you may learn their ways and get yourself ensnared."

There are things that we can pick up unknowingly, that can affect, taint and even damage our impact, character, charisma, connections and relationships by just hanging around the wrong people.

There is a saying that says, *"No matter how good a man smells when he enters a barn, when he leaves it, the barn doesn't smell like the man, the man smells like the barn."*

No matter how good you are or how good you "smell," being with the wrong people, being in the wrong places or doing the wrong things have the potential to leave residue.

Just because you don't see it or "smell it" does not mean it doesn't exist. Just like the man in the barn, it's probably not going to be instant that you realize that the "smell" has gotten on you.

You may have gotten so use to the smell that has been around you that you can become unaware that the "scent" has gotten on you. But, the ones who you come in contact with will notice it.

"A wise man foresees trouble and hides himself. A fool passes on and is destroyed... " Proverbs 22:3

"A prudent man sees danger and takes refuge; But the simple pass on, and suffer for it:" Proverbs 27:12

If this "brotherhood" or "sisterhood" frequently leads you into trouble, then it's time to step back and step away. If this "brotherhood" or "sisterhood" points you in the direction of sin instead of God, prosperity, and divine destiny, then it may be time to reevaluate your position and your mission as their friend.

2.EXAMINE:

Examine: Are they your stumbling block? Are you theirs?

If the answer is "Yes" in any way, then it's time to seek GOD for a change. It is important to allow the Holy Spirit to direct you throughout your friendships and relationships. It can easily become misuse and abuse when we do not understand the purpose for the relationship and the purpose of us in it.

Examine your purpose and your purpose together.

What were you born to do, be and become and how do they add to it? How do you add to them?

Every friend adds something to you, brings something out of you and feeds something in you, whether it be a positive or a negative. It is wise to look into how you are affected by them and how they are affected by you.

Examine your heart towards them.

Do they have more influence and get more attention than God? Your spouse? Your children? Than they should?

Do you have more of their attention than God? Their spouse? Than you should?

If any of the answers to the questions above is "yes," then there may be a need for a realignment of priority. If, as you examine, you find any area that is too much or too little, wisdom would confirm that it is worth fixing.

In order for relationships to be truly healthy, they MUST be in their proper place. It's always important to remember that no friendship is more important than the relationship you have with God.

3.BE...

BE good company.

1 Cor 15:33 "Do not be misled: Bad company corrupts good character."

Don't be misled or be misleading. You hear the phrase "be careful of the company you keep" but let's add "be careful of the company you are."

You do not want to make each other fall, so don't be the thing that causes them to "trip". Cover them. Protect them and their image. Be a man/woman of integrity and good moral standards. Don't belittle or lead astray. If you know what they struggle with, lead them away from it, not to it. Don't dangle temptation and sin in front of them and dare them to try it.

You are their friend, protect them and their integrity.

BE reliable.

Proverbs 18:24 "One who has unreliable friends soon comes to ruin, but there is a friend who sticks closer than a brother."

As a friend, people depend on you to be there for them to support and to listen. Yes, life does happen, and it is a known fact that you cannot spend 24 hours a day talking to or taking care of anyone, but there still are ways that you can be there for them as their friend.

Establish a system that works for you both. You can call occasionally and see how they are doing, include them and their families, businesses, etc. in your prayer and be there when you can, especially in times of loss. Remember, you can't do everything but you can do something. Don't let them "come to ruin" and you don't even know it.

BE a "brother" or "sister" and BE a strength.

Proverbs 17:17 "A friend loves at all times, and a brother is born for a time of adversity."

Life not always going to be easy. We will all face times of loss, frustrations, and times where we just don't know what to do. In these times, we all could use someone in our corner, know that someone cares, and know that someone is praying for us.

Rom 15:1(a) "We then that are strong ought to bear the infirmities of the weak..."

As a friend, sometimes you have to carry them to the altar. It is never meant for you to carry their burdens but there will be times when their burdens will be too much for them to carry alone.

This is the time when you hear them, support them, encourage them all while praying for them. Sometimes life may have beaten them so badly that they may be too weak and broken or can't find the strength to fight. You may have to stand proxy and intercede on their behalf. In their times of weakness and/or brokenness, they may need you for the GOD in you.

BE compassionate and patient.

We all have our areas where we are strong and areas where we are weak. It behooves us never to look down on others in their time of weakness or because we are strong. Inner Strength was never designed to tear down others, it was meant to build up and strengthen.

Strength is for service.

BE forgiving.

Col 3:12-14 "Therefore, as God's chosen people, holy and dearly loved, clothe yourselves with compassion, kindness, humility, gentleness and patience. Bear with each other and forgive one another if any of you has a grievance against someone. Forgive as the Lord forgave you. And over all these virtues put on love, which binds them all together in perfect unity."

You are not perfect and neither are they. Forgive as God has forgiven you.

Don't let things that don't matter affect relationships that do matter. Time is too short. Don't allow unforgiveness to steal what little time you have left. Tomorrow is not promised and neither is today. Anything can happen at any time. Forgive wholeheartedly and love like tomorrow may never come.

BE quiet.

Proverbs 17:9 "He who conceals a transgression seeks love, but he who repeats a matter separates intimate friends."

Don't spread their personal business. If they tell you something in confidence, unless absolutely necessary, keep it confidential. Use wisdom and discretion in cases of "absolutely necessary."

"Absolutely necessary" are times of informing the authorities on abuse, suicide, etc., or seeking wise, medical or spiritual counsel on how to handle a situation without naming names and pointing fingers.

Their business is not gossip material. They didn't tell the news, they told you. Friends tell you because it weighs on them, their hearts, and/or their minds and they trust you enough to share what they have to deal with or are dealing with.

It is a privilege to be trusted with their information. Pray for them, their strength, wisdom, direction, their minds, their emotions, and that GOD lead them to a place of peace. Pray for wisdom in speaking to them about or regarding their situation.

"You Shot Me. I'm Bleeding and You Don't Even Know It."

Sometimes, the biggest hurt that we feel can come from the people that we love. The closer we are to a person, the more we have access to their heart, ears, and lives. Our voices travel deeper and have more weight and influence than those on the outside, and, based on what is said, we could be killing our loved ones and don't even know it.

Always be mindful of what you say to your friends and loved ones. Just because you are friends or relatives, doesn't mean you should just say anything you want to a person. Words hurt and they feel even worse coming from a friend or loved one.

Even if you were playing or "just saying", words can hurt, damage and be building insecurities in the one you say you love. You could have shot them with your words, they could be bleeding and you may not even know it.

Don't be insensitive about the things friends are sensitive about.

If it is an "issue to them," **then it is an issue**. Don't discount how a person feels just because it affects you differently or not at all. It is also not a time to joke. If you really care about your friend, try being an encourager and supporter of their feelings.

Don't talk about their weight. Be productive.

- encourage them that they can.
- YOU eat healthier when you go out with them. Don't grab a burger and then start fussing with them about them eating a salad.
- Invite them to workout. YOU promote health for yourself and invite them to join you here and there.
- Remember it's their choice. You want the best for them but you never know what a person is dealing with on the inside. All the "you can's" may not be as loud as the inward "I can't." Pray for them, love them as they are, and encourage the "who they will be."

You don't know what a person is going through, has gone through or is dealing with internally when it comes to things like their weight and size. Jokes and hurtful statements dig deep wounds and have the potential to leave scars. You could be sowing seeds of insecurity, self-doubt, and loss of self-worth when you do not monitor the things that you say.

When you talk/joke about a person's weight, you quite possibly are planting seeds and trees of insecurity.

I say "seeds" because **something is planted**.

I say "trees" because **as it grows, it starts to develop other insecurities**.

When you say things about a person's weight or appearance, the mind is affected. They begin to wonder "if they are enough", begin to think about how others view them, begin to feel undesirable, unwanted and unloved and, in some cases, one can begin to compare one's self to others and in doing so, see themselves as "unworthy" and/or "less than".

70

Whether they tell you or not, it hurts to be teased and/or constantly reminded of size, and the last thing they want is to be hurt, especially by their friend.

Don't constantly remind them of past hurts or mistakes.

No one wants to have to re-live hurtful moments. As a friend, it is your job to protect as best you can and support where you can. It is not your job to replay negativity. God doesn't even do that. Once he has forgiven, then it becomes forgiven.

It is also not something to joke about. Pain is not funny.

Don't use private "jokes" to bring public embarrassment.

Not only is it rude, but it is also very hurtful. The information you know about you friend is not for the rest of world to know or to laugh at.

Watch what you say and who you say it around. This also includes asking private questions in public conversations or settings that can potentially cause embarrassment. If you want to know something that would be embarrassing if others knew or heard, ask them one on one, away from anybody else who could hear it.

Don't encourage them to settle.

If your friend has goals, dreams and/or standards, encourage them to go for it. Especially if it's morally, physically, emotionally, or psychologically the best things to do, you should be one of the main people supporting, uplifting and inciting them to do it.

Discouragement steals pieces of hope and can be damaging to the faith they have in themselves or their dreams. Discouragements, especially from friends, could also help them fall if they are trying to stay strong morally. There is power in what you say, be careful not to be the voice that helps them to trip or fall.

Don't belittle.

No one wants to be made to feel "less than" or spoken to as if they were incompetent. It is not always what a person says that hurts, it is how it was said, what was implied and/or the motives behind it.

When you are angry, be careful that you do not allow pride or vengeance to speak words that hurt. Be careful of name calling and demeaning conversations. Words like "Stupid" or "dumb" should not be in our vocabulary when talking to or describing someone we love.

Remember, a friend is supposed to love at all times, even in conversation. Love reminds you of the standard that GOD set out for you and says about you, encourages you, and prays for you to reach it.

Just because you are "cool with it," doesn't mean that the other person is cool with it or that it doesn't hurt. A person may NEVER tell you when you hurt them. Damages caused by words, often cut deeper than we think and often succeed at worsening self-image.

Think before you speak. Once words are released, you cannot take them back. Although "I'm sorry" is the right thing to say when you hurt someone, it does not undo the emotional and psychological damages that may have been done.

Acknowledgment

People in every area of our lives need to be and feel appreciated. No matter if it's a friend, sibling, parent, boyfriend, girlfriend, or spouse, people need to know that what they are doing is recognized and to hear you say, "Thank you."

There are three main acknowledgment areas that go lacking and cause the most problems.

1. Who a person is and what they mean to you.

2. What is done and the process it took to do it.

3. What is said and its importance.

Who they are:

This is a big one.

The people around you need to know who they are to you and that their position is recognized and respected. No one should have to fight for a position in your life that you have already given them the title to. Many have rough times in their relationships because they don't feel or receive the acknowledgement and respect that comes along with the position.

Parent: Acknowledge them as your parent. Treat them like a parent. Honor them. Respect them. Pray for them. Pray for patience. Hear them and pray for the wisdom in listening.

Real Friend: Acknowledge and respect them as a friend. Treat them like a friend. Call them. Check up on them. Pray for them. Encourage them. Make time for them. Be supportive in wisdom.

Associate: Internally identify them as your associate and treat them accordingly. Associate with them when the times call for it. They do not get full access to you and do not receive the same treatment and/or respect as those who are closer to you.

Boyfriend/Girlfriend: Acknowledge that you have a boyfriend/girlfriend. Acknowledge and respect the dating/courting exclusivity that comes along with being with this person. If you give them the title, then give them the respect that comes along with it. Acknowledge them in prayer. If you are together then you should be praying for each other. Acknowledge that they are your girlfriend/boyfriend and not your spouse. The acknowledgement of dating/courting differs from the acknowledgement in marriage. They do not have the covenant, so they do not get the marriage benefits package.

Spouse: Acknowledge them and respect them as your spouse openly, conversationally and privately. Treat them like a spouse. Respect them and their position. Don't give room or benefits that belong to your spouse to anybody outside of your spouse. Protect them. Protect their heart. Protect their name. Be trustworthy. Be respectful in thought, deed and conversation. Be thoughtful. Be mindful of those who try to separate you and those who speak against him/ her. Reassure him/her daily of their position in your heart and life. Make them your priority. Be accountable. Move with integrity. Acknowledge that you both are one and that you stand united when it comes to being a couple and when it comes to raising the children. Openly acknowledge what they mean to you **to them** and **to others**. Acknowledge what they do. Acknowledge how they have grown/matured.

Children: Need to be acknowledged publicly and privately **as loved, protected and respected by you**. They are people with feelings. Acknowledge how they feel. Talk to them. Share with them. Explain to them. Let them talk and share with you. Acknowledge their achievements and rejoice with them. Reward them for good. Correct the bad. Teach.

What is done:

When we are not acknowledged for the things that we do or are not acknowledged for the time, effort and process, it can make us feel taken for granted and undervalued.

It is important to recognize and show appreciation for what was done as well as the process it took to do what was done. If, for example, someone makes you a cake, just saying the word "thanks" and walking away with a slice is not enough.

You saw the cake and we're thankful for it but we're you **thankful for them**?

When we just acknowledge the cake, it gives recognition to the product but disregards and disrespects the process.

Keep in mind: The cake was made, not bought from the store, so it required the person who made it to give thought, time/hours, labor, and love. **What you received was not just cake, it was a "gift of them" that arrived in the form of a cake.**

What is said:

In conversations, when a person's feelings, thoughts, and views are not received, allowed, or welcomed, it can make them feel unacknowledged, unimportant and/or unaccepted.

Words are precious, especially when they come from the heart.

When people share, it's like they are choosing to share a piece of their heart with you. They are sharing because they feel that they can trust you with the thing they find precious.

When a person is met with a deaf ear or closed heart, it can cause them to stop bringing their heart because it no longer becomes a safe place. It says to them "You are not accepted", "You are not important" and/or "This person does not care about you" and it will eventually lead to no longer granting emotional access and creating emotional barriers which could also lead to mental, conversational and even physical barriers.

Remember, the power of life and death are in the tongue. When people who care about us speak, they are sharing their life and when we ignore it, we participate in the death of the relationship. People do not continually invest in places that they know they will get no return.

Lack of recognition in any area speaks volumes to those around us. Though it may not be done intentionally, it can make people feel and/or believe they are unnecessary, unseen, and undervalued.

People who feel as if they are being taken for granted will respond, but they will not all respond the same way.

You may see or experience:

1.The Conversation

It doesn't always start out with "We need to talk" but, no matter how the conversation starts, it a way of saying ***"Hey. I need you to hear me. There is something that needs your attention and/or action."***

<u>**Communicating what you feel**</u> and <u>**what makes you feel that way**</u> is sometimes not easy.

Depending on the person and their frustration, the conversation may go differently. Some people fuss. Some people are moved to tears. Some seem to be light hearted. Some come with anger and frustration. Some come peacefully. Some come quietly. Some get straight to the point. Some try to say it as nice as possible. Some could do it better. But, each one has a point that they are trying to convey and needs the person to hear them.

2. The Shut Down

Little by little the person stops granting access to places they once granted access to.

The thought becomes "I'm not appreciated, so why am I/they here?" and they begin to emotionally close the door. And, mentally, the process begins of placing the other person on the outer side of the "door".

The Shut Down could happen after "The Conversation" or without it.

3. The Eye Opener

When a person tries to give testers and subtle hints that they hope the person would eventually catch on to.

This happens more often than you think. From that subtle smile and blink when you are thanking everyone and forget to thank them, to that protest or mention of how much work things require when you ask them to complete a task, to when a person stops doing as much as the used to do, there are hints everywhere.

Oftentimes, the biggest hint that is most missed is a "no". It's not always because they can't, sometimes it's because they won't. They WON'T be disrespected. They WON'T be made to feel like they are taken for granted. They WON'T be made to feel like a doormat or floor to be walked on. They WON'T invest them, their time and their effort in something that is unappreciated and seemingly unnoticed or unrewarding.

4.The Walk Out:

It's the internal declaration of *"I'm done!"* emotionally, mentally, spiritually, conversationally and even physically.

Usually, this does not happen overnight. It often started with "the Shut Out" and repeated attempts with the "Eye Openers" before one reaches this point. Over time, the person closed door after door until there became no reason or place to stay.
Acknowledgment and a "thank you" goes a long way. If a person does something for you, they do it because they love/care for you, but don't let their love be the only payment of gratitude they receive. A lack of gratitude also goes a long way, it reaches deep and it tells the heart and mind that _they are the only ones willing to give._

Are You Preparing for Your Next or Are You Just Waiting for "Next" to Happen?

When it comes to dating, or seeking romantic relationships, it is best to know yourself. You should never build before checking your foundation.

Before you add anybody and anything else to yourself, take time out and assess YOURSELF. See where you are and then line it up to where you want to be and then you will see what you need before you get there.

Below is a list of questions that I would like for you to answer openly and honestly. I suggest writing each question in your personal notebook. Take as much time as you need to think about each question before you write your response.

- How are you financially?
- How are you emotionally?
- Is there space in your heart and your life for anyone else?
- How do you deal with frustration? Would you like to be dealt with in the way you deal with others?
- Are you occupying the "spaces" in you with people who are not supposed to be there?
- How is your health? And what should you be doing to be better?
- Do you have a "we" mindset or a "me" mindset?
- What does it take to be a good wife/husband?

- What would you say are your weaknesses?
- What would others say are your weaknesses?
- What do you bring to the table in relationships other than conversation and/or your body?
- How often do you pray for others?
- How often do you stand in the gap and pray for your spouse? (Single and married)
- What are your priorities?
- In what order are your priorities?
- Does your behavior and time reflect what you say is priority?
- How good is your word?
- Do you keep promises?
- Are you a "cheerful giver"? - (Do you give with regret or an attitude?)
- Are you a cheerful receiver? - (Are you grateful, appreciative, and do you say, "thank you?")
- How do you deal with anger?
- How do you deal with others when you are angry?

All of these are important to know in relationships. No one really wants to be with a negative person who fusses about everything and nothing and/or never says "please" or "thank you." It is not advantageous for a person to be with someone who is never there for them, emotionally dead and/or doesn't keep their word.

You want to be with and be a person you can trust. If you desire to have the best, then wisdom would say "be what the best deserves." It's only fair. Let what you expect to reap tell you the seeds you need to sow. You shouldn't plant apple seeds and look for cherries.

If you want someone who is patient, you may want to give patience a try too. You want others to be patient with you and how they handle you, so why not sow seeds of patience with others?

Get your prayer life in order.

Pray for your potential mate. Pray for their strength, endurance, power, authority, influence, their business, them on their job, their finances, their management of finances, their heart, mind, will, emotions, protection, growth, spirit, going out and coming in, that GOD would meet their needs. Intercede on their behalf against temptations, the attacks of the enemy, dangers seen and unseen, that their destiny will not be tainted, dismissed or destroyed.

Come against spiritual detours and road blocks, come against emotional detours and road blocks, come against physical detours and road blocks, come against anything that is being held up and held hostage that GOD has called to come forth.

Speak to dry places and command every place that God designed to live to live. Decree blessings, favor, and mercies their behalf. Speak into their existence what shall be in Christ and who GOD has called them to be in the home. Pray for the safety of their family and friends. Pray for wisdom and that they would receive knowledge and understanding.

Pray for peace in their mind, body, soul, spirit, and surroundings. Pray for the shift of God in their atmosphere and that God uses them to shift the atmospheres of others.

Even before you know them, pray. Establish a practice and habit of praying on their behalf. And when they get there, grow from there.

Prayer does not begin with marriage and/or dating, it intensifies. The prayers that you pray as a boyfriend/girlfriend will not be the only prayers you need pray as a husband/wife. No matter if you are single, dating or married, never stop praying. Even the strongest man needs prayer. The devil comes to kill, steal and destroy by any means necessary, so take up your armor and fight. Don't let them fight on their own.

Be careful what you practice.

The things or areas that you practice will be what you eventually become. Just like if you continually practice in music, you can become a musician, if you practice to lie, you become a liar.

Practice to cheat and you become a cheater. Practice to steal and you become a thief. Practice to forgive and you become forgiver. Practice to share and you become a giver. Practice to be lazy and your life will reflect laziness.

It is wise to only practice only what you want to be germinated in you, associated with you, and duplicated. Positive or negative practices condition, train and replicate in our lives and in the lives of others.

Children are students of the practices of the lives of the adults. Positive or negative, they learn by what they see. For instance, in order to adapt in their social surroundings, they often imitate the social practices of the adults around them. Whether they are a niece or nephew, kids from the neighborhood, or your own kids, you have the opportunity to teach what you practice.

Your practices can also teach people about how they should deal with you. If you practice to be pleasant, they will know you as pleasant. But, if you practice to be mean, distant and cold, people will know you as mean, distant, and cold and they respond to you accordingly.

"I Think I'm Ready."

All of us, in some part of our lives, start to feel lonely and desire companionship. When we get to the point of "I am ready," we often begin to search out that which we desire.

Wanting and desiring a mate is a common feeling and thought. Having a desire is not an issue, the problem comes when we don't know 1. Who we are 2. what to seek, and 3. Where and when to look.

> **When you don't know who you are, you don't know what you possess.**
>
> **When you don't know what you possess, you don't know what you need.**
>
> **When you don't know what you need, you don't know what you should be looking for.**

Many times, we are going "looking" when we should be "resting"...

Finding what was "made" may require you to close your eyes and relax.

"So the man gave names to all the livestock, the birds in the sky and all the wild animals." But for Adam no suitable helper was found. So the Lord God caused the man to fall into a deep sleep; and while he was sleeping, he took one of the man's ribs and then closed up the place with flesh. Then the Lord God made a woman from the rib he had taken out of the man, and he brought her to the man." (Genesis 2:20-22 NIV)}

Whatever God is doing, allow Him to do it. Don't rush it or spend your time searching for a mate. When it is time, HE will lead you to him/her and lead the person HE has for you to you. If the steps of the righteous man are ordered by the Lord, then it is going to take you to listen and walk out His instruction. You cannot follow steps if you are running in your own direction and leading yourself.

Always remember you can't do better than God. No matter what you "find" along your own way it will ALWAYS pale in comparison to what He wants to give you.

The rib came out of Adam to make Eve. There are some things that God has put in them that is "special made" for you and there is something in you that is for them. Only God knows what HE put in you and what you need. Trust Him.

As you "rest" be sure to:

- **Take some time to check "the me" before trying to introduce the "we."**

   Again, this is your opportunity to work on yourself while you pray and wait. Before you add someone else, take some time to look at yourself. You cannot expect to build a house that will stand, without having a firm foundation.

- **Set rules and stay there.**

  Boundaries are necessary when dating. Establish what you are and where you are and what comes along with the position of accompanying you.

- **Check your motives.**

  Why do you want to date? Why do you want to date that person? What do you want and what are really looking for?

- **Study the facts.**

  Who are you? What do you like and dislike, and what are you like when you experience what you like/dislike?

  Look and process BEFORE you leap. What do you attract? What are you attracted to? Why? Do you generally look at how a person looks or how a person really is?

- **Respect**

  Respect the process. Respect the person. Respect yourself. Respect God. Respect boundaries. And you should have a standard that says that they, whoever they may be, should be respecting all of them too.

- **Check yourself- Are you ready to date?**

  What do you bring to the table?

  Everyone has their ideal relationship in their heads. You think about what a person looks like, qualities that they have, how much they are worth, what they will do with and for you, but what do you have to give them?

  > *Are you broken emotionally or are you whole?*
  >
  > *Do you have the time to give a relationship?*
  >
  > *Have you given time for you?*
  >
  > *Are you mentally prepared to give up the single's mindset of one, for two?*
  >
  > *How is your name?*
  >
  > *How is your character?*

Healthy romantic relationships require that you have balance and stability. You should not build anything on a broken or shaky foundation, because eventually the "house" or structure will fall.

Relationship means responsibility. If you are having a hard time with you, how are you going to be able to carry the weight of someone else?

"Umm... Hey. It's Nice to Meet You, But Why Are You Here?"

People come into our lives for different reasons.

It is best to evaluate why they are in our lives and what they do for/to our lives, especially when it comes to dating. Not all people are bad for us, but they can become bad for us when we allow them in positions and places where they don't belong. It is wise for all of us to put things in the right perspective.

I heard a pastor once say, *"Good is bad when it hinders us from God's best,"* and that true statement should definitely be applied when it comes to friendships, dating and relationships.

There are quite a few key questions that you should ask internally when it comes to relationships.

- *Are you supposed to be here?*
- *Are you a distraction?*
- *Am I putting him/her first or GOD first?*

Based on your truthful answers, you should better see where you are and where you are with them being attached to you. **ANYTHING** that blocks you from hearing, seeing and knowing God and/or reaching your God appointed destiny needs to be **reevaluated, reassessed** and **repositioned.**

Reevaluate: Why are you here? Why are they here? Who sent them here? Did God send them to you or have they just become attached to you along the way? Is this who you are supposed to be with or be around? Is this God's plan and best for you? Were you meant to just be my friend/associate? Are you affected and/or infected by them or being around them?

Everyone has a purpose but not everyone is sent by GOD. Sometimes the enemy will send distractors and attractors to shift you from where you are supposed to be.

Be careful, everyone does have their place in the world but not everyone is assigned by GOD to be in your life. Just because they are a nice person, have potential, or have good qualities does not mean that they are the one. Just because you have or are developing feelings for someone doesn't mean they are for you either. Don't be so carried away with feelings that you do not take time to evaluate why a person is has come into your life. Is it ministry? Is it dating? Or is it distraction?

Reassess: What have you/they done or been doing here? What are you/they supposed to be doing here? Are you/they even supposed to be here?

Reposition: Where do you/they belong?

Sometimes the answer may be that they belong right where you found them and need to be released to go back.

Anything that God meant for you won't require you to exclude God to get it. Strength comes from God, not just yourself. Wisdom comes from God, strategies comes from God, peace comes from God and when you are detached from God, you not only are detached from the things that are attached to God, but also the fullness of the authority that goes along with it.

We must be careful when dating that the Spirit is not being removed in order to take advantage of the weaknesses of the flesh. When we honestly answer the question of "What position am I giving or am expected to give here?" and find that the answer includes things, mindsets, and practices that doesn't belong with a godly and healthy relationship, it is wise to step back and get things in order.

The Test of Knowing What GOD Said

"Now the serpent was more subtil than any beast of the field which the Lord God had made. And he said unto the woman, Yea, hath God said, Ye shall not eat of every tree of the garden? And the woman said unto the serpent, We may eat of the fruit of the trees of the garden: But of the fruit of the tree which is in the midst of the garden, God hath said, Ye shall not eat of it, neither shall ye touch it, lest ye die. And the serpent said unto the woman, Ye shall not surely die:" (Genesis 3:1-4 KJV)

Many times, we end up settling for the inferior in dating, relationships and in life when we do not know or believe in what we should be or what we should have.

One of the first questions we should ask ourselves is: **What has God said regarding me?**

When we don't know what HE said, and/or remind ourselves of what was said, we leave ourselves open to receive things, position, people, and priorities that weren't made for us.

When you know what God says about you and regarding you and your household, it is easier to identify what belongs with you and what hinders, distracts, or doesn't fit with you.

The fight to believe what God said.

Eve became tempted and did eat when she no longer believed in what God said.

Sometimes, we too find ourselves facing temptations when we no longer believe. No longer believing that he/she will come. No longer believing that we will reach our dreams or goals. No longer believing in having a standard because it seems no one will reach it. No longer believing that there is better or that we will reach it in time. No longer believing in ourselves or our gifts and talents, we settle and go for instant gratification, unfulfillment and for what we can get.

Remember, the biggest fight you may ever have is the fight to hold on to what God said regarding you. When the serpent came to Eve, he came right for what she knew God had said regarding her. It was an attack of the mind to change the position of her heart towards it. The bible says that when she "saw" it was good for food, she did eat. The question becomes *"What did she see before?"*

What did YOU "see" before?

What did you "see' before hurt? Before the bad relationship? Before the mistakes? Before the fear? Before the doubt? Before the pain? Before the age? Before the break up? Before (you fill in the blank)?

If it was the hope of a dream, a goal, a business, a relationship, a home, etc., before pain, hurt, or the enemy spoke to you, what has it become after? What caused you to "see" things differently?

Remember: **How you see is important.**

It doesn't matter what has come to shift and/or reposition your "view," how you "see" will <u>ALWAYS</u> be your choice.

- Will you choose faith or will it be fear or self-doubt?
- Do you see that you have value or will you continue to allow people who do not know your worth to define it?
- Will you walk in what God says about you or will you hold on to the negatives said about you or the negatives you think about yourself?

It's all about how and who YOU chose to "see."

Identify before you add or multiply

It is best to identify who you are, who you were called to be, and what you deal with before trying to involve anybody else. You have strengths and you have weaknesses. You have desires and you have lust. When you take time to identify what you do and look into why you do what you do, it will better prepare you for what is to come.

Who you are is not defined by who you date but, who you choose to date can be based upon who you are and/or what you possess.

What you attract and what you are attracted to are often a reflection of things we believe and/or are dealing with on the inside. For example, if I suffer with insecurity, I could be drawn to and/ or attract those who make me feel less insecure or I could attract/ be attracted to those who feed my insecurities. It could go either way. But, when I am aware of 1. my insecurity/issue, 2. my attraction and 3. my desire, I can better understand what I want, what I need and what I am willing to allow and/or pursue.

It could be lust, the need to be wanted, desiring to feel like a hero or appreciated, the need to be in control, the need to be controlled, fear, the desire to be rescued, desire to love, desire to be loved, lack of intimacy, desire of intimacy in conversation, loneliness, etc., whatever "it" is, "it" speaks.

When we attract, we knowingly and unknowingly call out to things from internal places, whether we like those things or not. The question is: "What am I calling? And why?"

Singles, When You Go to GOD for Your Mate...

Be empty handed.

God is not going to bless you with the person He has for you when your hands are full of someone else. When God places someone in your life as a potential mate, you must be ready to receive it.

It makes no sense to place someone in your hands when you lack the capacity to hold them properly and you could possible drop and "break" them. If your hands, emotions, or thoughts are already occupied, or you have a mindset that reflect or say, "I need a backup plan" when it comes to relationships, you are not ready to receive them.

The "back up plans" are weights that will keep you from fully being able to walk and carry the fullness of what GOD gives you. Lay them aside and don't pick them back up.

Although you may feel strong enough to carry it now, it is going to damage you and the precious cargo on your journeys. Whether it's dating, courting, or marriage, you cannot man or operate more than one relationSHIP at a time.

When God leads you to an open door it is not for you to walk in/through it looking for the exit or the back door. When we hold on to other "doors" or our plan B, C, or D, it says *"God, I do not trust that what you are going to give me/have given me is enough."*

When you are serious, you will know that there is only room for one. God will never give you double mindedness in relationships that can/will produce instabilities in your relationship.

Be mindful of your "oil"

In Matthew 25, there is a story of virgins with oil who were awaiting the bridegroom. The oil was used to keep the lamps lit so that the bridegroom could see them. Those with oil could be seen and those without oil couldn't.

There is something inside of us that makes us who we are (oil) that fuels what people see (light).

Many times, the "oil" could be our passions, our thoughts, our emotions, and our compassions. When we share our "oil" with others, we have to be careful that we are not wasting it, hiding it, or allowing ourselves to become empty or remain empty.

Intimacy can also be commonly defined as: "Into Me see". It is simply when you allow others to "see" into you, "see" who you really are, and/or know you and/or things about you that are hidden from the rest of the world.

Oftentimes, intimacy is associated with physical touch, but you most commonly become intimate through conversation and invested time.

We tend to have intimate conversations with friends, best friends, family and those who we are building, plan to build, and/or have potential to build a life/relationship with. Within the conversations, we share our thoughts, desires, passions, etc. This is where we must be careful.

As you open to "let out" be sure that you are careful of:

1. How much you let out.

2. Who you spend it on.

3. What/who you let in.

We must be careful of when, where, and with who we invest the essence of who we are.

When we allow others, especially those who turn out not to be for us, to **"see" us, receive our passion, thoughts, intimate conversation, heart, etc**., we can sometimes allow some of what we have for our ourselves and/or for our bride/bridegroom to be spent.

Often, we only realize that the "oil" was spent when certain parts of "us" end up in "dark places." And, by the time 1. we go to look for/at ourselves or 2. the one, who is for us, comes to look for us, it becomes a search to find "us".

Sometimes "who we were" was invested in who we used to be with.

Sometimes, instead of using the "oil", we can choose to hide ourselves so we don't get hurt again. Sometimes we used up the "oil" and feel that we can never find it again. Sometimes we spend the oil on people that only use us for the light. And, sometimes, due to fear of rejection, we take steps to put the oil on the shelf and go out into the world and, in turn, we become hidden, even to where we can't even see ourselves.

No matter what happened in the past, it's best to find and replenish your "oil". You are worth it. Never forget who you are and who you were made to be.

You are too valuable to be lost.

Never believe that 1. everyone is the same or 2. that no one will appreciate all that you are. Take some time to find and walk in who you are again. Your oil is not completely lost, it is just going to require that you go to the "Source" (GOD) to get it. You can love again. You can invest again. You can be open again... Find your oil.

Be patient.

What is for you will be for you in your season. Don't rush it and don't let age, loneliness, conversations, and/or envy of others in relationships be motivators to go and look for what has already been destined to meet you on your journey.

Every season of waiting is an opportunity, not a punishment. Sometimes God wants to grow you to the place maturity that can handle what and where HE is sending to you. Relax. Be where you are and do what must be done. If you need to work on your health, work on it. If you need to relax and strengthen your heart, mind, and spirit, then relax. Don't be so anxious to add on responsibility. Especially when the responsibilities you already have are in need of attention.

Relationships are responsibilities. They will require more from you. They will require more of you. If God is having you wait, then there is something HE is preparing. Be patient in mind, body, and spirit. "Mate shopping" at gatherings, church events and/or online is not you being patient. It is you checking door knobs to see what door will open.

Now, I'm not saying it's bad, I am saying to allow God to direct you where and when to look and, until then, keep your focus.

For all those thinking *"But it's been too long!"* You don't know what GOD has planned for you. Be patient. Believe me, it will be worth it. You, your destiny, and your legacy are worth the wait. Allow what GOD wants to grow in you and in them for you to mature, and then allow HIM to bring you together. Again, only HE knows what He put inside of you for him/her and what HE put inside of him/her for you.

Be kind.

Sometimes we can forget to be kind.

A heart felt *"good morning"* is not too hard to do. Smile. Encourage someone. Pray for someone other than yourself or the people in your circle. Whatever it is, show love by being kind. People are more attracted to a kind spirit than frowning faces, cold shoulders, etc.

You never know who is watching you. If the outside is a reflection of what is going on in the inside, then what do others see? Do they see love? Do they see peace? Do they see bitterness? Do they see your frustration?

Mean and surly are not great tools to help you meet/keep people around you. I am not saying *"Don't feel."* or *"Pretend that you don't have feelings."*, I am saying, **"Your emotions are a part of you, they are NOT who you are."**

Choose to be kind, even when you are not "feeling it". Kindness is a choice, not a feeling. It's the choice to put others above ourselves, and it quite often succeeds in lifting our spirits as well.

Be AWARE.

Not everyone that is sent to you is meant for you.

- **Be aware of who you invest your time, your money and yourself into.** Sometimes you will meet counterfeits before you meet the real. Always be prayerful and vigilant. Don't be caught up in what you hear or what you see, pray about what is REAL.

- **Be aware of your conversations and the real purpose behind you saying what you are saying and in doing what you are doing.** Remember to keep things in perspective. If you really want to be friends, then there is no need for romantic conversation or "jokes."

- **Be aware of yourself.** Be honest with yourself with how you are feeling or what you are thinking and if it is not right, hindering you from doing what is right, or treading in territories that you don't belong, it may be best to step back or step away.

- **Be aware by being prayerful.** Pray for wisdom. Pray for insight. Ask God to work on you, your attitude, pride, understanding, etc. and then let Him do it. You cannot do this thing alone and you don't have to.

The time you get to yourself before you receive your mate is a time to prepare yourself for the position you desire to walk in. If you want to be a wife, begin to pray for your husband, pray for his safety, for wisdom, for his health, for vision and provision, stand in the gap for him even before you meet him.

Men desiring to become husbands, pray for her mind, her emotions, her heart, etc., build a foundation of prayer that your house will be built on when she comes.

The Dating Prayer

Your prayer should NEVER be *"Lord send me a man!"* Or *"Lord send me a woman!"*

Yes, we can make our request known and we can tell God of our feelings, but we must remember that there is a season and a reason for it.

Occasionally, I hear people, especially older people, telling the younger, single people to "pray to get a husband" or "pray to get a wife" and to tell God that you are ready to start dating for marriage. Although the thought is good, ONLY God knows when we are ready to receive what He has for us to carry.

Dating and marriage come with responsibilities and their own share of work. Each person is different. You can try to humanly prepare as much as possible and still not be ready.

"A man's heart plans his course, but the LORD directs his steps." Proverbs 16:9 (NHEB)

Only God knows what He put and is working in you for the person He has for you, and what He is working and put in them for you. God also knows how much time it is going to take to ready you for your "NEXT". Allow Him to determine your seasons. Don't try to preempt God by filling your closets with "summer clothes" because you never know, your assignment could bring you to Alaska.

"What should I pray?"

I'm glad you asked. Whether you are single and looking to date, trying to date, or are dating, prayer should be a priority. What you speak about a thing, speaks to the perspective you have about that thing.

One of the best prayers we could ever pray and continue to pray, is found in Matthew 6:9-13. It's often referred to as "The Lord's Prayer" but we are going to make it the Dating Prayer. It may seem strange to use the Lord's Prayer as a foundation, but, it is something we can build relationships on.

<u>A prayer for you in dating...</u>

"Our Father which art in heaven,"

"Daddy, God, I come to you first."

"Hallowed be thy name." -

"I honor YOUR name and YOUR position in my life."

"Thy kingdom come."

"Lord, establish Yourself in every relationship that I have. Let my friendships, relationships and connections bring You glory."

"Thy will be done"

"Lord, let Your purposes be fulfilled in my life and in those You have for me to be connected to. Do not allow me to be fooled by my own thoughts and desires and put myself in places and/or with people I don't belong."

" in earth, as it is in heaven. "

"Help me to reflect Your heavenly design for my life and my relationships. Teach me to love as You love and give as You give and be an earthly reflection of You."

"Give us this day our daily bread. "

"Lord, You know what I need, I ask that you grant it to me. Feed me with food that is convenient for me. Give me a sound mind. Help me with my emotions, my thoughts, my words, and my desires. Help me to feed them things that are good and of a good report. Help my perspectives and my expectations that they are where they need to be today. Help me not to rush things, push things and/or overdo it. Help me walk in my today and not worry about tomorrow. Give me peace today. Give me joy today. Give me time with You today. Mold my day. Shape my day. I trust you to feed me and I believe that I will not go lacking. Help me to be balanced."

"And forgive us our debts,"

"Lord, forgive me of all my sins, wrong doings and ways of thinking that were not of You. Remove all hidden agendas. Break any self-doubt and hatred that I may hold against myself. Break defeated mindsets. Crush and destroy any ungodly soul ties and hindrances. Also, teach me how to better handle finances and be a good steward of what you have placed in my hands."

"as we forgive our debtors."

"Help me to forgive others and forgive myself. Help me to release every hurt, pain, and insecurity. Help me not to harbor and/or harvest unforgiveness, bitterness or strife. Help me to quickly release those who have offended and do offend me. Remove self-made walls of defense that I have built due to hurt, fear, and insecurity. You be my shield of defense. Let Your ministering and warring angels be my border protection that protects me and my heart.

Lord, let your love override any offense and defense that I may encounter. Teach me how to release others when they have offended me. Teach me how to love in spite of. Let my heart of forgiveness be a reflection of Yours."

"And lead us not into temptation, "

"Lord, don't let me become a victim to my own lust. Keep my paths straight, my heart clean and my thoughts pure. Help me to walk the path you laid before me and not my own. Continue to lead me and guide me."

"but deliver us from evil:"

"If this is not of You, remove it and remove it quickly. Reveal the enemy and his devices and teach me how to bind them up in Jesus name and send them to the pit from which they came. If I have chosen to go down a road that will lead me or has led me to evil, get me out of it. If this is not Your plan for me, please help me, show me and give me the strength to do what must be done."

"For thine is the kingdom, and the power, and the glory, for ever. "

> "For it is Your purpose that I want to follow; it is Your destiny for me that I desire; and it is Your glory that I want to shine in my relationships, from beginning to the end. Have your way."

"Amen."

> "Let it be as I have prayed. Amen."

Proverbs says, *"In all thy ways acknowledge HIM and HE shall direct your paths,"* and when it comes to dating, you definitely want God to direct your paths.

When you pray about any relationship, you should not just pray for yourself and leave it at that. You are not and will not be the only one in the relationship. Once you have prayed for you, you need to pray for "them" and the "us". Praying for him/her is just as important as praying for yourself. It is always good to honor God in every way, FROM THE BEGINNING.

Praying for "Us."

Here is a useable sample of a prayer for "Us" that still uses Matthew 6:9-13 as its foundation.

"Our Father"

> "Lord, You are our God. You are our Father and I thank You for increasing our individual relationships with You. Increase our hearing and our listening for

104

Your voice as our Father. Instill Your wisdom in us as our Father. Let our actions be of those reflecting actions of Your children in honor and obedience."

"Which art in heaven"

"We know and understand that You see all and that You know all. Allow our thoughts, conversations and actions to be pleasing to You."

"Hallowed be thy name"

"We reverence Your name and Your position in our lives first, above all things, above all people and above each other."

"Thy kingdom come and thy will be done"

"We agree with Your purpose. You know the path that You have laid out for the both of us and the purpose for which we have come together. Let Your plans be established with us and within us. Let Your will be done. Let this relationship be for Your Kingdom. Let it reflect Your glory. Let it honor You.

If this relationship is not what You have planned for us, please end it. We want Your best, and if we are not for each other, then we would not be receiving or giving Your best. Help us to understand Your purpose for us meeting and walk in that purpose only. Don't let us be taken away with our own ideas. Help us to remember that even our best ideas are nothing in comparison to the blessings, peace and success that comes with our obedience to Your will.

Don't let us settle. Don't let us be weary in waiting. Don't let us allow people to occupy spaces in our minds, hearts and schedule that do not belong. Grant us peace and wisdom to walk out Your plan for our lives, even if it means we will walk separately. If we are to be together, let us be together, You, me and them, with You as our leader and You as our keeper. Help us to follow You completely."

"In earth. As it is in heaven"

"Lord, we are YOUR earth. You have created us from the dust of the earth and filled us with the purpose and sound of heaven and we ask that You establish it. Let us reflect You in every way, in every day. And we come against ANYTHING that would block, hinder, detour or devour what You have set out for us to do, in Jesus' name."

"Give us this day our daily bread"

"Lord, don't let us rush things or give titles and positions prematurely. Help us to share what you have given us to share and to keep what you have given us to keep. Give us balance and give us patience. Help our perspectives and perceptions. Show us what you have created for us together and as individuals, and let us walk in that, wisely and righteously."

"And forgive us our debts"

"Forgive us for any ungodly thoughts and practices. Forgive us for speaking unjustly about and/or to others. Forgive us for any disobedience in the slightest and help us to hear and obey. Forgive us for harboring any ill feelings towards You, people, our families and/or each other. Help us to better manage time, money, and self-control. Break every bad and hurtful habit and practice that we may have picked up in our individual pasts. Break every curse and soul tie that has connected itself to us and our bloodlines. Break every negative word that was spoken over and to us that has come to hinder who and what You said we should become. Please cut off any weight that would set or is setting us back."

"As we forgive our debtors"

"Help us to forgive. Help us to release the pains of the past so that we do not injure each other with the weapons we made from it. Help us not to see people as our enemy. Help us not to give out or serve each other consequences based on the actions of others who have hurt us in the past. Give us grace for love and for life. Help us not to harbor ill feelings for things that we say we have forgiven. Help us not to bring up the past to hurt, distract and/or destroy each other. Help us to use our words to build and not to tear each other down. Help us to let go of the things that weigh us down and place them in Your hands. Please, help us to come to You before we come to each other. Break every barrier that blocks us from reaching You and reaching where we are supposed to be individually.

Please, help us to forgive completely and love as You love. Teach us mercy, so that we may give mercy as You have given mercy. Teach us compassion, not just for each other, but for others."

"And lead us not into temptation but deliver us from evil."

"Help us in times of temptation. Let us not be subject to or give in to lust. Help us and this relationship become acceptable in Your sight. Save us from ourselves and give us wisdom. You be our strength and keep us strong in times of weakness. Do not allow fleshly desires to override Your will. Give us strategies and follow through for safety and purity. Keep us accountable. Keep us trustworthy. Keep us aware. Keep us. Lead us on the path that You put us on and please help us do what is necessary to stay on it."

"For thine is the kingdom, and the power, and the glory, for ever."

> "Let our relationship and friendship be for Your glory, and reflect Your Kingdom. God, we give You all authority over it."

"Amen."

> "Let Your will be done. Amen."

Prayer is not hard. It's just conversation with GOD. Think about it: *As much as you think about your relationship and talk about it with others, how much more should you talk to your all-knowing GOD and FATHER about it?*

Whenever you pray, the key things to remember are:

1. **Acknowledge God** (Our Father...)
2. **Pray HIS will** (Thy kingdom come/will be done)
3. **Make your request known** (give us this day our daily bread)
4. **Acknowledge/Pray for/Understand/ Ask for forgiveness for your part and purpose** in it just like you **Acknowledge/Forgive/Pray** about their part and purpose (forgive us our debts as we forgive our debtors) Note: We should also keep in mind that many times we can be guilty of the same PRINCIPLE we are complaining about. It better puts us in perspective of forgiveness and compassion
5. **Ask for help and wisdom continuously** (And lead us not into temptation but deliver us...)
6. **Put things in HIS hand and in perspective** (For THINE is the KINGDOM/POWER/GLORY)
7. **Leave it in HIS capable hands and go on in peace, wisdom, obedience** (Amen- So be it)

Whether you are just starting out on this dating journey, have been dating for a while, and/or are considering marriage, prayer is a necessary part of your relationship. It refocuses your minds, hearts and thoughts to help you better see where things should and/or shouldn't be going.

Praying for "him/her."

Here is a useable sample prayer for "him/her." It still uses the Lord's Prayer format, but this time it is without the parallel. Feel free to insert the person's name in the blanks. If you do not have a name to put in the blanks yet, it is okay, just replace the blanks where there would be a name, with "whomever You bring/are sending to my path."

> *"Father God, I come on behalf of _____, reverencing Your name and Your position as my God and his/her Father first.*
>
> *I ask for Your Kingdom to come and Your Will to be done concerning _____. In his/her life, on their job, in their home, and his/her relationships, let Your Will and only Your Will be done. Allow their eyes to become open and them to see what You would have for them to see. Even in our friendship/relationship God, whatever you deem it to be, let it be.*
>
> *Lord I honor Your purpose for this. Let this friendship bring Your glory. If this is not Your plan for him or us break it up. Let YOUR KINGDOM come and YOUR WILL be done. Do not let him/her be led by emotions, ideas, or impatience.*

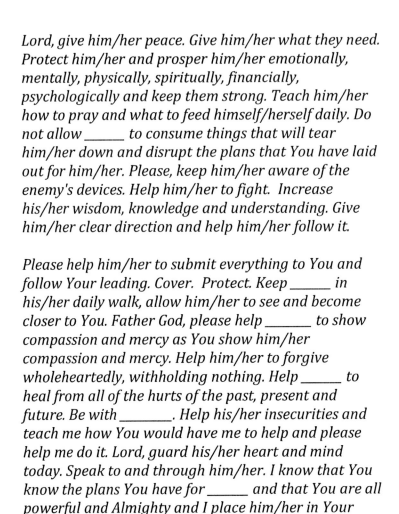

Lord, give him/her peace. Give him/her what they need. Protect him/her and prosper him/her emotionally, mentally, physically, spiritually, financially, psychologically and keep them strong. Teach him/her how to pray and what to feed himself/herself daily. Do not allow _____ to consume things that will tear him/her down and disrupt the plans that You have laid out for him/her. Please, keep him/her aware of the enemy's devices. Help him/her to fight. Increase his/her wisdom, knowledge and understanding. Give him/her clear direction and help him/her follow it.

Please help him/her to submit everything to You and follow Your leading. Cover. Protect. Keep _____ in his/her daily walk, allow him/her to see and become closer to You. Father God, please help _____ to show compassion and mercy as You show him/her compassion and mercy. Help him/her to forgive wholeheartedly, withholding nothing. Help _____ to heal from all of the hurts of the past, present and future. Be with _____. Help his/her insecurities and teach me how You would have me to help and please help me do it. Lord, guard his/her heart and mind today. Speak to and through him/her. I know that You know the plans You have for _____ and that You are all powerful and Almighty and I place him/her in Your hands. Amen"

Whether you are dating or waiting to date, this prayer covers a lot. Even if you have not met him or her yet, you are still praying for his/her holistic well-being. Whether he/she will become/remain a friend or become something else, your prayer should always be God's will for his/her life.

If you are in your waiting season, don't worry, don't rush it, and don't settle. Don't get discouraged and stop praying because it seems as if nothing is happening. Allow God to present them to you and you to them.

Finding a Balance: Dating/Courting

Balancing Family and Relationship

When dating, it's good to understand that although your attention is being held by another, there are others who love you and you love them in return. Sometimes, we can be so engrossed with building our lives around someone that we can forget or begin to tune out the life that we already have built.

If you are going to be there, then BE THERE.

If you are doing or attending something to support your family or close friend, and you have set time and space for them, then grant it to them.

Do NOT double book yourself.

If you are there for their birthday, be THERE for their birthday. If you are there to celebrate someone for their graduation, then be there to celebrate them. If it's their wedding day, then celebrate their wedding.

Remember you are there to celebrate THEM, not just an event. Whether your significant other is there or not, enjoy the person you came to see. If your special someone is there, you both should enjoy who you came to see. Eat with them, talk with them, dance to the music and enjoy them. One day is not too much to give.

Seeing it from the other side: It is rude and can be hurtful when a person says they came for you, but they are consumed with their cell phones and/or others.

Teaching Relationships

*"Train up a child in the way they **should** go..." –Proverbs 22:6*

Teach your children the requirements, expectations and reason for dating, courting and marriage.

What do you expect to see?

Parents, when children are born, you know that they are going to grow up, but deep down they will always be "your babies". It is ok to see them for what they are, but you should also be preparing them for where they are going.

Children become teens that become adults. It is important that you tell them and teach them what dating/courting looks like. The world around them is always trying to teach them something. Don't let their communities, friends, social media, and the media be the ones that define what a healthy relationship looks like. We all want to avoid that "talk", but conversations of just "the birds and the bees" are just not going to cut it. There are so many more things that needs to be discussed.

Here are some wisdom discussions for healthy relational growth. Think of them as the seeds you will plant for the trees they will become. It's a given that not all of these conversations should happen in one day. This is a tool to be taught throughout their lifetime.

When choosing where you have these conversations and when you have them, use wisdom. Know your child. Speak to them in love and as a person. It may be uncomfortable, but that's ok, you are training and training is often uncomfortable. Meet them where they are but do not under estimate them. They may know more than you think. You would be surprised to know how much relational things they see day to day. Your voice needs to be the one that not only instructs but resounds.

1. **How to add a person while protecting your family unit**- Discuss the do's and the don'ts; What is important to you as a parent when it pertains to family; how the significant other should deal with family; teach them to accept someone who is not only respectful to their family and yours, but, will protect, nurture and provide love and support for them and their family in the future; What info should be shared and what is private; How to conduct themselves in and out of public view;

2. **How to protect the addition while protecting and respecting your family**- Discuss the role of having a significant other as a girlfriend/boyfriend, as a wife/husband; their responsibilities in being a boyfriend/girlfriend, the journey, and in being husband/wife.

3. **When to introduce**- Discussing the qualities that make up a boyfriend/girlfriend; The qualities to look for in a wife/husband; The right times to pursue, entertain, and/or introduce a significant other; The

stages of relationship, seasons and when to identify the next seasons.

4. **What to introduce**-Identifying what the person is to them and if that person fits the requirement to be in the position given.

5. **What are the qualities and responsibilities of good character -** In friends, in women/young ladies, in men/young men, in themselves, in a best friend, in those they seek for counsel, in groups and group settings, etc.

6. **What is expected in relational behavior in and out of your sight-** Explain the expected guidelines for behavior.

7. **What you feel disrespects you and your household-** Identify and explain what is disrespectful to you as a parent and what brings dishonor to you and your household; What is not to be tolerated in or around your home (in many cases, its ok to include why you feel the above is disrespectful and dishonorable).

8. **Understanding the benefits of dating VS. the benefits of marriage AND how they differ-** Help them identify and understand their "ships" and what belongs on each boat. You don't want them capsizing before they even hit the water, so don't let them travel unaware.

These are just a few key areas to discuss that can help establish a foundation for what you expect to see and in what they should expect to receive/look for.

Without a vision the people perish, and many of our youth and young adults are dealing with the vision of what they "think" the outside world deems acceptable. But the truth is: its unhealthy. It's unhealthy for the person, it's unhealthy for the family unit, it's unhealthy for the significant other, it's unhealthy for the communities, and it's unhealthy for legacy.

Your voice, as a parent, creates a vision that is worth being seen. You may not have made all of the right choices, but, knowing what you know now, you can impart life changing and destiny changing words by just taking time to shed light. Even when the world is saying something different, it is your responsibility to show your children a better way. Don't be afraid to have the necessary conversations. Pray for the what, when and how.

Do not talk to your dating adult children as if they were married already.

Be careful of the things that you say. Certain conversations can communicate acceptance and silent approval of certain practices. When talking to single people, **you must remember that they are single people.** Acknowledge that they have found someone, but always keep things in perspective.

Relationships Are Not Exchanges, They Are Additions.

Although things may shift when gaining a relationship, the people in your life still need to know you love and respect them.

Guys:

Your mom, sisters, grandma, etc., may not be #1 women in your life anymore, BUT they are women in your life. Your brothers are still your brothers. Make time for them. Special son/mom lunches or even an occasional flower or card is helpful to remind them that you STILL love them. Make time for time with siblings, one on one. Talk to them, with them, about them. Have a family get together, go bowling, see a show, but whatever you do don't completely forget them.

There is a time for everything; a time to do things collectively AND a time to do things individually.

If the brothers are having a guy's night out and you choose to go, then let it be a guy's night out. The men want to bond with their "brother" and talk about personal and private guy things that they want to share with YOU. It's not that they want to alienate her. They want to share this portion of their "life" (time and words) with their brother.

Use wisdom and pray about what to share.

Not everything that is shared with you by your siblings, family and/or friends is to be shared with her. When in doubt, ask. Some people have certain levels of privacy and only feel comfortable sharing with those who they have confided in.

If you KNOW your girlfriend/fiancé cannot hold water, keep your mouth shut. What hurts you may be different from what hurts your family member, and to share something personal that was told to you in confidence could come back and badly affect your siblings, friends, family and/or close relationship.

One never expects to break up when you are in the "process of building." Unfortunately, and in some cases fortunately, break ups happen. Be careful. Information that was shared privately can quickly become public knowledge. Vendettas, anger, and sheer pettiness can fuel the fire within. And that person, the one you KNEW would keep your secret, will spread it like the 6 o'clock news. How much more could they use the information about your family members against them?

Women:

Everything that was told to you has a place, and sometimes that place is a vault that only you and God visit. Whether it's your best female friend, your mom, dad, sister, brother, or husband, pray about what to speak and what to release. Sometimes things are said from a place of feeling and not a place of understanding. A person can see things one way and then, after receiving information, see it another. When you share it prematurely or as a complete story, you can paint unnecessary pictures in the minds of others.

Know the difference between private and public information. If your best female friend or sister tells you something in confidence like they have a yeast infection, keep that to yourself! That is not anybody's business. If it's something about abuse, rape, drugs, alcoholism, and anything that puts her in danger, pray about who to tell. Don't just share information, pray. If you must put her on a prayer list, don't use her full name. Put "friend" or "relative".

Don't broadcast the family's "off the records". Some private family business may need to stay private family business. Business ideas, tentative plans, travel plans, personal funny stories, etc. may need to be held in confidence. The right hand may not need to know what the left is doing. You never know who is listening to attack. There are many people who have gotten their houses broken into, music and business ideas stolen, and road blocks put in place to hinder them and/or others because of shared private information. If your family is starting a hair care line, it may be best to wait until the hair care line is finished and ready to be sold before discussing it. If it is profitable, then the information is profitable. Protect the people, thoughts and things that have value. Before you speak, think and before you think, pray. Pray for clarity, understanding and wisdom.

Be present. If you are having a girl's night out, please don't stay on your phone all night. The gathering is a time set aside, designated for "girl time." Your friends are not alienating him; they just want to share their female hearts with a friend who understands and guards their female hearts.

Be where you are. Be careful that you are not just granting them your attendance while withholding your presence. If you are going to spend time with them, then spend time with them. You will not have them forever. Make the time you have with them count. Be present in conversation. Be present in listening, BE present. Don't be so consumed with what HAS happened or what WILL happen and miss what IS happening.

Men and women:

Balance Time.

It is important that we make time not only for the people we love, but for the things that need to be done. You cannot spend all your time in love and not take care of the responsibilities of reality.

You are living a real life that requires real attention. Whether it's work, school, business, etc., you must take the necessary time to be present and do what needs to be done. You cannot pay your rent with love. You cannot earn your degree just by having love. You cannot fulfill your dreams, goals and destiny by just being in love. It requires action, work, perseverance, focus, drive, and determination and it will require: **Time.**

Understand your journey.

Whenever you embark in love, please understand it's a journey. Each part of the journey comes with its own responsibilities and benefits. Many times, when dating/courting, we can end up giving benefits that belong to another position or don't belong at all.

Even though you are building a relationship, he is not your husband yet. She is not your wife yet. You are NOT "one". You are in the process, and it's best to understand the difference.

Balance Goals.

God has given you a vision; whether you define it as a dream or a goal, it still belongs to you. Whatever you are supposed to do in life, with life, and for life, do it.

Relationships are good, but relationships are better when the people in them know who they are and why they are. Only then, can they begin to better understand what fits with them and how they fit with others.

Make decisions.

There will be decisions that you will have to make about an individual but there also will be decisions you will have to make regarding destiny when it comes to relationships. The question that SHOULD be in everybody's mind is: *"How will this effect, affect, or infect my God given destiny?"* Based on your answer, you must make a decision to **"Allow it."**, **"Reposition it."** or **"Stop it."**

When you allow it, you are deciding to let things run its course. When you don't "reposition it" or "stop it", you are choosing to allow it. Choosing to do nothing, hiding or ignoring it, is still a decision made. The choice of doing nothing ultimately says, *"I choose not to change it or its course".* Evidently this decision puts you in the position to accept whatever outcome that will come from it.

When you choose to reposition it, you are choosing to prioritize, resize and/or reset things as it should be or in a way that puts things 1. In place and 2. In perspective. Repositioning often restores order. Regardless of what your specific circumstances are, GOD and HIS plan for you should be #1 on your list. I'm not saying church. I said God. There is a difference.

There is nothing greater than God. Let me say that again: "There is nothing greater than GOD." If you look at your significant other, job, money, issues, etc. as being bigger than or more important than God, then they are your god.

Prioritize.

First, it's knowing "What is important", then it's understanding, establishing and implementing the order to where its/their importance coincides with your God given destiny and/or assignment.

For example,

> You have a boyfriend/girlfriend/significant other and you are in college. You know you have exams and need to study. Wisdom would say studying to pass,

succeed, and graduate is the priority. It's not that the person you are with is not important, it's that the assignment/goal/task requires it be given the priority.

Establishing priority does not mean that the people, places and things are not important. It means that you are maturing in being responsible with what and who GOD has put in your hands.

Resize.

There will be things in life and in relationships that will need to be resized.

Sometimes there will need to be a **resize in quantity**. There will be things that you will need more of and there are things that may need to be less. You must determine what that is and what needs to be adjusted. If it's things/people/places that are negative, cause drama, cause tension and dissention, cause strife, stress and unnecessary worry then it may require you to lessen it, and the power, attention, and time you give it. If it is prayer, peace, faith, focus, etc., then these are things/actions/principles/behaviors/mindsets that may require increase.

Sometimes there will need to be a **"resize" in view**. How you view a thing is important.

Sometimes we see things as bigger than what they are. Sometimes we make things smaller than what they really are.

And sometimes, we successfully give unnecessary attention to things we shouldn't and we fail at giving attention to what is necessary.

When we see things as "too big", we worry and when we see things as small we tend to ignore, discredit, devalue or dismiss it. Even when it comes to our own position, we can find ourselves doing it when it comes to our goals, dreams and/or visions.

When we see things as "too big," we often become concerned that it's not going to happen or we allow our worry to entice our fear, which often results in us running to others, to "fast track alternatives," and/or running away from it.

When we see things as "too small," we can 1. put down or reject the very thing God wants to exercise so that it can grow for your destiny and/or 2. begin to ignore what needs to be changed or removed.

Nothing is "too big" and "too small"; it just "is."

See it for what it is. See you for who you are. Where you are going is not where you are, and where you are, is not the only place you are going. If God, is showing you something, acknowledge it. Never dismiss something that is damaging as "small" and discredit it. It could be about you, or an issue, or with a friend, relative, boss, co-worker, girlfriend/boyfriend, etc., if He is showing you something, see it for what it is and see it for what it is through prayer.

Once you see it, seek GOD for wisdom in handling it accordingly.

Reset.

There may be things in your life and/or relationship that needs to be reset. If things have gotten off course, the worst thing you can do is allow it to continue. You cannot make it 100 miles east if you are set to travel 1000 miles west. Sometimes you will have to reset the sails for the destination you are trying to go to.

If you find yourself in the wrong place mentally, emotionally, physically, sexually, and spiritually, then it's time for a reset. Reset the course of your thinking. Reset the course of your position. Reset the course of your "SHIP."

It may be time to go check and see if God is still the Captain of the "SHIP." Sometimes we end up rerouted because we allow other things like lust, pride, and fear drive our boats. Mindsets and behaviors that reflect *"I'm afraid I'm going to lose him/her if I don't do this." "I know it's not right but..."* and *"I got this."* often leaves us to skipper or sail our own SHIP's. Oftentimes those ships/boats end up capsizing, crashing and/or sinking and it's not just because we allow other things to steer our Ship and "they" don't know where we are going or how to drive it.

Crashing is often inevitable because our boats weren't made for travel in certain areas. Captain God "charted" our course for a reason. It's so that the "Ship" travels the path that best serves it and its destination.

Sometimes a "reset" may require that you travel back to where you are supposed to be without that extra passenger.

Especially in cases where they refuse to allow the dating/courting relationSHIP or friendSHIP to be reset, or for you to be reset, it may be time that you exit the "SHIP" and head back to your dock called "YOU."

With or without your extra passengers, it is important that you make it to your own personal, God-given destiny and/or destination.

Are You IN Love?

"God is love" 1 John 4:8

If God is not IN it, then what do you have?

"Love is patient, love is kind. It does not envy, it does not boast, it is not proud. It does not dishonor others, it is not self-seeking, it is not easily angered, it keeps no record of wrongs. Love does not delight in evil but rejoices with the truth. It always protects, always trusts, always hopes, always perseveres." (1 Corinthians 13:4-7 NIV)

Now that you know what the definition of love is, use it to define what you have and/or answer the question of "Are you in love?"

Ask questions of Love according to 1 Corinthians 13:4-7:

Is ____ patient? Is _____ kind? Does ____envy? Does _____ boast? Is ____ proud? Does _____ dishonor others and/ or me? Is _____ self-seeking? Is _____ easily angered? Does _____keep no record of wrongs? Does ____ delight in evil or rejoices with the truth? Does _____ always protect me? Does _____ always trust? Can _____ be trusted? Does ____ have hope God, in you and in themselves? Does _____ persevere?

The blanks above can be filled with their names or yours. Use it as a tool of introspection, reflection and inspection.

Love is: Taking responsibility.

No matter what relationship you are in, do your part. Even if you have a working relationship, you take responsibility and do your work. Don't leave your part on anybody else when you are fully capable of doing it yourself.

Every relationship, single or married, comes along with its own set of requirements, obligations, and duties. Whether is a friendship that requires support or a dating relationship that requires time and attention, it all comes with responsibility. In order for the "SHIP" to move, everyone must do his/her part. Excuses do not excuse responsibility or help the others on the "Ship".

If you are married, then it is imperative that you do the responsibilities that goes with the position you vowed to take.

Husbands, lead, love, provide and forsake all others. That might include the abundance or placement of video games, hanging with the boys, football games, time in the "man cave" and sometimes yourself. Sometimes you will need to forsake or put certain things away so that you can be or do what is necessary for the needs of your wife and family.

Wives, follow his lead, love, support, uplift, cherish, encourage, be the helpmate, oversee the home, bring things to his attention and work with him on what it lacks, and do your part in providing the needs of your husband and children, forsaking all others. Sometimes it may require that you not be so focused on the intimacy of conversation, work, time with your girlfriends, talking on the phone, watching your favorite show, etc., so that you, like with the husbands, do not miss the needs of your husband and/or your children. **I am not saying that you cannot expect, need or desire those things**. I am saying, "You too, just like the men with their "caves", may have to sacrifice what you want at times, in order to care for the needs of your spouse and children"

Love is: Sacrifice.

For both men or women, loving relationships will require sacrifice. You are going to have to do some things that you don't feel like doing.

You are going to have to go to places you don't feel like going.

You are going to need to help when you don't feel like helping.

Responsibility is real and feelings do not erase what must be done. You can pretend that it's not there and may even keep your eyes closed to reality, but reality is still there, eyes open or eyes closed.

Love comes in many shapes, sizes and forms. We must be careful that when we love, we do it genuinely and not because others are watching or it's what we think people want to hear.

Love is: Genuinely aware.

Be conscious not to allow yourself to become:

- **The talker, but what is being said does not reflect your actions or heart**

  "If I speak in the tongues of men or of angels, but do not have love, I am only a resounding gong or a clanging cymbal"

- **The head smart but empty hearted**

  "If I have the gift of prophecy and can fathom all mysteries and all knowledge, and if I have a faith that can move mountains, but do not have love, I am nothing."

- **The attention seeker**

  "If I give all I possess to the poor and give over my body to hardship that I may boast, but do not have love, I gain nothing". (1 Corinthians 13:1-3 NIV)

Although there are many love languages, the purpose of love is never to boast on what you have, what you've done, or what you spend. Love requires a balance and follow through of action and words. You never want to be known as one who loves with words only.

Don't Just Date, Learn.

Take some time to get to really know a person. Learn his/her likes and dislikes. Ask questions and take note of the answers, SPOKEN and UNSPOKEN.

Take note of signs of jealousy.

Jealousy is real. Don't ignore it. Jealousy is an outward sign of inward insecurity. Based on what it's coupled with, it could determine if the relationship should continue. Rage is never a good thing in relationships and it could be a clear indication that things should end. Rage is when anger or the need for revenge exchanges logic for emotion. Anger and/or vengeance without logic is a bad combination.

Without logic, there is no thinking rationally. Irrational thinkers are dangerous.

Know the signs of certain behaviors.

It is very important to pay attention to behaviors. Certain behaviors can reflect deeper issues, some of which may require medical assessments and/or medical attention.

Emotion needs to be balanced out with logic and awareness.

It is understanding **what is happening VS what is happening in the mind** and how it affects/could affect them and others. Sometimes it is wise to pay attention to how deep the mood swings and emotional whirlwinds go. Certain things may be learned behavior and other things may be cause for alarm, and in some cases, separation. Be watchful and prayerful. Ask God to allow you to see what needs to be seen and remove you from what is not for you.

Be Watchful.

There is a difference between being emotional and bi-polar behavior.

There is a difference between a person being sad and a person that is clinically depressed.

Violence is not ok. Violence, mental abuse, verbal abuse and any other abuse are not tools of love. God is love and things like these that hurt, harm and wound the mind, body or spirit is not of God.

***Also, be mindful of yourself and others when it comes to playfighting. Sometimes things that may start off or seem to be "innocent" are gateways to progress and/or may be or reflect something deeper.

Take note of those who become "different personalities."

Be watchful of those who practice to be one way/personality with you in public, a completely different way with you in private, a completely different way with others in public, and/or a varying personality day to day. They may not really know who they are or how to be. Be very careful if the personality switches become dark, full of rage, violent and/or possessive.

Oftentimes, a switch in behavior or conversations in social settings could become a social challenge because we are unsure of how to be, so we ***become in order to adapt***. But, it becomes something bigger when a person does not realize, know, or accept that a negative shift in personality is happening/has taken place.

When a person **becomes to adapt,** they <u>are only becoming what they think is socially necessary</u> to adapt to their surroundings.

When a person has **adapted to becoming,** the settings does not determine who they become, it has already become a socially developed personality. Especially in social settings or everyday behaviors where an individual **routinely becomes negative, vengeful, narcissistic, or violent,** the person may have already developed and has already determined the person they want/are going to be socially.

Whether or not the individuals know WHEN they are becoming the who or what they become, is something within itself.

If they know, and have or are trying to identify and/or correct it, it may be a behaviorally developed issue. If they don't know when they become the alternate personality, even when addressed, or do not see that their changing personalities as an issue, it may be something that would warrant the wisdom of professional counsel.

Whether it's dating, courting or marriage, the person you get with should not be a daily, emotional, mental, physical, or psychological box of chocolates, where you don't know what person you are going to get.

We all have our areas that need work. No one is perfect, but consistency and mental/emotional/psychological stability is a must.

Listen to what is being said.

When beginning and in going through the dating process, it is important to listen to what the person is saying. Listen and take note of what is being said to you, about you, about him/her and about his/her lifestyle.

<u>Some may be honest</u>.

Honesty is great. You want to be with someone who is honest and has integrity. Keep in mind that not every honest person is open to discussing everything, especially in the beginning. In the beginning stages, you may find that some places, details and conversational topics are reserved or off limits. As time goes on, and when more trust is established, you may find that they may begin sharing more.

Some may keep it "too real."

Know your boundaries. If something is being discussed that makes you uncomfortable, it is ok to politely say that you are uncomfortable with discussing that subject. A quick change in subject matter also works, especially when the subject is being changed to the topics of what they like or dislike.

If you or he/she is the "keeping it real" type, then it's good to remember that although "Keeping it real" is good, it also requires tact, respect, and self-control. When you speak the truth, speak it 1. In love, 2. In wisdom 3. With understand and 4. In season. Just because you CAN say something does not mean that you necessarily should. Let wisdom guide you.

Some create lifestyles of grandeur in conversation.

Listen closely. Is this reality? If not, it may be wise to find out if: 1. This is "wishful thinking" of what the person desires to be or become in the future, 2. Is he/she blatantly lying, or 3. If this is something that only his/her mind sees as a reality. **It is one thing to be attached to life and believe in your dreams, but, it's another to be attached to dreams and believe it is life.**

If a person is not aware of where they are or refuse to identify where they are, then they are not capable of telling you where they are taking you.

Disappearing Acts

Dating, relationships and friendships

Men:

They say, *"if you know better, then you can do better."* This is a chapter that may give insight and an opportunity to do better by understanding how disappearing without warning or communication affects women.

Picture this:

> **A guy walks into a room and notices that a movie is playing in the VCR/DVD player. The movie seems interesting and now, wanting to know the name of it, he takes it out and looks at it...**
>
> **After inspecting the ejected DVD, the guy:**
>
> 1. decides he no longer is interested and walks away, leaving the DVD ejected
> 2. pushes the movie in but then hits pause, OR
> 3. watches the movie and seems to be enjoying it and then, all of a sudden, loses interest in it and turns it off.

In many ways, this is how it is sometimes with women. The woman is living her life when a guy comes along, notices her and finds her interesting.

Wanting to know more about her, the guy takes her out. After taking her out or dating her, he may realize that she is not who he sees himself with or he wants to explore other options. He doesn't tell her; he just walks away. Without communication, the woman has more than likely stopped life as she knew it, paused waiting for his return, or is restarting/playing unnecessarily to an invisible/nonexistent "audience".

How she is affected:

With each ending scenario, she may come to wonder *"What did I do wrong?"* , *"Why did he walk away?"* and *"What is wrong with me/why didn't he want me?"* And, for a long time, she may have to deal with the unfinished pieces he left behind.

Besides being made to feel like she has been set back and/or betrayed, due to the time and pieces of herself that she invested, she now has to deal with trying to understand what happened.

Like the movie, her life was not only paused, but she also now needs to be rewound and has to restart her journey of singleness from the beginning. Depending on how long or how far she went, the longer it may take for her to get back to where she started emotionally and psychologically.

Some women even become damaged in the process and are not able to return to the beginning.

Guys, if you need space, change your mind, or decide to go another route, communicate that.

No woman wants to be held in limbo or held hostage. When a guy, who has her interest or has expressed his interest, just disappears, it is NEVER good for her.

When a man walks away without communication, he:

1. Puts the woman in a mild panic.

2. Feeds her seeds of insecurity.

3. Stirs negative emotion and evokes negative thoughts.

4. Denies closure.

When a guy just disappears, it equates, communicates, and imparts **rejection** and/or **abandonment**. It causes a woman to question who she is, her place with him, and what she has to offer.

Even though it may not be your intent to hurt or damage her, stepping away in silence can be damaging.

Communication is necessary. Although you may not see the need to say something, feel like it is necessary, don't want to hurt her feelings, are trying to avoid drama, need some space to think, etc., the effects of NOT communicating are worse than communicating. At least she knows.

It is not ok to just walk away/disappear without saying something. It's not that women do not respect or want to respect your process or decisions; we just ask that you consider us and the position that you leave us in.

It is important that both parties involved know where they stand. Unfortunately, many women only find out that the guy has "moved on" AFTER he has moved on, she sees or hears he is with someone else, or when he no longer responds to her or her position, not because he told her directly.

COMMUNICATION IS KEY. Tell her, in the nicest way possible, that you are leaving. Don't just walk away. Walking away is going to affect her either way, but communicating the "what" and "why" with compassion could help her heal faster.

Don't have her on "hold" while you are on "play" trying to "figure it out" or watch other "movies."

You are dealing with a woman and she has feelings. No woman wants to be or be made to feel as if she is an option when she knows she is a choice. You should not be entertaining other women if you already have, expect, or requested a woman to reserve a spot in their lives, heart, and schedule for you. It is selfish and unfair.

Don't press play or touch the queue if you do not aim to watch the movie.

We know and understand that things may happen, and this "movie" may not be for you, but communicate that, don't just disappear. It is never ok to play with her emotions.

Think about what you are doing before you do it. If she is not what you want or who you want to be with, then be honest and respect her enough to value her feelings.

Always be honest.

Women appreciate when their feelings are considered and respected. She may be hurt that things have ended, but at least she knows and she can process it.

Now, if she is a bit "clingy" after you tell her, that's a different story. You may have to ask yourself "why is she clingy?" And, based on the answer, one might better know how to handle her in this situation.

Be sure you are not telling her something opposite with your actions

You cannot say *"No, I don't want to date you"* and then reach for her has if she were a woman you are dating. If she is going to be a cool friend, then treat her like one. Don't call her every day, hug and kiss on her, and have girlfriend expectations from her without giving her the position of girlfriend. It doesn't work like that. There should be no benefits if she can't have the job.

Are you still making investments into secret accounts?

Do you knowingly or unknowingly fill the role of boyfriend or significant other for her? Sometimes we can consciously and subconsciously fill the empty spaces with someone and expect nothing at first but then, as time goes on, emotion and a sense of ownership can begin to happen. It doesn't just happen with people we like or date, it can also happen with Best Friends and friends. That inner sense of ownership or entitlement is often something she may not even realize she is doing or exhibiting.

If you guys are friends, sometimes, in order for you and her to reach a better understanding, it may require an in-depth talk. She may not even realize that she is being this way and may just be used to you being in or occupying that space. A conversation where she is able to be brought to a place of understanding, may be good.

The conversation may also give you an opportunity to hear her side or view of things. Sometimes, what seems as if she is being "clingy" may not be what you think and could be her way of being there for you or protecting you. Women know things about women that men will never know or identify, and men can see and pick up things about other men that women will never know to see or recognize. It is good to be able to come to a place of understanding for both parties, and these conversations could also help define and redefine boundaries lines.

If you have had the conversation and she clearly knows her behavior, expectations and/or conversation crosses boundary lines or makes you uncomfortable but she doesn't adjust or refuses to accept your chosen boundaries, you may have to use wisdom and give each other even more distance.

The "Safe Haven"

Be careful of who you run to in difficult times.

Single or married, it's important to know where and why you are running when things go awry, or become difficult.

Why we run...

1.Running: From Danger or Injury

People typically think to run when they are being hurt or think that they are in danger. Whether its emotionally, physically, or spiritually, when there is perceived danger, a flight or fight mode kicks in within us. It's a defense mode that helps us to self-preserve.

Sometimes choosing flight, especially in cases where there is physical abuse, is the most beneficial thing we can do. Just because you run, it doesn't mean you didn't fight; it means you chose to fight alongside wisdom on a different plain.

Sometimes choosing fight, can be beneficial. It doesn't always mean you are physically throwing up fists, but that you are going to not only do what it takes to overcome and win, but also that you will not stop following God until He leads you to victory.

And then there are times, more common than we think, that we use the flight or fight mode unaware. Whether it be with our spouses or loved ones, or in conversation, we can often choose to mentally, spiritually, emotionally, and conversationally leave and hide when we perceive that there is danger.

Emotionally, we can run when we feel there is or will be injury.

When we feel or perceive that we are under attack emotionally, our defenses can go into fight or flight mode. If we feel that we are being done wrong, frustration says, *"I do not agree with this, this needs to stop"* so, internally we choose to combat it or walk away from it.

But, when it comes to our emotions, it is important that we know that we are not only limited to 1. Fight or 2. Walk away, we have a third option: to seek wisdom and get understanding.

Sometimes the appearance of "attack" is not really an attack from the person, it's the position of perception. Sometimes we just do not communicate well. And, what people think we are saying, is not what we were trying to say at all. Now, there are times when you are under attack, but understanding the who and the why better shows you how you should deal with it.

If your emotions are under attack, you must understand who is causing them to be.

Ask yourself: Is the person/are the people trying to be mean and hateful? Why? Could it be that they do not know the effect of what they are communicating? Could it be that they know what they are saying, but not the way it affects you? Could it be that they were taught to respond that way? Could it be that they are in pain and the frustration is causing this hurt person to lash out? Could it be that they are broken?

Could it be you? Could it be how you are seeing it or are choosing to see it? Do you see it that way because you are used to or conditioned to see things that way? Do you think offensively? Defensively? Do you see the complete picture, from all sides before you make your conclusions? Could it be another way?

Could it be a trick of the enemy to try to separate you?

These are all good questions that would bring about different answers. Not every battle we encounter is the battle that we see. Many times, in relationships, misunderstanding is the tool used to keep people separated.

Without the using our third option of seeking wisdom to get understanding, we can fight or run from things, people and issues that need us to understand.

Emotionally we distance ourselves from others because we no longer perceive it to be a safe place. Whether it a step back to swing or a step back to run, it still distance. If you are going to step back, use it to look at what is really happening, not just respond to what you "think" is happening. Pray for clarity and examine. Even if you need to pause the conversation for a minute to diffuse, think, and get your thoughts together, make understanding your goal.

Sometimes you will find that what you thought is really what happened. It is still an opportunity to find understanding the "why?" in what was happening. Things happen for a reason. It could be to grow you or to show you.

Sometimes the reason can be that it's because of you. Sometimes we can set things in motion and we don't see that its moving until it hits us. Sometimes we are the one who has had a bad day and have unknowingly come home and taken it out on the ones we love. Sometimes, what we think is their actions towards us, is really just a reaction towards what we are doing or have done to them. Now, not everything is going to be your fault, but there may be things that are.

When there seems to be danger, we can run physically.

If it is physical abuse, I agree that you should run. If you are being beaten or physically abused, run to the police, file a report and stick to it. Then don't go back unless there is a real change. A promise that "I won't do it again." Or "I will go to counseling" is NOT enough. You must take measures to protect yourself and, if you have any, your children.

Having children around an abusive relationship is an even more pressing reason to leave. Whether a person knows it or not, the children see and they are affected. Even when the children are small, they may not know exactly what is happening yet but they know that something is not right. Abuse is never the answer. If you are being abused, seek help and get out. Do not stay in places that are dangerous for you and can potentially kill you.

You don't deserve to be beaten, no matter what you have done. You are valuable, are loved and was born to be loved. Love is not abuse.

We can also run spiritually.

It could be **running to or with purpose** or the assignment that God has placed inside of us.

It could be **running from** the things that we know we should be doing, because of how much we "think" it will cost or "injure" us.

It could also be **running to the things we shouldn't,** because of how we "think" it benefits us.

Whether we run positively or negatively, we all have the capability to run. Fight or flight takes on two different meanings when its positively and negatively motivated.

Positively, you begin to fight for purpose, in order to achieve and run with fire and fervency to accomplish things. A dream, a goal, a vision could become greater as you run with passion. Positively, we can begin to run away from, or begin to remove ourselves from the things, people and places that defeat, hinder, distract, reroute, and kill our purpose and our passion.

Negatively, you can begin to fight against and fight with your purpose/assignment /instructions and run from it. Sometimes, we can run when we know that what we are doing or are not doing, is wrong. And we, like Adam and Eve after they sinned, go and hide. We can begin to do things like stop picking up phone calls from friends who we know would probably remind us of what is right, we stop going to church, or even walk away from God.

Negatively running, we begin to embrace the things, people, and places that keep us away from God, purpose, and assignment.

2. Running: Looking to fill a void

Although explaining areas of void is multisided, it can be defined as **any** emotionally, physically or spiritually unfulfilled or empty space that we desire to be filled knowingly and unknowingly.

The "Proxy"

A "proxy" is someone who is used to fill a position, space, substitute or stand-in.

Many times, we can find and/or use "proxies," to fill in spaces where we feel there is a void. Now, not everyone can identify with just one specific type of "proxy," but we may all be able to identify with proxies in other areas.

Whether it's a conversational void, an emotional void, relational void, physical void or spiritual void, we must be careful. Oftentimes, the voids that we try to fill are the very places where God wants to fill, fix, or bring it to your attention, but we try to fill it with people, conversation and/or activities.

Unknowingly and knowingly looking for a proxy.

Don't expect relational things from friendships. Whether you are married or single, male or female, you have got to be careful of filling the "empty spaces". Sometimes we can fill the empty spaces with proxies and call them "friends". Sometimes we can knowingly and unknowingly, deem or get people as a "fillers" to our voids.

Don't believe me?

- Are you looking for or desiring someone to talk to when you feel alone?
- Do you already know who you want to talk to/call/ see when you are lonely, both male and female?
- Do they both serve the same purpose?
- Are their conversations and/or the conversations you desire from one, different than the other?
- Are all of your conversations and jokes, conversations that all of your friends can hear?
- Do you use anyone, that you are not dating, to go on dates...umm... I mean...cuddle or snuggle with...hmmm, no, that's not right... I meant kiss, talk romantically.... Umm... I still don't think I said that right.... I meant, "hang out?"

When you, single or married, are missing the presence of your spouse emotionally, mentally, physically, or conversationally, who do you call? Why are you calling them? Should you be calling them?

Both men and women, can find proxies. It is not limited to one gender. Though men tend to think differently, it is still important that both men and women take the time to ask the necessary questions that bring clarity and a reality to where you are and what you are doing.

A note for men:

It's not always about the effect they have on you or the intent you have with them, but the effect you have on them and the intent they have with you.

Sometimes jokes, are not jokes and games are not games. Be careful of the roads you choose to travel. You are a leader, she may be thinking you are leading her somewhere that you may have no intent of going. You are a pursuer. Your conversation and/or action may be speaking a language that could be interpreted to her that she is being pursued. Be careful. Be aware. She is not built like you and she does not break like you. The heart is never something to play with.

Especially in the cases of married men, be careful of **1. the conversations that you keep, 2. the timing of the conversations that you keep,** and **3. the message of the conversations that you keep.** No woman, outside of your wife, should ever know that there is a void.

Women are natural born help mates, we are design to see and help to fill your voids. **It doesn't just work on the men we are married to, it works with men period. Be aware.**

Information is data when it comes to the female mind. Be careful of what you say. Even jokingly, you can cause things to happen in places you have no idea existed or that she could feel/develop/become that way.

Be careful, married men, that you are not filling the voids of another woman. Always remember that **conversation is intimacy.** Cover yourself and your spouse.

Be careful single and married men, that you are not filling the voids of married women. Sometimes a woman with voids can use her time and conversation with you to fill the voids she feels in her own marriage.

A note for women:

We must be careful not to get or create a proxy, especially in places where our husbands should be, whether we are married or unmarried.

Those *"he is just a friend that I call when I need to talk"* and *"He is a good listener"* mindsets and people can get you in trouble!

You must be careful of where you sow your emotions, they are attached to you.

Where you invest your time, thoughts and your conversation will be where you will become invested. When you are lacking in areas like quality time, you must be careful not to go to people and places in order to fill it. When you are lacking in the areas of conversation, confidence, intimacy, affection, attention, affirmation, and validation you must be mindful of YOURSELF. For you it's not about what you attract; it's about what you start to seek and seek out.

As a woman, you are not only vulnerable but predatory in nature. Our self-defenses allow us to search out that which we seek, in order to survive. It happens knowingly and unknowingly.

Sometimes things that start out innocent, could end up deadly for you and your relationships and one of them is conversation. Especially in the cases of married women, when women have a void of intimacy through conversation, we seek it and seek it out. What could be an innocent beginning of light or joking conversation with a male co-worker/friend/etc. could, over time, cause emotional disasters. It is also wise to be careful of yourself when you see or know that the guy is lacking in areas of intimacy or validation as well.

When you are lacking, you look for it. When he is lacking, you can become it. It's a part of being a "help mate", which is why we have to be careful. **We ARE logic and emotion.** Where we go, even in conversation, our thoughts and emotions go with us. We are a packaged deal.

When we converse, we begin to emotionally attach ourselves to the individual, whether it be our best friends, friends, spouse, associate, etc. We can begin to bond and/or share a bond with them knowingly and unknowingly. You may know that you esteem or hold in higher regard a person above others, but you may not know how much or why. When you emotionally attach, eventually your mind, body, and its property, become assessable to it.

3.Running: Out of fear of the unknown.

Sometimes, people, both men and women, can begin running because they are afraid of what could happen. It may be due to past hurts or broken relationships or it could be due to a deeper seeded issue. Sometimes things can stem from our own insecurities.

> *"What if I'm too fat?" "What if I am not attractive enough?" "What if I am not enough?"*

These are just some of the things that we think could disqualify us. So, instead of allowing it any opportunity of potentially hurting us, we disqualify ourselves in order to save ourselves a potential heartache.

It's another form of self-preservation. A way of subconsciously protecting ourselves. But, it's not a protection, it's a prison. It not only keeps people out but it keeps you trapped in. What was built as a security measure or "self-defense," becomes a self- destructive barrier, which keeps its captive behind a wall of insecurity.

Where you run...

Be careful where you run, especially when you are feeling emotional or are trying to fill a void or running out of fear. Not all comfort is real comfort and not all counsel is wise counsel. Don't choose people that will soothe you when you are wrong and coerce you when you are right. Make wise choices. Chose those who will seek only to get a prayer through, impart Godly wisdom, direction, instruction, and encourage you in what is right and what is wise. You do not need "yes men" that will just tell you anything you want to hear or encourage whatever you decided even when it or you are wrong.

Search for people who speak wisdom, and not just someone to talk to. You have to be careful of what you allow to be poured into you, especially when you feel "empty". Again, everyone comes with something and leaves with something. You don't want anyone to come with drama and leave with information. They will fuel the fires that already burn.

You want to make sure that the people that come, come with wisdom and leave with a heart of prayer for you and the issue. You don't want someone to just make you feel better, you want someone who can, through wisdom, help you become better, so that you can "see" and produce better.

If you are married, you have no business running to private counsels of the opposite sex, especially as it relates to your marriage or your spouse. It will get you in trouble. Even if it's the pastor, then it should be a counseling session of the pastor and their spouse, never alone. If it's "just a friend", make it a group of wise counselors, not a private one on one thing. Use wisdom. Cover yourself and your spouse.

Before you decide to share, ask yourself if the conversation you are having with the outside person is the conversation you should have been having with your spouse first.

If the answer is that you should be talking to your spouse," then you may need to pray for wisdom and then have the conversation with your spouse before you involve anyone else.

Sometimes things can be rectified with communication and conversation. Conversation presents information.

Communication, seeks out, embraces and does what is necessary in order to bring and ensure clarity to what has been said.

It may often require that you lay down "how YOU think" and "how YOU process" and communicate in a way that the other person can process and understand. Just because you speak, does not mean you are relating to others what you think you are saying.

If it takes time to explain, then take the necessary time to explain it. Your marriage is worth the investment of time. Never see it as a "waste of time" or as unnecessary to communicate to one another.

At times, it will be hard, but that's ok. Do it. Communicate by aiming to reach the place of understanding for him/her and for you. Don't just talk, listen. Hear him/her. Let him/her speak. **Communication is not one sided.**

Many times, things and situations can cause us to be separated. And, it may even lead us to a place where we don't hear, we know what details to be listening out for, or we don't care when the other person is trying to communicate. Sometimes a person could just be blocked by offense, being shadowed by distrust, or be standing behind a wall of hurt or misunderstanding.

It is not always that the other person is choosing to walk away from us. Sometimes it's us who are the ones putting up invisible barriers that we expect others to see and cross to get to us. Communication is like the telephone, and it often requires conversation to relay what needs to be communicated.

In communication, one side calls in and the other side receives the call. One side listens and the other side speaks. Both parties are needed. Communication is NEVER just a speaker, because there would be no need for it if there was no one there to hear/receive it.

Even if you feel that he/she isn't listening, relationships, especially marriages, require that you still make the call.

Communication is NOT: Limiting yourself to acting out when angry or frustrated.

Never assume, married or single, that a person just knows how you feel, or how what they did or didn't do caused you to feel. In the relationship, the walls and barriers, although often felt/interpreted as distance to them, can only be seen by you. They won't know what "it" is until you shed light to show them.

If you find that a conversation, issue, or situation is something that requires outside help or influence, then it may be time to get counseling.

Choosing to go to counseling, grief counseling, or marriage counseling is not saying that you are "broken"; it speaks to how much you value yourself and your relationships and what you would do to keep them from being damaged, broken, or destroyed. Counseling is an investment in what you have, not a punishment for what you've done.

When it comes to being married, counseling is often beneficial. Marriage does not come with a step by step instructional, and you will often find out that, what you are going through, other marriages have gone through it.

Counseling just helps you to better see ways to get through it and get through it together. Marriage counseling, groups and retreats are often good refreshers for the marriage. It's a place where you have support and opportunities to gain wisdom and insight when dealing with what makes you "you" and what makes them "them" and how both can live, grow and work together.

Counseling does not have to start after you are married.
One person put is as "Knowing what to do before saying 'I do'." Pre-martial counseling is a major plus when going through the process of engagement. It helps you identify things about them and things about yourself that you may have missed or didn't know to understand. It can also teach you ways to change or remove that which could hurt your future, and teach things that would help build, secure and ensure your future.

Whether you are dating, courting or engaged, it is good and beneficial to attend and glean from Christian relational classes and groups. There is so much that you could learn that would prepare the way for the future. Never look at these classes/groups as *"a waste of time because I already know!"* Remember, as much as we know, there will always be 1. Things that we don't know, 2. Things we can learn, and 3. Unexpected people who hold unexpected information.

You do yourself a disservice when you think you already know or that there is nothing anyone can give or tell you. Don't judge a book by its cover and don't judge a class by its size or its reach. Just because it's small, doesn't mean it doesn't have value.

Where to go: In physical abuse

There are many places that have resources to help you escape to safety. Your local police department should be an advocate for safety and may have more information of what is available in your area. There is also a National Domestic Violence Hotline and a host of other domestic violence services and hotlines that have ways that they can help.

Sexual assault is another type of physical abuse. No one has the right to touch you in areas that you do not want them to. If you are, or anyone you know is experiencing or has experienced sexual assault, there is help available. There are a host of agencies that have resources available to discreetly help victims see victory.

The "EX"

Not everyone that breaks up becomes enemies. Some people actually become good friends. If you happen to be one of those people who ended a dating relationship and entered a platonic friendship here are a few things to remember:

1. They are human and do not process like you.

One of the worst things you can do in ANY relationship is expect others to think and process like you, and then punish them or think less of them because they don't. It may take someone more time to get over a break up than the other person. It is not that they don't or didn't care. They may just process differently.

2.Know when it's time to be friends and when it's time for space.

Communication can be good but sometimes some space to heal is even better. Sometimes, TIME is a healer and it may require not talking and/not being around each other. Depending on how it ended and why it ended, it just may need to end.

3.If they or you need time, understand it and respect it.

4.Understand your position.

When you break up, you forfeit the rights and benefits of being a boyfriend/girlfriend. The things you were expecting as a boyfriend or girlfriend, stop expecting. You no longer hold that position.

5.You cannot have things "your way."

If you have an event or situation and call them, it is a possibility that they may not show up or arrive on time. Your position of priority now rests amongst the other things that they have going on, have to do, and/or the places they need to be. The position of "first priority" is a benefit of a romantic relationship that you both no longer have. So, "if" he/she is not able to make it, don't be upset. Remember it their right to say "no."

If they do show up at a later time, it's not worth you becoming angry. You may not like that he/she didn't come when you wanted, BUT they did come. Remember he/she doesn't have to. Anything someone does for you, is them doing it for you. It's not that a benefit for them, especially when it's added time and work to their schedule. Allow them to decide their gift and say, "thank you."

6.If he/she cannot do what you want them to do or run when you call, it's ok. Again, it's their right to say "no."

If they say "no," respect it. Whatever their reason, it's still THEIR reason. They don't owe you an explanation. I know you probably don't like me saying this BUT... It's the truth. Singleness is not only their status, but it is their reality and anything they do for you, at this point, is voluntary and subject to conditions. They are not obligated to anything they do not want to do for you or with you anymore.

7.One thing mature people don't play is tag and hopscotch in a relationship.

Together. Not together. Together. Not together. Together. Stop the cycle.

Either you are going to be together or you are not. There should be no benefits given for a person who does not hold the position. There are no "interims" in dating relationships. They should not be sitting in or warming a seat that you have purposed for somebody else. Depending on how and why it ended it, the truth may be that you 1. Need counseling or 2. Need to be over. If it is meant to be or it is going to be, then run the process that is needed to keep it together.

8.You cannot disrupt consistency and expect things to stay consistent.

If you are one of those people who cannot make up your mind if you want a relationship or not, then you need to make a decision and honor it. A doubleminded man is UNSTABLE in all his ways. You cannot have a stable relationship with unstable behaviors and mindsets.

9.Don't be a stalker

If it's over, then it's over. Don't go on Facebook or social media pages trying to see what he or she is doing. And if they block you, stop using friend's pages to bypass the "block". If they want to move on. Let them. Don't stop your life, even for a minute to chase information on how they are moving on. It keeps you stuck. Stuck in the past. Stuck in your feelings. Stuck on them, when your focus should be you and what God has for you. Give yourself a break.

10. Understand that he/she WILL date again and maybe even get married.

If he/she starts dating again, it's ok. If he/she gets engaged, it's ok. If he/she and the significant other decide to get married, it's ok. It is their life and their choice.

Whether you are friends or not, their relationship is between them, the person, the person they are with, and God. Give them respected space. It's not a slap to you, it's just called respect.

When in doubt ask yourself "How would I feel and respond if the person I am with, had an Ex that did/is doing, what I am doing?" If the answer is not good, then you need to stop.

11. Friend means friend.

That is NOT your boo, your boyfriend/girlfriend, your wifey/wife/husband/future baby daddy, your baby, your boo thang, or anything other than your FRIEND. Remember that. It's not time to rekindle old flames when you are bored or lonely. This is a friend (an in some cases an associate).

"Friend." "Associate." Or "This Needs to End?"

Not everyone is meant to be friends after dating. If you find yourself in a negative place, in a place of sin, or in a position of any type of abuse, it needs to end completely. Don't tell yourself *"I got this,"* when you know that you don't.

Sometimes an acquaintance is all an "Ex" needs to be. Sometimes, just giving them a "hello" every 1-5 years is ok.

Either way, be sure to put it in its place. Assess what and where you are and then address it as such. Boundaries are necessary in all relationships. Even sin is a boundary for God, it's the thing that keeps YOU separated.

Remember that a true friend prays.

If you are going to be friends then be a real friend. Above all else pray for them, their protection, guidance and wisdom. Pray that God's kingdom, will and plan for their lives, reaches them and brings them to a place of purpose. When you pray, don't give God ways to fix them. Pray that God would help them become who they created to be. Only He knows His plan for them, you just seek the Holy Spirit on how to pray for them, others and yourself.

Are you rekindling a fire that should be put out?

Single guys and girls: Sometimes the "break up" is God doing you a favor....

"Stand fast therefore in the liberty wherewith Christ hath made us free, and BE NOT ENTANGLED AGAIN with the yoke of bondage." Gal 5:1

Ask yourself "what is real?" and deal with the realities. If that relationship brought out the worst parts of you, negatively affected or altered you, or was not God's best for you, LET IT GO.

The worst thing you can do is try to go back. I know you probably miss him/her and the voids that they filled, but remember: Just because you are used to him/her, it doesn't mean you're in love with him/her. You could've just made him/her a habit.

"Can a person become a habit?"

Yes, people can become habits. Habits are things that we practice doing, being, or being around. When a person has a habit, good or bad, it becomes a part of his/her life. When you are used to being around a person/people, talking to them, holding them, etc., you can develop a system of habit and feel a void when they are removed. Why? Because life has made room for them and when they are gone the empty space is noticeable.

It is often perceived that a "break-up" takes away from who you are, but it really takes away from what you do. You have to make the mental, physical and emotional adjustments from 'two' to 'one' and it is a process. During that process, it can be painful and the immediate voids will be noticeable. Sometimes, to avoid the pain and/or the process, we can return to the very thing that bound us in the first place.

The good thing about life is that, even though the space is noticeable, it is still able to be healed, filled and/or adjusted. Empty spaces or voids do not often feel good, but sometimes it's necessary. If you know that this relationship, in any form, is unhealthy for you, seek counseling or cut it off and leave it alone. Don't worry about the "hole". Anything that is killing you from the inside or has the potential to kill you should be removed.

Sometimes we can confuse the feeling of being "in love" with a habit. Just because a person likes/people like being around someone or they miss the presence of someone, does not mean that they are in love with them. Like cigarettes, people can become an addiction. And like cigarettes, even though people know it can kill them, give them health problems and is bad for them, the knowledge that this is not good is not enough for "it" to be broken.

Just because you know that a person is not good for you, doesn't mean that the knowledge is the thing that will break your habit or soul tie. The soul is defined as: the mind, the will and the emotion.

If your thoughts, your desires, your heart, your voids, or your sinful nature are still calling for, connected to, or enticed by them, and you know that this is not for you, **then wisdom says that this is may not be something that you need to pick up.**

Don't be distracted by emotions.

Don't get caught up in **_how you feel right now_**. Be honest with yourself. Take time to answer questions like,

- "Who was I when I was with them and what did I become?"
- "Am I better and better off without them?"
- "What did they really bring to the table?"
- "What did I invest?"
- "Was it a good investment?"
- "What did I walk away with, good and bad?"
- "What did I lose?"
- "How long did it take me to recover?"
- "Did I recover?"

After you ask and answer these questions, it should help you determine if you should allow, what was an unhealthy relationship, to become another relationship. Whether it's friendship or reigniting a dating/courting relationship, it is still a relationSHIP.

Is it REALLY a friendship?

You must identify if that is how you or he/she **really** feels. Even when you tell yourself *"I'm ok. We are no longer together but we can be friends."* you have got to be careful.

Feelings are real and they can be used to "trap" and "entrap" you again. Watch your thoughts. Stay away from dwelling on the "what if's." Sometimes, when dwelling on the *"what if's,"* it starts to become *"Maybe if."*

"Maybe if we tried again. Maybe this time it would be better. Maybe, now that we are older, things would be better..."

If there is any part of you that wants to be back together, and you know that it was not good for you or is not good for you, watch it. Don't rely on your strength to resist. Many times, it's that "natural strength" that can and will fail you.

Beware of the Stockholm Syndrome

The Stockholm Syndrome is a survival strategy of emotionally bonding with an abuser or as a prisoner, hostage or victim by allowing intimidation or a perceived threat of a person's physical or psychological survival or existence. In relationship, the threat of being alone may look scarier than being in "bondage". You will find that many of us, choose to go back, not because we want to, but because of our perception of life without them. Even when the relationship hurts, it is the enemy that we know verses facing the world that we don't know without him/her.

Be sure to understand why you desire to return to any relationship. Sometimes we can revert to what we knew when we step into "survival mode." Be aware. Be careful. Deal with reality. And if reality says, *"it was not good for you,"* don't return. Stay free.

Heal before you hurt again...

Again, take the necessary time to deal and to heal. When we do not assess and address what was done to us and how it affected us, we can develop in ways that we do not know or understand. Besides returning to an abusive place with an "Ex", we can begin to search and seek out new things and/ or relationships that can continue or enhance the abuse or imprisonment you came out of.

Sometimes, people will begin to search for others to abuse them or others for them to abuse, when they do not deal with the emotional, physical and psychological bondage that they faced in the past. Oftentimes, it's the things that made the person a victim, calling out to those who create victims. It's like the prey to the predator. The victim becomes visible to the victimizer.

And then, there are also times when the experiences of the past, that are left unidentified, unhealed, and unchecked, develop into hatred for what people have allowed themselves to become, and they become the predator. They can begin to take vengeance on those who remind them of what they once were.

If it is meant to be "just friends," then be sure that you keep it just friends.

You cannot get anywhere in your friendship journey by incorporating conversation, baggage and maps/charted courses of a dating, courting or marriage relationSHIP. If the person is "just a friend", then what you say to him/her and the time you spend with him/her should reflect that of a friend. Kissing and intimate conversations do not belong to friends OR to those you say you no longer desire to be with. Don't make investments of YOU in places you have no intention of building.

Be real with yourself.

If you start to feel like you miss being around and with him/her and you KNOW that this is not good for you, it's definitely time to distance yourself from him/her and his/her conversation. Take time in silence. It may be hard, but it's more than likely necessary. Every conversation feeds something. Identify what that "something" is and why that "something" is. Then assess "Should that 'something' be?"

Don't tell yourself that you can handle it, when you know that you can't. Don't tell yourself you can handle it alone, even when you think that you can. If you have wise and praying counsel, it may be wise to call them. Accountability partners are good to have and solicit for continued prayers BEFORE you allow yourself to go too far.

In some cases, silence might be necessary for an extended period of time. While you are silent with your "friend," be in communication with God. Talk and Listen. Not only is it good for direction, but it can also help you gain strength and help you reposition.

Sometimes, we can spend so much time talking to people, that those people become a part of who we are. We begin to process life including them and often excluding God. They can become an idol or the most important thing/person to us. We can wake up thinking about them, spend hours talking to them, and go to bed missing them and go through a whole day without actually spending time with God.

Quiet time with God often refocus our eyes and resets our view of realities.

Ladies, there is no ownership with friendship.

If you start to feel a bit jealous when it comes to him or upset that he isn't calling, texting or spending time with you, then you have already gone too far. Catch yourself and regroup.

We do not place ownership on things that we do not feel belongs to us. You must be careful. Subconsciously we can begin to attach our emotions and claims to people, especially the opposite sex. Once emotion is attached, we begin to hold that person in a higher regard. The higher the regard or the closer we view them, the more the attachments.

When we are not careful, we can often attack or become defensive over anything that we feel belongs to us, even when it rightfully belongs to someone else. It is also one of the reasons how a single woman can end up feeling no regard for a married man's wife. This is something you have to watch, whether you or they are single or married.

When we, as women, invest ourselves in something, we expect a return and feel entitlements. It is not often something that many women plan or begin with intent to do, but, every position, emotionally, verbally, mentally, and subconsciously comes with its benefits and entitlements. When a woman shifts in conversation and is allowed to become comfortable in that "shift", she shifts. Again, repositioning does not always happen consciously.

Many times, the shift happens in and because of conversation. It can be initiated by both men and women. Sometimes certain topics, seeds of emotion, and/or "jokes" are thrown out as testers. If it's received and/or continued or allowed to continue, guards can come down and we feel "it is safe or good to be here" and we know that there is not boundary in this area.

If a topic, emotion or "joke" is thrown out and not received, we see there is a boundary and we are not welcome there. Some women see the boundary and respect it. Some may even try find another way around or a more subtle way to enter by testing the boundary lines. Be aware and be careful.

Beware of interim positions.

Any position you assume, man or woman, you also assume the responsibilities. Your "title" of friend means nothing if your position or your duties say "girlfriend" or "boyfriend". You have to be careful that you are what you say you are, whether he/she is married to someone else or not. A friend does not think, act or respond like a "boo".

Don't let "habits" lead you to an unhealthy life or into an unhealthy relationship. Bondage is never worth it.

Remember conversation is a form of intimacy. If you have no desire to allow them "in" again, then it may be wise to limit or cut the conversations. If you do converse, try to avoid certain topics that **open old wounds** and **invite old feelings**. Either way you can become vulnerable. Emotions can sometimes overshadow reality.

Children Are Not Tools for Revenge.

Children are a blessing. They were never meant to be a weapon or a tool to be used to hurt, coerce, or gain information about an "EX". Children do not deserve to be punished for their parent's mistakes. Whether it's in wars of parent against parent, parent against in-laws or family, child against child, or any other war that includes them to inflict pain, bargain or teach a lesson, it causes damages to children when they are caught in the middle.

Parent Vs Parent

This is the most common war that affects children. This battle causes children to struggle to know what to do and how to handle what they see/experience/gather from watching leadership fight against leadership, in attempt to prove ownership, distribute responsibility, rekindle partnership and/or seek revenge for past and present wrongs.

When parents fight each other, no matter the reason, it affects the children. It affects how they process, how they feel, how they view things, how they learn to deal with other, and what they believe about themselves.

In many cases, parents fight more about their issues with each other than they do about what is best for the child. The arguments and yelling tend to be mostly regarding what the parents feel and/or think, and not so much about the child themselves.

Be sure you are not trying to hurt the parent through the child.

Both men and women have been guilty of knowingly and unknowingly doing this. Whether it's denying visitation, withholding child support, removing perks and/or physical involvement, it all hurts the child.

You never want children to feel like they have to choose sides, choose who to love, fear that if they mention or talk to the other parent that there will be repercussions, or believe that they are the cause of the problems. When children are forced to choose, or are made to feel as if they are the reason for the division and/or problem, it plants seeds of rejection and abandonment in them.

If there is a fight, contain it.

You came together once to make the child, you can come together to protect and raise the child. As the parent, it is your responsibility to work as amicably as possible to ensure that your children learn that they are loved and that they do not have to choose which parent to love back.

You are not going to agree on everything, but you don't have to be disagreeable. Do what you can do to make things work without attacking each other, disrespecting each other or walking in defensive mode. There are things you can do apart and there are things you can do together. Choose your battles. Not everything is grounds for a fight. Try talking and listening and praying for wisdom, understanding and execution. You may want to even try writing down what needs to be done and come together to see what is able to be done. Make it your goal, as parents, to reach understanding every time you speak.

Child support vengeance

A child is a person, not property. You cannot hold your children hostage until a person pays up. Ladies, I see this a lot from us. When a father does not pay child support or do what we want, he is banned from seeing and/or talking to his child. This is not always a wise decision to make because it hurts the children.

If he is not doing what he should be doing to support his children, take him to see the judge. A court will order him to pay or deduct it right from his check. You don't have to fight with him. Let the courts do what they can do, and you do what's best for your children.

Understand why you are really angry and/or angry with him.

Is it really the child support or do you feel abandoned? Do you feel he has wronged your children or do you feel that he has wronged you? Are you feeling frustrated with having so much of the responsibility?

It is good to identify why you feel what you feel. When you know "how you feel" and "why you feel" you can better communicate what you feel, and what you need and/or need to do in order to feel better.

The end of the relationship with you is not the end of the relationship with your children.

Just because you broke up, it doesn't mean that it's ok for him not to see or be around his children. You should not restrict the parent from seeing his children just because he no longer wants to be in a relationship with you.

You may be hurt and angry that the relationship is over or at how it ended, but, don't let how you feel overshadow what is best for your children. Forgiveness is some of the best medicine you will ever take when it comes to healing a broken heart.

No amount of revenge is going to cure or undo what has happened to you. You are worth your freedom. When you choose not to forgive, you become a hostage to your past. And, as long as you hold on to it, it will affect your future. Every bad seed that a person sows will come back to them, and if you continually plant bad seeds it will come back to you as well. Choose to stop the cycle of hurt. Choose to let the past be in the past and allow the future to become the future.

Arguing is not always the best to get your point across.

When you yell, scream, curse and/or argue, he sees your frustration and not your point. It is not that he doesn't care about what you have to say; it is just that your own anger and frustration overshadows and blocks him from being able to hear what he needs to hear.

Think about it ladies. How much work could you get done if someone continually yelled orders at you, told you what a horrible job you were doing, did not allow you to speak, comment or defend yourself, and created a hostile environment every time you came around? Not much, right? It is the same for guys. We have to be careful of how we deal with each other, especially when we are frustrated and angry.

Respect goes a long way.

How you deal with each other is important. He may not be doing all that he could or should be doing, but that does not mean that you have to alter who you are to belittle, disrespect, and bad mouth him.

Always remember that you do not have to lose who you are and/or your peace for anybody. If he is being unbearable, put him in the hands of God and let God deal with him. Maintain your self-control and remember who is in control. Bad attitudes, words and behaviors tend to promote bad habits. Not only will it affect you but it can infect your children. You are the standard and are training your children to respect or disrespect not only their father, but those who they do not agree with.

Guys:

If you are a guy who does not support your child because you 1. Don't want to deal with her 2. Don't see where the money is going or 3. *"Didn't sign up to be a father,"* stop that.

If you have children, it is important and your responsibility to help take care of the children. Do what you are supposed to do. Don't worry about her and what she is doing.

You may not see where she is spending the money, but it does take money to provide the household that your children live in. Don't be upset if you see her with her hair done. It is more than likely NOT your money she is spending on it. She probably is finally able to use her money to do something nice for herself instead of having all of her money go to responsibility.

Don't look too hard at what she is doing with "your money." Look at how you are investing into your child.

"But she argues with me all the time!"

She may not be a peach to deal with. That's okay. You cannot control anyone other than yourself. You still be a gentleman, be patient, be kind and be responsible. Do not fuel her flame, seek vengeance or argue back. Hear what she is saying, gather your truth and discard the rest. She may not know how to communicate how she really feels or what makes her feel that way. She just knows that she is angry and frustrated and that you helped her to feel that way.

Sometimes the anger comes from her feeling that you do not care or care enough about her and her child's well-being.

It may not be what you feel but it may be what she perceives. If she says something like *"I am doing this all by myself"* what she really is saying is that **she needs you to step up quite a bit more**. Don't be so turned off by HOW she said it, that you reject what she is saying.

Want to help?

Try finding out what she needs and contribute to it.

Give her a little extra money here and there to offset some of her bills and living expenses. Often, the money that she receives from child support is helpful but it is not enough to cover what she and the children need. A little extra can go a long way and help her see that she is not doing everything by herself.

Give her a break from having the kids all the time. She could be frustrated because she has no time for herself anymore or to do the things that she needs to do. Try adding in more or random days that you spend with the children so that she can do something for herself.

Do something extra that says *"I see your effort and what you do for our child. I appreciate you."* Whether it is a gift card, gas card, birthday card, or movie tickets for her and 2 friends, do something that says, *"I appreciate you as the mother of my child."* Mother's Day is also a good day to show her honor. If you can, invite her and your children out to breakfast, show them that, although you guys aren't physically/romantically together, you are united in the care and well-being of your children and you treat each other with respect. If you can't, do what works best for the both of you. A card and a gift in the mail or having something delivered may work as well.

Parents, be careful where you "vent."

Children are sponges, not garbage cans. Parents must be wise about the things they say regarding the other parent, all those connected to the other parent, and the children. You paint pictures and plant seeds when you speak to and over your children.

Be watchful of curses.

If you, as a parent, see a behavior or mannerism that is negative, harmful or reflective of the opposite parent, it is not time to speak things like *"You are just like your, no good daddy.", "You are going to grow up to be just like your mother/father,"* etc.

Watch what you say over your children. Words have life. If you see a negative, counteract it with a positive. Pray for them, encourage them to be better, talk to them and help them to understand why doing or being "this" is a bad or unhealthy practice. Teach them that it can affect them, their lives, and/or others.

In all things, stay prayerful. Pray for and over your children. Don't speak negativity over your children. Negative words are not something to speak over or to children, especially as parents. You are the ones who are supposed to see the best in them even when the world sees the worst. Be the parent, not the bully.

Be careful of what you show your child.

Children are always watching and they are always learning. You must be careful of what you allow them to see when it comes to how you deal with or are affected by the other parent and/or their family. Children need to see a united front.

You may not know that they are watching you when you hurt or get hurt. What they see becomes what they learn, then they begin to process, and eventually, as they grow older they develop from what was learned in childhood. And, by the time they reach maturity, they adapt and take steps to run from it or to it.

Allow room to "talk."

Allow children to express how they feel. Hear them out. After you listen, take time to explain to them that although you, the parents, are no longer together, you both still love them very much. Kids need to know they are loved. Kids need to know that you make time and care about their feelings. It can get pretty hard when you have a break up, especially when you include children. There is no situation that is exactly the same as another. Every situation has different people, different circumstances and involve different children. Here is a basic recap of things to remember:

- Anger, strife and revenge are never tools to happiness, peace and positive growth
- Your children are learning. Watch what you do and how you treat each other.
- What you say to and around your children about their parent is important.
- Be mindful of what you say to and over your children
- Your children are the priority. Do what you can to work together as peacefully, wisely, and amicably as you can.

You must be careful of the seeds that you sow into your children. They are very impressionable. The seeds that you sow can cause your children to either imitate, assimilate, or regurgitate. Imitate the behaviors they see, assimilate for survival, or give out a worse version than what went in.

Remembering that children are like sponges, we must be careful of what we give them to take in. It's not the children's fault that you two are no longer together. Do not take it out on them. Children need to know they are not the blame. Tell them with your words as well as your love.

Women: *Are You the Reason He Loves You but Doesn't Want to Marry You?*

The contentious woman:

"It is better to dwell in the wilderness, than with a contentious and an angry woman." Proverbs 21:19 KJV

The main things that a man/husband looks forward to coming home to is the love, peace, and rest of his home. When you behave in this manner you say to him "You will have no peace." Nobody wants to argue all the time or be reminded over and over and over again of what was said 10 minutes ago.

If you are the wife, your job will include creating atmospheres of peace. If you cannot do it before you marry him, you won't do it on your own after marrying him. Marriage is not a fixer of bad behaviors; it actually amplifies them.

Be mindful of how you deal with your anger and frustration in your relationships and friendships.

Familiarity and frustration can bring platforms of 1. Multiplication and 2. Amplification. In other words, what's in you will have the tendency to come out "bigger" and worse when you feel comfortable or frustrated enough to "lash out".

Usually, it is the ones in the home or the people closest to you that get it the roughest. There is a sense of openness and nakedness that comes with close relationships. The closer you are, the more that you see. We tend to reveal more of ourselves than we would with strangers and associates. When we begin to get familiar we tend to take off the "masks", both negatively and positively.

The quarrelsome woman:

Proverbs 25:24 (NLT) "It's better to live alone in the corner of an attic than with a quarrelsome wife in a lovely home."

Ladies, if you always like to argue and get your point across, stop that. If everything that he or anyone says is grounds for an argument, cut it out. I'm not saying, "don't stand for righteousness," I'm saying to "EXERCISE SELF CONTROL."

The home should be a place of peace. No one wants to live in a hostile environment. When a man sees you, he sees potential. Besides seeing your good qualities, he also thinks about your behavior, thoughts, and practices that will affect him and his household in the future.

The potential to act out, cause him stress, take peace, create hostile/negative atmospheres, potentially cause him and others to be or live in defense or with his guards up, and the potential to magnify and multiply the negative words and behaviors being practiced in the dating or friendship **are not motivators for him to move forward towards marriage.** If you steal his peace as a friend, what will you do if he makes you a wife who he has to see and be around every day?

The woman who forces entitlement in position:

Women, for us, every position comes with responsibilities but it also comes with position and entitlements.

With every new position/title in relationship, we expect a certain level of respect, consideration, and openness. To us, each position is like receiving the keys that open doors that gets you closer to his heart. And, for us, marriage is the final key. We expect him to completely be OPEN and unhindered with us. Things that you tolerated in silence, as a girlfriend, you may not silently tolerate as a wife.

Never try to force a man to meet your entitlements. No man wants to be made to feel as if he has no choice. It is ok to talk to him regarding your relationship and expectation, but it is never ok to force him. Even God gives mankind the option of choice, and, based on our own choices, it determines what position we get to walk or stay in.

It is true that no one knows what you are thinking or how you feel until you tell them, but your job is to present him with the information, not an ultimatum.

Expectation varies with each person and each position and does warrant a conversation of information from both parties involved. You will find that his view of things may have similarities and dissimilarities to your view.

The goal is to get understanding of the views, position, and consent (or lack of) in honoring those expectations.

The dishonoring woman:

Men do not want to be or feel disrespected. A man sees his wife, not only as something that he protects, but also as something that reflects.

As his wife, you would carry his name, which also means you help in carrying his vision, possessions, influence, and passions.

- **Dishonor shows that you do not value that which you carry.**

- **Disrespect shows that you do not honor those who trust you to carry it.**

Your words and behavior have the ability to infect his mind, soul, and spirit. You could be killing him and you don't even know it. Men don't easily identify how they feel, but when they love you, they love you. They may not know how to show it completely, or as you would like them to, but, when they give their hearts, it is something valuable that they put in your care.

A man does not walk around freely investing his heart into places that he does not intend to stay or build. If he is investing his time, it may be that he is trying to see if this is a safe and nurturing place to invest his heart.

Dishonor and disrespect are sure fire ways to say "YOU AND YOUR HEART ARE NOT VALUED HERE". And wisely, he does not invest in pursuing a deeper relationship with you.

The overly needy:

He may not mind the "Damsel in Distress," but he doesn't want a distressing Damsel.

Allowing him to be the hero every once in a while, is not bad, but making him your savior is. No man wants to carry all of your burdens while carrying his own. God said Adam needed a HELP Mate, not a mate that was always in need of help.

Our design, as women, is to help him, not become a hindrance or another burden to him.

Granted there will be things that you need him to be and/ or do. I am not referring to those things. I am, however, referring to situations, conversations, and other things that are excessive, unnecessary, and avoidable that are done 1. To get his attention 2. To cause him stress when you know it could easily have been handled by you or by using the wisdom, resources and knowledge that you already possess, and/or 3. That is not really as major as you portray it to be.

<u>Never forget: You are in this together. You are in this together. You are in this together.</u>

Being "in this together" means that you both are working for the common goal of achievement. You are carrying what you can so that he can carry what he can. He cannot carry what he needs if he his hands are always filled with you, drama and/or "baggage."

The overly independent woman, the boastful woman and the competitive woman:

Sometimes our quest to show "we can do it all," causes him to see *"There is no room for me..."*

This is the other side of the spectrum from the "overly needy" woman. This woman doesn't need a man, or anybody for that matter, to do anything for her because she "has got this". And even when she doesn't have it, she still "has it."

You never want to consciously or unconsciously do, say, or imply that *"I don't need you. You are just here."*

We all have needs and the desire to be needed. Whether it's man or it's woman, we all have areas where we need each other. We all want to feel like we belong, whether we choose to admit it or not.

Receiving help, love, advice, etc., does not mean that you are not independent or cannot stand on your own. If anything, it speaks to how much you value those who see your hard work and want to ease/lighten the load or assist by giving you a break. Sometimes we need it.

Find your balance. It's ok to need people. Its ok to need him. It's ok to relax sometimes. Its ok to let him be him.

There are things that you can do and there are things that he would like to do for you. Allow him to do them. Don't allow fear to tell you, *"you have to do this alone,"* and don't let pride keep you from receiving love or allowing him to show his love to you by doing things for you.

As a man, he was created to be the head of his home, and as the head he is wired to provide, protect, cover and go before all who is "in" his house. When he dates, he looks for the potential to build a home and that also includes looking for the potential to provide, protect, and cover.

He is a provider. Do not remove or reject his ability to provide. He is a protector. Never tell him or imply that you don't need his protection. He is a leader. Do not fight him to be in the lead.

No man wants to have to continually fight with a woman to have the ability to prove that he is the man. It's not about him making her feel like less of a woman, but about her respecting him and his position as a man and allowing him to be.

In many cases, you will find that a man likes to see his woman be strong and confident and walk in her God given authority. Men, for the most part, don't usually have an issue with his woman/lady walking in her God given authority; his issue often comes when she begins to cross over into his God given authority, comes against his God given authority or when she wants to control or command his God given authority.

Its ok to be a strong woman, but we, as women, must be mindful that we do not use our strengths to overshadow, belittle, control, intimidate, ridicule and/or compete.

It's one thing to be competent but it's another to be competitive.

You never have to compete or crush with your "strength". If you make more than him, have more than him, or know about more than he does, it's not time to flaunt it, crush his spirit with it, or make yourself his superior because of it.

Strength is a weakness when it is not use in the right place, the right way, and at the right time. Many times, the reason we try to show our "independence" to others, is to prove to the world, *"See, I can do it on my own."*

No matter where that strength came from, whether it came from a place of overcoming an obstacle we or others thought or said we would never make it through, or from a place of self-awareness, self- belief, or self-efficacies, it is something that we may need to identify and deal with. Accomplishments are not tools that build pride or to harm others. Pride is a killer of relationships and can also be a killer of those in the relationship.

The immoral or unfaithful woman:

Proverbs 5:1-23

It is hard for a man to build trust with someone who is untrustworthy. He needs to be able to trust the woman who he will share everything in his life with. A man will emotionally, conversationally and even physically avoid and/or run from women that he does not trust or feels that he cannot trust. Even if he loves her and loves being around her, there can be parts of him that remain or become "closed off" to her.

In simple terms: **1. Beware of things immoral** and **2. Beware of doing things that intentionally and unintentionally betray trust**.

You don't necessarily have to do something to directly betray him for him to not feel as if he is able to trust you. Never forget that he is watching, and he is learning from what he sees. He watches you with others, how you relate to others, how you are with your parents, how you treat the men in your life, etc. and he is paying attention.

Ladies, men look at you and your life because they want to see how you react and act, and often use that gathered information to see how you will eventually treat, talk to, or deal with them and/or those who are connected to them.

For example, when a guy sees, dates, or entertains a woman who has a father who has been a father to her, active and caring in her life, but she disrespects her father and his authority, it is a clear indication and red flag that she has the possibility to treat him the same way or worse if he were to become her husband.

There is no man who wants to be disrespected in his relationships and in his home. Many men, even though they may care for the woman, will walk away. It is not that they are weak or uncaring, it's that they see a problem that will more than likely sink the "SHIP" and kill him in the process.

Cheating, lying, or inviting in other partners are common ways of betraying trust. Even in conversation, whether its intentional or not, you must be careful that you are not giving others information that was told in confidence and should remain private.

Honesty is the best policy. If you hide things that he should know or are not being honest with your feelings, intentions, or information or if you share private things about him or your relationship unguarded, it may be best to stop. These things do more damage than good.

The manipulative woman and the controlling woman:

No man wants to be manipulated or taken advantage of. Manipulation may last for a while, but when a man comes to the realization that he has been used and manipulated, it will not end well.

You will find that a man who finds he is being manipulated, will, in some way, walk away, whether it's emotionally, financially, or physically.

Deceit will eventually lead you to defeat. Be careful that you do not use manipulation to get what you want out of him.

You are an instrument of love, not a tool to use people in order to get what you want. Keep that in mind when you prepare your mind for marriage. Manipulation removes one's ability to choose by presenting lies and false hoods and/or to cleverly exploit or influence a situation or way of thinking. Manipulation is a form of control. That is not the way or the plan of God. Even God allows us to choose if we will serve, if we will obey, and if we will follow.

A common act of manipulation is the use of threats.

If you are a woman who uses threats in her relationships, stop it. Threats should not be a part of a loving relationships. They are used, knowingly and unknowingly, as tools to control and manipulate.

Threats don't always have to sound dangerous to be a threat, and are often pitched as ultimatums. **A threat can be simply be identified as: Telling someone that something needs to be done, said or rectified or it will constitute in a disciplinary action or consequence.**

If you give or imply a command and attach a personal consequence to it if your command is not obeyed, then it is a threat.

"If you love me you would do___"- indicating that he doesn't love you if he doesn't do it.

Or

"If you do not do or give me _____, I'm going to _____."

"If you don't _____, then you (insert a consequence)".

"If I don't get ____, then _____." - giving him a choice of doing what you say or receive punishment.

All of these examples are threats. It pretty much says to him that he will lose access to you if he does not give authority, control to you, or acquiesce. That is NOT a good practice, behavior or mindset. Control and mental/ emotional/ and psychological imprisonment is NEVER something that accompanies love and relationships.

Many times, a person's aim may not be to be intentionally controlling. The intention could be to help or guide someone into what he/she "should" do, but we must realize that there is a difference in **bringing assistance** and **being controlling**.

Assisting is offering to help and/or helping others, including those who are in leadership, through submitting ideas, views, and support. When you assist, you present a plan, idea, etc. and then let him/them/others CHOOSE if he/they will use or accept it.

Being controlling is the fight to have leadership. You present a plan, idea, etc. with the expectation of it being completed and/or no intended option of choice. What you say, needs to happen when you say and/or how you say (and sometimes, because you said it).

God has called husbands to be the head of their homes. And, God called for us as wives to be under their leadership. If you "run him" as a boyfriend, you will try to "run him" when you are married. What you practice, grows.

Ladies, if you refuse to submit to God and your husband in the future, then stop desiring to get married. When you get married, it's a covenant to keep what God says about marriage; not just a free pass for sex. If God has called him to be the head, then he is supposed to be the head.

Your husband/future husband should not have to fight with you to do what he was called to do: LEAD.

Leadership is responsibility and it has already been ordained. Now you will have some strengths and he will have some weaknesses, that is why you were created as a help mate. You help and support his leadership. He needs you, but he needs you to be with him and follow him, not stand in front of him, block him or lead him.

The practice of control and manipulation has cause many relationships, including mother and son relationships, to end or to make a turn for the worse. If you value your relationships, then value and respect the people you are in the relationship with.

The uncooperative woman:

How can two walk together except they agree? -Amos 3:3

It's a given that there will be times when you both will not agree on something, and that is okay. You both bring ideas and perspectives. The goal is that you both reach a common place with a common goal to get clarity in wisdom and get understanding.

Unfortunately, there are some women who, no matter what the guy asks, the answer and behavior is going to be "no".

Now, if the questions or requests reflect things that go against moral judgement and Godly principle, then that answer should be "No" and should remain there. But, if it's a request to assist with something you can do and are fully capable and free to do, and you see they need it, why not do it? A "no" is not always necessary.

In relationships, romantic or otherwise, it will eventually require that all parties participate. The "SHIP" cannot be operated by just one person all the time.

People have many reasons that they say "no" when they could say "yes", but the most common reasons are **1. Fear, 2. Being uncomfortable 3. Self-focus and 4. Offense.**

1.Fear

Fear is a big motivator, and many times it motivates us "not to do". Whether it's fear of failure, the fear of outcome or fear of doing or becoming, it is still fear. Oftentimes we can unknowingly redefine and/or camouflage the things we fear as us "being uncomfortable." In these instances, we become uncomfortable with taking action or being associated with something that "could possibly fail".

Now, you cannot constantly be led by fear and continually give "no's" just because of it. Be prayerful, use wisdom and branch out. Don't use a "no" as an escape from trying. When in doubt, ask for help. You may not know the "how to's" but someone does and God can also give you strategies. Again, be prayerful, use wisdom, and don't be afraid to branch out.

2.Being Uncomfortable

Although fear can cause a person to be or say they are uncomfortable, they can also become uncomfortable in doing certain things when those things conflicts with what they know, saw, or have experienced.

If you are uncomfortable with doing something, it's ok. It is not uncommon to feel uncomfortable. Identify how you feel and then look at why you feel that way.

Silence is not always the best move when you are being asked to do things that make you uncomfortable. If something makes you uncomfortable, tell them. Granted there may be times that it is best not to explain or it's not the time to explain but don't continually just leave people, especially the ones you love, with a "no" and no explanation.

Relationships require communication. No one just "knows." You may have your reasons why, but without you sharing them, the people in your "SHIPS" may feel like you are abandoning them.

Wisdom says, "invest in what builds your relationship." Sometimes you will need to take them to the side and share what's on your heart and allow them to talk to you about how they feel. Help them understand your boundaries and feelings and the reasons why you have come to feel that way. Take time to speak and listen. Hear them and how they are affected by your "no."

If it's something that goes against good moral judgement, a *"no"* may be in order, accompanied with an explanation of *"this goes against my morals and I will not be doing/participating in _____,"* when an explanation is necessary.

3.Self-focused

Whether it's behaviors or mindsets of things like *"I don't want to."* or *"I don't feel like...,"* it still focuses on you.

Relationships require that your focus be balanced with God at the center. One cannot have a balanced and healthy relationship when all he/she sees is himself/herself.

Granted there will be times when we are tired and need/have to take a break, but we must remember that love itself requires sacrifice. Whether it be romantically or otherwise, relationships require sacrifice. There will be things requested of us that we will not want to do. Do what you can in wisdom and with patience. Don't practice to sacrifice only when you "feel like it".

Everyone in relationships, both men and women, want to know that they, their time, and their part in the relationship have value and are valued. Ladies, men are no different from us when it comes to needing to know that they are investing in **us being a part of their "Ship"** and **that we are willing to do what it takes to keep the "Ship" going,** even when it means doing jobs that you don't want to do.

Men, like women, also desire to be considered and to know that you have their backs and support them, and that that support is not just predicated upon how you feel but how you feel for and towards them and what you have.

4.Offense

Offense can cause defense.

That "no" could be a defensive move. It can also be used as a punishment for doing or not doing something, whether it was knowingly or unknowingly. "No" is denial.

Women, we can use the defense of "no" to deny access to us, our thoughts, our participation, our hearts, and more. It's a mental statement of *"you don't belong here"* or *"you don't or no longer have access to this."* Be careful with this type of "no." It is often caused by pride. It's our silent "stand" in response to an offense to us. Ever forget that pride is a killer of relationships.

Even when he asks you "what's wrong" and you say "nothing," you have not granted him access to your thoughts and are 1. keeping him out or 2. forcing him to try to find another door to reach you. Forcing him to find another, more acceptable door to "find you" is not good. Ladies, that is manipulation.

The constant "hide and seek" is not a game that men want to continuously play.

If he is reaching out to you or for you, it is because he cares about you. Don't continually make him "pass tests" and jump through hoops to prove that he cares for you.

And ladies, just because he didn't "just know" or automatically "notice or address it," does not mean that he doesn't care or that he is purposely not being attentive. Please give him a break. He is not you and doesn't live in your head.

If you need a hug, sometimes you are going to have to tell him. If you need to talk or have some quality time, sometimes you are going to have to initiate it. **Don't use your "no" as a way to hurt him or get revenge.** That is NOT profitable to him or you. You are not only hurting him, but, you are hurting your relationship. Believe me, your revenge is not worth losing your relationship.

The rebellious woman

The definition of rebellion is - the disobedience and/or defiance against authority.

"For rebellion is as the sin of witchcraft..." 1 Sam 15:23 (a)

This is a behavior and/or mindset is one that goes way further than just being uncooperative due to fear, self-awareness, not being comfortable, or offense. It is a direct attack to anything he says **because of his position or authority.**

Disagreeing with a decision or opinion is not rebellious. Being disagreeable only because it was him who said it, is an act of rebellion.

If something inside you says, *"You ain't gonna tell me what to do!"*, no matter what he says, then you have a problem on your hands.

If something inside you says, *"No **MAN** is going to tell me what to do!"*, then you have an even bigger problem on your hands.

How can one defy authority and then expect the one who is being defied to remain in or become more in authority?

A man does not want to pursue someone who fights or is going to fight him tooth and nail on everything, or fight him for his position. Again, God has called the husbands to be the head. He should not have to fight with you about him having a position or with you about his position. If he sees that **his biggest fight will be in his home if he has you there, then there is big possibility that he will not invite you to be a part of it.**

As a boyfriend, he is interviewing, training for, and learning if he is best fit for the position of husband and you are doing the same for the position of wife. When a woman is rebellious, she shows him that he will never be in the position to lead her because she refuses to follow. Her own actions can tell him that she will be one who will be fighting against him, instead of beside him.

Women, wives and girlfriends, when you take on rebellion you become his enemy. He may genuinely love you but may not trust you with his heart completely because of it.

***Disclaimer:** Disagreeing with a boyfriend/man you are in a relationship with does not necessarily constitute rebellion. Men, please do not manipulate with this principle. It is not a free pass to get what you want or press her on her strong moral judgement. There will be things that she can and will be willing to do and then there will be things that she cannot and won't be willing to do. In either case, if you want her to follow you, please be sure you are 1. following God and 2. escorting her to places God desires her to go.

The *"You'd better take me as I am. I have no desire to change or be better/Don't expect me or things to change or be better"* woman:

Ladies, sometimes we need to get past the *"that's just me"* and the *"I like me"* phases that cause negativity.

It's not about liking yourself, it's about you loving God, them, and yourself enough to aim for God's best in you. Strife is not your portion. Confusion is not your portion. God is not the author of confusion, so you must ask yourself "Where did it come from?" in your relationships.

If the answer continuously shows that you or your behavior cause or contribute to confusion, it is time to make a change for the better.

We must be careful that we are not confusing strife with attention. Sometimes we knowingly and unknowingly create stress, drama and can use strife to gain attention. We can cause a ruckus so that he will pay attention and see us. Ladies, believe me, that is not the attention you want or need.

You never want your man to associate you with problems and issues. The more you are associated with problems and issues, you begin to look like problems and issues.

The bible says in John 13:35 (NIV) *"By this all people will know that you are my disciples, if you have love for one another."* This should apply to relationships as well.

Ask yourself: ***"How does he know me?"***

Let him know you by your love. Let him see you as love.

Love is a safe place.

According to 1 Corinthians 13, "Love is patient. Love is kind. It does not envy. It does not boast. It is not proud. It does not dishonor others. It is not self-seeking. It is not easily angered. It keeps no record of wrongs. Love does not delight in evil but rejoices with the truth. It always protects, always trusts, always hopes, always perseveres..."

If you love him, then exhibit love to him and others. Let him see the light in you, not the shadow from you that makes everything around it dark. Love purposefully. Love intentionally. Intentionally be patient and not quick to anger. Intentionally be kind. Intentionally choose not to be dishonoring. Intentionally choose not to be self-seeking or delight in evil. Be intentional about how you love.

Remember that no man wants to build a house with a woman that he KNOWS is going to tear it down.

Sometimes a guy may genuinely love a woman and being around her, but he may choose not to take the relationship further than friendship or casual dating. It's not always about a guy being immature, indecisive, or intentionally playing with her heart, that causes him to pause "steps," step back or step away.

His stepping back may be that he sees potential, but is waiting to see if she will become the woman he can safely build with and store his treasures- his heart, his home, his future. Every guy has his reasons for going forward in a relationship, going backwards, standing still or stopping.

Though the reasons vary, some of the most common reasons (outside of the cases of personal insecurities, fears, and lack of commitment) are often due to **who she is and who she chooses to be** VS **who she is and what she can become.**

Often, we can classify ourselves as being a "good catch" or a "good woman" and that very well may be true. We do have our good qualities, but sometimes, who we say that we are is not always reflected in how we act, process or speak.

Being a "good woman" does not necessarily mean the woman is good to be around, good for him, good to him, and/or good to build with.

Although you may have good qualities, you may also have some not so pleasant qualities that make frequent appearances and can affect and/or infect those who are close or around you. **You could still be a good woman and have a bad attitude.** Now, no one is perfect, and honestly no one expects you to be perfect. All that many men ask for is **1. Respect, 2. Honor and 3. that the woman they love tries to aim for her best self.**

Aiming for your personal best, is something that says, *"I acknowledge I am also a work in progress and I choose daily to aim for progress."* instead of the typical *"Take me as I am. I'm finished and if you want me you'll deal with it."* Ladies, if you see that how you deal with anger is not the best, work on it. If you see that you could be nicer, choose to be nicer. If you see that you could be more encouraging, be more encouraging. If you could be more attentive, then become more attentive. If you see that you have an issue with saying "I'm sorry", then work on it. If you allow your jealously, frustration, rage, fear, etc. to lead you, then it may be time to change it. Whatever it may be, work on it.

If you are "worth it" then he is "worth it" too. You cannot demand respect and you are disrespectful. You should not demand that he hear you, but you don't have to hear him. You cannot require your significant other to give his best while holding onto or refusing to be yours. It is selfish of us to require that he be better or aim for his best, yet refuse to make any adjustments, modifications, and/or changes when it comes to ourselves.

Fix "It" Before You Bring It Together...

One of the biggest misconceptions in dating is that marriage is going to be an automatic fixer of bad habits, practices, mindsets and behaviors. The truth is: **Marriage is not going to fix what is broken in your relationship nor is it going to automatically transform, correct, or reset your mindset or the person you marry**.

Don't think that everything is going to be "fixed" when you get a ring and say, "I do."

- If they are a cheater as a boyfriend/girlfriend, marrying them is not going to make them not cheat.
- If they are a lying fiancé/boyfriend/girlfriend/friend, marrying them is not going to stop them from lying.
- If they are mean and abusive as a boyfriend/girlfriend, marriage is not going to change that.

Never think that marriage is a fixer to relational, emotional, psychological, and physical problems. You must deal with reality BEFORE you join realities. Marriage is not going to magically change bad behavior. A person needs to want to change, make a change, and walk in the consistency of change.

You cannot hold marriage expectations with people who don't really want to be married or want you as a responsibility.

Marriage is not just a ring or a title; it is a joining of two lifestyles, two mindsets, two goals, two hearts, in the process of becoming one. Marriage is the covenant of realities that embrace the possibilities. If his/her realities don't line up, don't join up.

Don't ignore principles. Don't dismiss the warning signs.

If you see that there is something that will potentially harm you OR your relationship, pay attention to it and handle it accordingly. Do not proceed just because you don't want to be alone, you feel as though you are getting older, or because it is expected of you.

You have a choice, use wisdom.

If he is uncappable of leading, then don't willingly or hastily make him your leader. If she has habits, mindsets, practice, and behaviors that tear down who you are or has the potential to destroy you and/or your household, re-evaluate what you are about to make a part of your vision, your future, and your legacy.

Choose wise counsel. Choose to see the relationship for its realities as well as its potentials. I would recommend that every couple go to counseling before getting married.

Why Marriage?

Marriage is a representation of Christ and His church.

What did Christ provide to His church that should be reflected in marriage?

Covenant- a contract, legally, relationally, and life binding vow that one belongs to the other in deed, partnership, title, hand, heirship, companionship, and has been granted position, authority, exclusivity, and priority above all others. Without a covenant, you hold no legal claim to ownership, authority, or position.

Joining/Unity-*Two to be one flesh*

In marriage, there should be a continued process of becoming one. Unity is also a must. The goal is not just walking, the goal is walking together, walking straight, and walking in power.

Heirship- In marriage a name grants not only position but in the authority and possessions that accompanies it.

Accountability-*Ecc. 4:9*

Husbands and wives support each other, especially in ways that others cannot. They have a position that is so close to their spouse that they have access, information, and vantage points that others are not privy to. This better allows them to see, protect, cover, and stand in the gap for each other.

Legacy: *Multiply and Reproduce*

From the beginning of time, we were called to be fruitful and multiply. Even if you were physically unable to have children, you still have the opportunity to teach, train, and be an example of what a healthy marriage relationship looks like. We all have the potential to lead just by being who we are. You never know who is following, so be the spouse/ married couple that is a prototype that should be reproduced.

If there are children, marriage should provide not only a foundation, but a structure and balance that nurtures, guides, protects, trains, and provides. Both mother and father play vital roles in the bringing up of legacy and in teaching to continue legacy.

God can also use you and your relationship to re-set your legacy, the legacy of your children, and even the mindset of others when it comes to legacy, by combatting generational curses and familiar spirits that have come from or travelled through bloodline.

The Role of the Husband

Responsibility

When you accept the role of husband, you accept the role of responsibility and all that comes along with it.

"Husbands, love your wives, even as Christ also loved the church, and gave himself for it" Ephesians 5:25

Jesus was the ultimate example of God's definition of husband. He assumed the full responsibility of His bride and gave His very life for her. All that HE possesses belongs to her, and all that He does is for her. Jesus did all that was required to bring His bride blameless access to His Father, His possessions, and Himself.

As a husband, you are to daily bring her to a place where she has free access to your Heavenly Father, all that you possess, and all that is you. When you become a husband, it says *"I give you all that I am, all that I have and all I am going to be"*. There is nothing that you have that she does not have access to.

Responsibility of standard

John 10:10b "... I have come that they might have life and that they might have life more abundantly"

As the husband, the reason you have taken a wife is to "create life". You both put life, as you knew it, down in order to come together to create something new. Life is no longer what is was, it is now what it is and will be, together.

In creating something new, you must be careful of old and "single" mindsets. It is no longer "I". You now hold the responsibility of establishing what that life should look like. And it should be better, in all aspects (naturally, spiritually, financially, physically, etc.), than where you took her from. Her life and the lives of your children should be more abundant.

When pursuing a wife, it's important to meet and grow from the standard in which she is accustomed to. Never take on a wife and give her less than what her father gave her. If she is covered spiritually, naturally, physically, emotionally, and financially, by her parents, then it would be only right that she be placed in capable hands that can provide the same and more. She and her guardians, whether it be father, mother, grandparent, aunties, family, church family, etc., need to know that she is covered under your leadership.

It is important that the life that you live be a good reflector for the life that you lead. Integrity is a must. Truth is a must. Love is a must. Accountability is a must from the head down. The standard in which you live will be the standard in which you lead. The standard that you set for your home not only affects the life of your wife, but it also establishes a standard that your sons will continue and your daughters will expect.

"Unto the woman he said, I will greatly multiply thy sorrow and thy conception; in sorrow thou shalt bring forth children; and thy desire shall be to thy husband, and he shall rule over thee.

And unto Adam he said, Because thou hast hearkened unto the voice of thy wife, and hast eaten of the tree, of which I commanded thee, saying, Thou shalt not eat of it: cursed is the ground for thy sake; in sorrow shalt thou eat of it all the days of thy life; Thorns also and thistles shall it bring forth to thee; and thou shalt eat the herb of the field; In the sweat of thy face shalt thou eat bread, till thou return unto the ground; for out of it wast thou taken: for dust thou art, and unto dust shalt thou return." Genesis 3:16-19

Responsibility to be the leader

"...and he shall rule over thee."

You are the head of your household, which means you establish the standard in God in which your household will run. As a "Ruler" you assume the responsibility of caring for those under your leadership.

It also means that God holds you responsible for the care of those he placed in your hands to care for. You can only "Rule" what He has given to you. And you should only "Rule" with the rules God has given you.

Please note: She is not your slave and should not be treated like a slave or spoken to as a slave. She is still to be respected and loved as Adam did when God presented Eve to him.

Adam's response to receiving her was one that understood that although she was his, she was also a gift from God to him. From the moment he saw her, he recognized that she was a part of him, bone of his bone and flesh of his flesh and to damage her in anyway is damaging to himself.

Responsibility of being the Provider

In addition to being a "Ruler" you must be a provider. It is a part of caring for those you lead. As the head, you also provide the standard of lifestyle.

It can be tiring and hard most of the time, but that is your responsibility. When Adam sinned, he and all men who followed suit were given the task of hard work to obtain food to eat and means to live.

"In the sweat of thy face shalt thou eat bread..."

The bread that you worked so hard to eat is not just for you anymore; it's for the house that you lead. It is a part of your responsibility as a husband to provide for your family.

1 Timothy 5:8 KJV "But if any provide not for his own, and specially for those of his own house, he hath denied the faith, and is worse than an infidel."

As you can see in the verse, God does not take a lightly view of a man providing for his household. The bible often equated the role of the husband to the example of Christ with His bride. Christ was the ultimate definition of Husband and provider.

Responsibility of definition

"And Adam called his wife's name Eve; because she was the mother of all living." Genesis 3:20 KJV

Adam identified her as **"who she was" when God presented** his help mate to him, but then, **when he assumed responsibility, he spoke to "who she was going to be."**

As a husband, it is your responsibility to speak what she is going to be in the position God is sending you to. Speak to the path she is going to lead. Help her to understand who she is and how important she is to you. Your assignments are intertwined. Though the steps you get to take there may be different, you still walk together.

It is important that what you say to her is what God says about her. The very fact that Adam called her Eve was a support to what God had just said to her. When Adam called her Eve it said *"I recognize, agree and support the assignment that God has given you, and I will call you 'by your name'."*

Responsibility of stability

"Thy wife shall be as a fruitful vine by the sides of thy house..." Psalms 128:3.

Vines cannot grow on things unstable.

Responsibility of ensuring she remains fruitful

"Thy wife...Thy house"

Sometimes you have to cut away things that would harm, kill, or injure the vine and its ability to produce fruit. Cut away any actions, behaviors, criticisms and conversations that create insecurities in her, because it limits her "fruit" production and chokes out the vine.

Feed her what she needs to grow: Affection, quality time, conversation, intimacy, planned time with her, planned surprises for her.

Find and create ways to make her feel special. Tell her she is special. Tell her you love her. Consider her. Ask her what she likes and then do what you can to use the info she gave you to please her. Pray for her. Let her hear you pray for her, words of affirmation, encourage her, ask her how you can help and then do that. See how you can make her job and/or responsibilities lighter even for a moment, give her a break and some time for herself to rest and regroup. These are just some of the ways that you can keep your vine healthy.

Water her with love and prayer. You are the head.

Responsibility of being the "Keeper of the Gate"

John 10 "I am the door..."

Spiritually and naturally you are the gate keeper. Nothing should have access to your family unless it comes by you. You must beware of what you let in and what you let out.

Anything that cannot be announced is probably something that shouldn't be in your house.

"Verily, verily, I say unto you, He that entereth not by the door into the sheepfold, but climbeth up some other way, the same is a thief and a robber." John 10:1 KJV

Unclean thoughts, suspicious conversation, lack of integrity, dishonesty, laziness, unforgiveness, are just some of the things that can rob your family of time, togetherness, oneness, and can destroy your home altogether.

As the keeper of the gate, you must be spiritually watchful of what spirits, things, practices, behaviors and/or mindsets **that you allow to be brought in** and **what you allow to remain**.

What you allow in, will have access to lead your children.

"But he that entereth in by the door is the shepherd of the sheep." John 10:2 KJV

- Infidelity leads your children to know infidelity and suffer the effects from it.
- Dishonesty leads your children to know dishonesty and suffer the effects from it.
- Drunkenness leads your children to know drinking and drunkenness and suffer the effects from it.
- Drugs and substance abuse leads your children to know drugs and substance abuse and suffer the effects from it.
- Verbal, physical and mental abuse leads your children to know verbal, physical and mental abuse and suffer the effects from it.

Things like corrupt communication, backbiting, lying, pornography, sexual indiscretions, lack of discipline, greed, rebellion, etc., once allowed inside the doorway, will begin to lead your family into places they need not be and down paths they should not go and can eventually control their destiny.

You are the gate keeper. Lock the doors.

Be sure to allow the Holy Spirit and the word of God to live in your home. God should not be a frequent visitor. He should live there. Which means your family gets to build a relationship with Him and HE is a part of your family.

"How do I build and teach relationship with GOD in my home?"

Conversation: Prayer is talking to God, wisdom is listening for an answer.

Teach your children how to pray. Pray as a family. Pray individually. Pray from your heart. There is no reason to say words that you, yourself, don't believe. Be honest, be open, be real. God loves you and He hears you and He is concerned with everything that has to do with you, as an individual and as a family.

Obedience: You cannot teach your kids to be obedient when you, yourself, are not obedient.

If God says "no," then you should say "no". If God says "yes," then your answer should be "yes." Whatever He says is what you should reflect and obey. You cannot teach a double standard and expect a solid lifestyle.

Education: Teaching how to guard the door with the "sword."

Do you know how to use the word and apply it to guarding your home? Do you know what to look out for and how to attack it when it comes?

It's not just enough to gain knowledge at a Saturday or Sunday Church service. You must study the word daily. Get life books that will build you up in God and the word, in addition to your studies. There are many Christian books of wisdom out there written by Generals in the faith. Dr. Bill Hamon, TD Jakes, and John Bevere are just a few of the many authors who write books that can help grow you.

Be sure that when you read, you read with understanding and not just trying to hurry to the next page. It will not help you to say, *"I finished the book,"* if you have learned nothing.

Husbands, you also have the responsibility of vision.

"Where there is no vision, the people perish..." Proverbs 29:18a

You are the leader for your house. You need to have a God-given vision. Your family should know where you are going and how you want to get there.

If you are going to "move as one," then it would be wise to inform the people that they are moving. It is not wise to just get up and do some life changing things without informing the ones that are with you that life is about to change. By doing that, you can cause confusion, resistance, mutiny, and cause damage to their sense of stability.

The Role of the Wife

Along with supporting him and his vison, being in unity, and supporting and encouraging him in everything in the chapter "The Role of the Husband," there are a few more key things that may need to be touched on or reiterated in this chapter.

There is a difference in you taking position and in you accepting responsibilities. When you accept the title and position of "Wife", you are responsible for respecting and reflecting his authority. When you accept the position of "Wife," you not only have position, but you also have authority and you become his "favor."

You are: Favor

"He that finds (obtains) a wife, finds (has in his possession) a good thing and obtains (gains) favor with the Lord." Proverbs 18:22

When your husband marries you, he stands to inherit the favor of God that accompanies having you.

Man obtains wife -> Wife is a good thing -> Man gains favor with the Lord

A wife is only accompanied by favor when she is a wife. A girlfriend will not do. No matter what you bring to the table, it will always be lacking when you do it your own way. Favor does not accompany disobedience, consequence does.

You <u>ARE</u>: Good

The same verse (Prov. 18:22) applies to this principle.

Let "good" be defined as and reflect anything that is: above reproach, above standard, of a Godly nature, virtuous, righteous, moral, honest and has integrity, has quality, commands peace, allows harmony, and has merit.

The definition is WHO YOU ARE and what you were called to be.

As a wife, you:

> Bring "good". Accompany "good". Respond with "good". Impart "good". Love by doing and being "good". You are a "good" listener. You follow "good" and teach "good". You require "good". Invite "good". Delight in "good". You are called "Good". Influence "good" and attract "good".

All that you are, becomes **all that you are to him**. You <u>ARE</u> a good thing. It is your job to <u>BE</u> "good."

You are: His treasure

- Worth is far above rubies -*Proverbs 31:10*
- Husband's crown- Prov. 12:4

"For where your treasure is, there will your heart be also"-
Matt 6:21

In giving you their name, husbands invest all that they are
and all that they have so that they can invest in the treasure
of their heart that is you...

You are: A helpmate

Genesis 2:18

Eve was created as a helpmate for Adam.

**God saw that Adam needed help, not that he could not
function.** Adam was already up and working when God
presented him with Eve. Helpmate does not mean boss. You
were meant to help. You see what he cannot see, and be
where he cannot be. You cover him in prayer. You encourage
him. You are right beside him in battle, covering things that
would attack him, his God-given vison, your marriage, your
home, and your children. You are under his leadership to do
what you can to help him as he leads.

Understanding and operating in the power of vision

"Where there is no vision, the people perish..." Proverbs 29:18a

You are a reflection of your husband, which means you
operate in his vision. You are necessary. It is important that
you not only see his vision, but understand it and work with

him to build it. There is power in your position. He needs YOU, to see his vision AND he needs you to SEE his vision. When he sees you, he should be able to see his vision, and when he goes to look at his vision, he should be able to see you.

Wives help maintain and regain his "sight."

"Where there is no vision, the people perish..."

Sometimes life can cause him to forget or be discouraged, and he can lose or give up on the vision. You are his life partner, his rib, his help mate. Help him with encouragement, affirmation and assurance. Speak what God says about him into him. Remind him of his God given vision. Pray for him and over him daily. He is under attack, and what affects him, affects you.

The children of Israel kept what was called "frontlets", to remind them of what God has done and His promise towards them. The frontlets said, "God blesses, God guides and God delivers." Let that be a continuous frontlet that resonates throughout your home. Be the reminder that says "God blesses. God guides. God delivers." Encourage him through the word, that he can do it, that he will make it, and that you support him.

He needs to know that you support his vision, that you can see what he sees, and that you are behind him.

Train your children to follow, understand, and to have vision.

"Where there is no vision, the people perish..."

You are the nurturer and the re-enforcer of the home. It is your job to teach the vision to your children. You both are training them in the way they should go and you are also training them so that they will be able to train others. It's a two-fold goal. What you do today, affects not only today, but also tomorrow.

As you and your husband align yourselves with God, be sure not to leave your children behind. Vision often requires sight and almost always requires some insight. Don't just teach what you know, teach what you show and why you do it.

Ladies, dating and looking to marry:

Before you become a wife, be sure you see the vision and that it's a vision that you are willing to support and follow.

Let's define "people" in the scripture verse as: You.

"Where there is no vision, you will perish..."

Women who desire to get married should never get with a man that has no vision.

When you align yourself with a man, you align yourself with his vision. Men were designed to lead and you were designed to be a help mate. In order for you, as a woman, to flourish in your role as wife, there must be a "vision" for you to "help".

If he does not have and refuses to have a vision of marriage, then there is no reason to waste your time. You will never be helpful there.

If he doesn't have a vision for the future and is complacent with doing, being and having nothing, then you will be aligning yourself up with nothing.

If he just talks about vision, but never puts any real action towards it, then it might be wise not to align yourself with it. A double minded man does not bring stability. A man who believes in his vision will take steps towards it.

In Our Nature

Men:

When it comes to women, it's in her nature to want to help. We were born that way. We do not, for the most part, try to step on your toes or into your lane on purpose, but it can, and more than likely will happen from time to time.

In our efforts to help, we can often be focused on having your back and still miss the *"I don't need your help"* signals. Be patient with us. It's often hard to balance the *"I'll wait for him to ask for help"* and the *"take initiative."*

Our *"take initiative"* approach is not to slight you. It's our way of not putting added loads on you when we know you are handling so much already. Many times, our "initiatives" are meant for good, and can happen in subtle ways.

For example,

- She may have known you were going to have a long day at work, so she packed your lunch.
- She knew you had an appointment so she washed your shirts and helped prepare your clothes, or
- She saw you needed some "you time," so she stayed out or took the kids out for a while so you could have a little time to yourself.

All of those are examples of initiatives. She is thinking of you and preparing for you. She does these things to help take the burden off of you, even if it's only for a little while.

Although she may have good intentions, those "initiatives" may not be appreciated or welcomed if it is not understood.

When misunderstood, that lunch could be viewed as her controlling his diet.

When misunderstood, that wardrobe "help" could be viewed as *"She is trying to tell me what to wear. I'm a grown man and I know how to dress myself."*

When misunderstood, the going out, expressed or unexpressed, could be viewed as *"She is avoiding me."* or be seen as if she is making executive decisions without your consent or approval.

Women:

It's not always ok to take initiative. Sometimes he just wants to do it himself. It's ok to ask if he needs help sometimes, before just jumping to do things.

Sometimes, it may require a subtle "heads-up" to let him know what you are doing, just to let him know he is being considered and that this is not a "hostile take-over."

Don't stop helping, just use wisdom in doing it. If you are going to set out a shirt, ask him what he would like to wear. He may have a picture in his head that you can't see. If you are going to pack a lunch, pack it and occasionally let him know (if the money is there) that he has an option, in case he wants something different. Allow him room to say what he wants. Try seeing his vision and then you will better know how to proceed.

The "initiative" is good but it's going to take wisdom in application to be effective.

The "what to do" never comes before the "what."

The bible says that only a fool answers a matter before hearing all the sides. We are not foolish women. Take some time to hear before you answer. Sometimes your husband may be speaking louder than you think.

Sometimes it's difficult to find that balance, but never give up. Always continue to try. In all things pray and pray for wisdom. You are a HELP MATE, you can do this!

Men and Women:

How do we reach understanding?

- **Communicate with the intent of reaching understanding.** Nobody just KNOWS what you want to be done or how you want it. It can be difficult to find the balance from either side, male and female. The human condition doesn't always know what we want. In many cases, we just know what we don't want when we see it or are experiencing it.

- **When communicating, it's best that we gather our thoughts before we present them.** If you don't understand or know what you want, what makes you think they will?

- **When he/she comes to you to ask a question, don't be upset saying *"you don't have to ask me,"* then turn around and get upset when they do something without asking you.** It's confusing and frustrating. Let them ask. It's not because they are incompetent; they are just getting your view on things before creating/executing their plan.

- **Understand that there will be times he/she may not be able to ask or give you an answer.** Sometimes, based on the time sensitivity and/or circumstances, they will NOT be able to ask your consent or thoughts on the matter. It is not something that should happen every single time, but it is something that is prone to happen from time to time. If there is a need or desire for information, discuss it when the time is right and/or allows for it.

Men:

It's good for you to take initiative but do not forget Consideration.

Never bark orders, especially to plans that only live in your head. We do not automatically know what to do.

Be aware of the details. It is frustrating to us when you come up with plans and expect us to execute them quickly and efficiently, without you having an understanding of what it is going to take to get it done.

Example 1:

A husband wakes up his wife to be ready for church in 30 minutes...

From his side:

> The man wakes up and then wakes up his wife to be ready for church in 30 minutes. He gets up, showers, shaves and gets dressed. He looks for his wife and finds her just getting in the shower. Frustrated, he goes to eat breakfast so she can have a little more time. After he eats, he goes to find his wife so they can leave. When he enters the room, she still is not even dressed yet.

> **His response: Anger and Frustration.**

From her side:

> Husband wakes her up and says be dressed and ready for church in 30 minutes. She has to scramble to fix breakfast, get the kids cleaned and ready, iron clothes, help her husband find his socks, fix his tie, and search for his cuff links. Twenty-five minutes has passed and she still has to shower, do her hair, and do her makeup. She finally jumps in the shower when in comes her husband fussing about not wanting to be

late. She hurries to try to dress and *"oh no!"*, she just got a run in her stockings from trying to rush. They are past the 30 minute mark, her husband is upset, the kids are crying and she hasn't even dressed yet....

Her response: Frustrated and feels like crying.

Consideration is important. In cases like these, you must make allowances and adjustments. If you are late, then you are late. You cannot expect everyone's process to fit within your limited span of time. If you are limited in time, then they are limited.

Teamwork helps.

If you are going to need her to help you or see that she has a lot on her hands, then you might consider helping her. In the example, she had responsibilities to take care of and then she had to get herself ready. If she had help, it would have been less stressful on her, less frustrating for him, and they would have been able to leave the house sooner.

Preparation helps.

If you know you have to go somewhere in the morning, 1. Prepare your clothes, 2. Prepare yourself and 3. Prepare your clock. Having your clothes ready before hand eliminates the need for rushing and ironing in the morning. Having your mind and things prepared for what needs to be done the next morning can help with making the mornings run a bit smoother. Set your clock to give you and your family enough time to get themselves ready.

Time Management helps.

Waking up late is going to happen, and that is okay. Things will happen that we cannot prepare for. Just don't make it a habit. Don't knowingly wake her up with just enough time to get YOU ready, when you know she has to get herself ready, and, if you have children, get them ready too. Allot for who you have and what they need. If they need an hour to get ready, wake them up 1 ½ hours before you need to leave. That way you allot for what needs to be done and incidentals, like in cases where there is an accident and there needs to be a wardrobe change, so that people are not rushing or feeling rushed.

Example 2:

Husband invites friends over to eat and fellowship/hang out.

His side:

> He thinks, *"They'll come over it will be good. I'll order some chicken. Yep. This is a good idea. Let me tell my wife."*
>
> He then calls his wife and says, ***"Honey I invited a few people over later. Don't worry, I'm going to buy some chicken. I told them to come around 5."***

Her mind when he tells her:

> "ok... Let's see... I have to clean the house up for company...He says he is buying chicken... What about the drinks?... I will have to make some sides.... We may need paper plates because the dishes are going to be overwhelming... Can't forget the cups... If we have something to drink, then we are going to need ice...Wait... Do we have anything here to drink?... Are they bringing kids? How many will be there? What will they do and where will we have them?... Is that area kid proof?... Is it teenager proof?... What about the clean up afterwards?... What am I going to wear?..."

What started as a good idea for him, became a job for her.

It's ok to invite, but it may be wisest to ASK HER FIRST.

1. You never know what she is doing already or has planned to do. She may not have the time to accomplish everything.

2. There might be an appointment, assignment or event that you are forgetting that was already scheduled to take place at the same date and time.

3. She may need time to complete the details it takes to accomplish what you are asking.

You are not asking for permission, you are asking if this is the best course of action for your team. Don't forget you are not alone in the decisions you make. Your decisions affect her more than you know.

Ask what time is good for her.

She knows what has to be done and the estimated time it will take to complete the details. Again, you are not asking permission, you are just being considerate of her.

Picking up chicken is good, but she may still need your help.

She appreciates that you tried to help out with the work load by stopping for chicken, BUT she will also need your assistance in getting things together. Do not just come in and kick back and feel your job is done. Ask her where you can help.

Although these were just examples, the principles remain the same. Many initiatives require her to have an added work load and require more details than you know. Be considerate of her and what she may be feeling when you do what you do. Lend a hand wherever you can. Try not to always make last minute decisions. When you can, plan ahead and give her time to accomplish what she needs to do.

Dealing With "Them"

Wives, remembering that man was created in God's image and likeness, we can better understand there are things that can be reflected in the nature and desire of our husbands.

There quite a few things we can learn from the nature and desires of God that can be applied to how we should also deal with nature and desires of our husbands.

- **Have Faith**-You must have faith in your husband.
- **Praise**- Tell him how good he is. Speak to his strengths and accomplishments.
- **Give thanks**- No matter how small, say, *"thank you."* No matter how big, say, *"thank you."*
- **Honor**
- **Do not complain. Ask.**
- **Don't be afraid to ask.**
- **Spend quiet time, listening.** Use this time not to ask for anything, especially attention. Your focus should be him and him alone.
- **Take time away from everything and everybody to spend quality time, just you and him.**
- **Do, give and say what pleases him.** - If he likes chocolate bars occasionally give him a chocolate bar. If he likes football, take him to a place where they

have sports and food, throw him a tailgating party, or take him to a game. If he loves a certain type of food, fix it, order it, take him to a restaurant where he can get it. Etc.

- **Acknowledge him**-Don't just make a decision that affects the household, talk it out first.   Recognize, consider and communicate with your husband. His views and thoughts are important too. He may know and see another side of things. Discuss it first, listening to the pros and cons and be sure the both of you pray for wisdom.

- *"In all they getting, get an understanding..."*- **Get an understanding.** Listen to get understanding. Try to hear his point.

- *"Thou shall have no other gods before me..."*- **Be care of entertaining, befriending and communicating with other men AND be careful not to make any person more important, more valued, or give "more affections" than your spouse.**

Husbands:

Woman was created out of man, so the same attributes that you have, she has them and then some.

The same principles written for her in the section above, still apply to you. **<u>In addition to those principles,</u>** don't forget that the word says, *"Husbands love your wives as Christ loved the church and gave himself for it."*

Be like Christ,

- **Give of yourself**

- **Take time to talk....** - Jesus took every opportunity He could to talk, share and impart.

- **Take time to listen**

- **Be patient.**

- **Speak in love.**

- **Don't throw stones, save her.**

- **Be open for the children to come.** Don't deny access to you. Your children need to see that they can come to you and your wife needs to see/know that it's not only she, but also your children, who can freely come to you.

- **Walk in your authority.**

- **Speak to the storms**- Use your voice. Speak what SHALL BE in the midst of the storms. Don't speak out of fear or out of what you see naturally. She needs your confidence. You are the leader. What you say, they not only follow but they also believe. Speak faith, not fear.

- **Pray with her, for her, and over her.**

- **When tempted, resist and rebuke the devil.** If you see the enemy, do not entertain him in any way, whether it be in thought, pride, the things that you allow yourself to see, lust, sin or any temptation that could harm you, your character, your name, her, her emotions or anything that is connected to her, your children and/or legacy. If the enemy comes to kill, steal and destroy, then what do you think he wants to do with you, your wife, your household, or your marriage?

- **Teach how to build kingdom.** -There is a vision for your house, know it and share it, and then pray for wisdom in achieving it. It will not happen in a day but it will happen. Remember you are a team and can only reach this goal together.

- Jesus fed, taught, and healed the multitudes but he did not live there...- **Ministry and fellowshipping with others is good, but even more of your time should be being invested in and set aside for your bride.** You MUST come away. There will ALWAYS be a multitude.

- *"Come now let us reason together..."*- **Talk it out.** You and she are one. Hear what she is saying, don't assume you know what she is going to say. When you do this you subconsciously shut down and shut out what she is saying.

- *"Jesus wept..."*- **Go ahead and feel. It's ok.** If she is crying, hurting, broken, be there with and for her. Don't rush her in her pain or rush her to get over it. Go to her, to where she "is." Understand with her, be patient, and allow for there to be tears. You just wipe them away and speak life to her until there is a "resurrection".

- **Be and give living water.** - If she is the vine, then she needs water. It is your job to nourish her and give her what she needs to grow. Remember "vines" grow with water and SON light.

- **Be the Bread of Life.** - Feed her physically, emotionally, romantically, psychologically, and spiritually. You be the bread that brings life to her, not take life from her. You must watch what you say to her and about her because it's feeding her. You have to be the one that is careful that your "food" doesn't get her "sick."

In knowing that she is an extension of you, bone and flesh, you must be careful that what you are doing and saying is not cutting her flesh and damaging her bone.

Bone is structure. A damaged structure could make the whole house fall down.

Be careful with your words. Think twice before speaking in anger and frustration. Ask yourself, *"Will this break her bones or heal her?"*

If it's something that will break her, don't say it! It's ok to be angry, but how you react in anger is important. Be intentional with your words.

Communication is a necessary part of a woman's composition. It is an entryway and doorway to her heart. Her heart is one of the most delicate parts of her. You as her husband, have the ability to go right passed the door and straight to her heart. You must remember that the power of life and death is in the tongue. What you say goes straight to her heart. Be careful of what you speak, you could kill her...

Ask yourself *"What would my words make my wife's heart look like?"*

Now, how can it be better?

In Time of Grief

In relationships, you will encounter times of extreme loss and grief. Everyone deals with grief differently, but it is important that we become aware of **1. the needs of others** and **2. the affect it may be having on you and/or your relationships.**

Men:

You deal with loss and grief differently than women do. It is important to BE AWARE when it comes to yourself and to BE INTENTIONAL when it comes to the women in your life and around it.

Be intentionally patient.

She will not know how loss and grief affect her before it affects her. She may tell herself she is going to be alright, but when things actually happen, she may be torn to pieces. Her emotions are open. She may lash out, become frustrated or frustrating, she may cry, she could shut down or shut up, and she could be holding in everything and tell herself things are "ok," all while, piece by piece, she is breaking down on the inside.

Be intentionally sensitive.

You process differently. Don't expect her to be "ok" with her grief and don't give her a time limit to grieve. Her process is her process, and your process is your process. Especially in cases of death, you must watch what you say and how you handle her.

Be intentionally wise when speaking.

Don't use clichés to convey your thoughts. They can come off insensitive and not genuine. Be careful how you express your feelings. If you were "prepared for it", it's ok not to announce it to her. No matter how long she had "to prepare," she will never be prepared. Emotion never gets fully dressed before the party.

Be intentionally prayerful.

While she is going through her process, she needs you, above all else, to pray. Whether it's your mother, daughter, wife, other family members or friend, she could really use prayer. It brings strength and comfort in times of chaos and stress. Prayer helps calm the noise. Only God sees the areas where she is broken and can heal them.

Be intentionally careful.

It may be your instinct to "fix it" or try to "help," but don't set yourself up in a trap. Friends do not get an all-access pass to you when they are grieving or otherwise, especially when you are married.

This is often a season when the "outside woman" will try to make her move. Whether she is grieving or you are, it is important that you pay attention, set strategic boundaries, and guard your heart and mind. When certain women see emotion, they play on it to their advantage. BE CAREFUL.

Your emotional state is your vulnerable state. Because you are no longer thinking "logically," you are more open for attack. Remember: Men think logic OR Emotion.

Be mindful of hurtful words.

Hurt people tend to hurt other people. Be watchful of what you say to others when you are grieving. Grief is not an excuse to be mean. Emotions may run high in time of grief, and that's okay. It is ok to feel but be mindful of how you speak and treat others.

Don't refuse to grieve.

It is a myth that men are not supposed to cry and/or feel emotion. God gave you tears and feelings for reason. Don't be afraid to allow grief its process. It can help you heal and find a sense of release. When we hold grief in and refuse to process, we can become stuck and/or bitter at what has happened. And, life for you becomes stuck in the moment of loss. Grief is a natural process that allows us to release emotion and helps us regain our bearings. You need it as well as women need it.

Women: Be mindful when you and/or others are grieving.

Be mindful of how you "pick up."

You are a sponge. Things go in and things come out, but you must also remember that sometimes it leaves residue. Emotionally you can feel when others feel, and often sympathy becomes empathy and, when unchecked, it can wreak havoc on your emotions.

When something is being deposited, we feel **as** we process. For example, a girlfriend comes to tell you about how her husband has been mistreating her. As she speaks to you, you may hear words but feel 1. Anger at him for what he is doing, 2. Sadness for the sorrow she feels, 3. Contempt for what he has done to her, 4. Vengeful for the emotional and internal scars you see on her, and 5. Compassion/ judgement for her allowing herself to go through it. All of these emotions continue to grow and may even pick up other emotions as the conversation continues. And next thing you know, you are harboring unforgiveness towards him for hurting your friend.

Many times, it happens just like that. Frequently, the funny end to the story is that the friend and her husband have gotten it together, forgave each other and moved on, while you are standing there with your bags of emotion, still carrying them with you.

You must be careful of what you pick up emotionally. It can become baggage and it can become heavy.

"Cast your burden on the Lord, and He shall sustain you; He shall never permit the righteous to be moved" (*Psalm 55:22*).

Sometimes you are going to have to throw it as soon as you get it. Only God knows the whole story and HE knows what should and shouldn't be done. Seek HIM first, then release it/her/him/them into God's capable hands.

No matter how "light" the burden is, if it's causing you to carry more than God intended, release it to Him. There is nothing you can physically do about it, other than pray and receive His wisdom and direction, anyway.

Be mindful of what and how much you "put down."

There is certain information you should not share with everyone. Granted, you will have things and feelings you can share, but some information is private. There are also some parts of you that you, yourself, may not understand how, what or why you feel?

Be mindful of where you "put down."

Where you release your thoughts and feelings is important. Not every place is good ground to plant your "seed."

Seeds carry potential, but they also carry DNA. In this instance, it tells more about you than the words you are actually saying. Your tone and choice of words can speak to frustration and unhappiness, showing others ways to "get in" and ways to get you "out."

242

When we speak, we share secrets about ourselves that we do not even know we reveal. Predators, both male and female, seek weaknesses and search for, knowingly and unknowingly, vulnerabilities and accessibilities.

Some women hear your information, your problems, and your heart and will pray for you, with you, give you sound advice, and be there for you in their own way.

And then there are some, who use the information as Intel to gain access into your marriage, your relationship, and/or your position.

Women, we don't just talk when things are bad. We talk when things are good, giving others an inside view of an intimate/ private life. It can also be the same or even worse when we carry our burdens to men outside of marriage.

When we speak, both men and women, we show which doors are locked, which are broken, and which ones are open. Many of the access points become vulnerable and visible when we share the part of us that is emotion.

The difference with women sharing "us" with men outside of marriage is that we can begin to use them as a crutch, a savior, and make them our go to person or personal "boo." We will invest emotion where we think it's safe, and it's often to our own demise when we do not filter what we say and to who we are saying it to.

It's not wrong to share certain things, but PLEASE BE ADVISED: Share in wisdom.

Sometimes, the person you really need to talk to is God. Prayer is always in order. It helps you not only get things off of your chest, but you can also find a sense of peace, and often walk away with knowledge, wisdom and a better or different perspective than when you came in.

Begin with the end in mind.

Have conversations that evoke and involve solutions and the process of reaching it. It makes no sense to only release words and walk away with no direction, strategies, wisdom, sense of peace, etc., given to or about it. Talk in purpose.

Be mindful of who you hang around when you grieve.

Negative habits, behaviors, words, and dispositions can affect and often "IN-fect."

Healing is a process.

There is something to be said about the healing process. We all experience it, in one way or another, but no person knows how long a wound will actually take to heal. We may know seasons, and we may even know how to help the healing process, but there is no one but GOD who can tell you the specific date and time.

Grief is very similar to an open wound. It can often resemble or be categorized as "bleeding internally."

Some cases of grief cut deeper than people can see or understand. And then, there are some "cuts" or "injuries" that hit arteries, where our hearts are not only affected, but it brings us close to death in certain areas, when it's not identified and treated.

Men and Women:

Sometimes you may need to be heard and need help.

In times of grief, it may be wise to speak to those with wisdom. In cases of extreme grief (divorce, death, extreme loss), it may be wise to seek counsel from those who wisely use their professional experience to help you heal healthily. It could be a wise pastoral team, a grief counselor, a Chaplin, a psychologist, financial adviser, Cleansing Streams, or other effective faith based grief ministry groups. The goal is to speak in a safe environment and know you are receiving Gods wisdom, direction and love throughout and through those who have been trained to not only listen but give sound advice.

We may have friends and love ones that want to help. That's okay. We tend to want to help and heal those we love and care for. We all can be guilty of trying to help even when we don't know how.

Don't be discouraged or discouraging when someone comes with a "band-aid" trying to fix your wound.

A "band-aid," although something that was meant to and designed to help, will not really help in closing or covering deep wounds. Even though the thought or gesture is nice, we must still be careful with the wounded areas. The area needs to remain "clean" or it will become infected, worsen the wound and/or prolong the healing.

Whether it is you or them, care must be given when applying anything to a wound.

Beware of "infection."

Generally, those who can become infectious, don't do it because they are malicious or hateful, they just might be bleeding too. Usually when people offer help, they really have a genuine desire to.

The term "hurt people hurt other people" can also be applied in times of grief. Those who are bleeding can sometime hurt those who bleed. Sometimes people can even reopen old wounds and/or cause wounds to those who weren't bleeding before.

Damages can happen from something we say, do, don't say, don't do, etc., both knowingly and unknowingly.

It could be as simple as something like withdrawing your support because you are angry, that causes things like insecurity, distrust, sadness, and brokenness in others. Your one action (withdrawal) from a reaction (anger) caused reactions. Whether you knowingly withdrew or unknowingly withdrew yourself, it still had an effect.

Try to understand where you/they are.

Usually, we mean well, but we may not be in the physical or emotional position to carry the burdens of ourselves or others any further than to the throne of God.

Whether is your time of grief or others time of grief, give and receive in wisdom. Take time to gain wisdom to know what is a closure, a balm, a band-aid, and what has the possibility to infect.

Sometimes, we or others will bring a balm or something that will soothe for a moment. Sometimes, it will be like a band-aid that may cover just a part. There may be times where there is God given healing words and/or loving deeds that may help reach the place of healing. But, each time, we must be careful to not infect or become infected.

Grief is a natural PROCESS. It's something all of us will go through, whether it be from death or from any other emotional or physical loss.

Ecclesiastes 3:1-8

"To every thing there is a season, and a time to every purpose under the heaven: A time to be born, and a time to die; a time to plant, and a time to pluck up that which is planted; A time to kill, and a time to heal; a time to break down, and a time to build up; A time to weep, and a time to laugh; a time to mourn, and a time to dance; A time to cast away stones, and a time to gather stones together; a time to embrace, and a time to refrain from embracing; A time to get, and a time to lose; a time to keep, and a time to cast away; A time to rend, and a time to sew; a time to keep silence, and a time to speak; A time to love, and a time to hate; a time of war, and a time of peace."

Seasons require time.

Grief has its season, allow it time.

A time of silence:

Silence can be a part of grief. There may be a time when you are a loss for words and just want to be alone. There is a time for that, and it's ok.

Just remember:

1. Although this moment may call for you to be away from people, you are not truly alone, and

2. This is just for a moment.

You cannot truly enjoy the fullness of life by living in isolation. Life connects us to others. We need others and others need us.

You have a purpose and so do your friends. Even if it's a shoulder to cry on or a listening ear, it's good to have someone that you can be yourself with. It doesn't make you weak to speak, and it doesn't make you strong to be silent. Even Jesus had His alone time with God, but He returned to His disciples, His friends, His assignments, and His call.

A time of war:

- **<u>The internal war</u>**: There will be times when you may be at war with yourself, your emotions, your thoughts, your goals, your past, your present, your hope for the future or lack of. Don't worry, life is just "recalculating". The road you are on just took an unexpected turn. The cause of this grief has made you feel lost. Emotionally and mentally you are trying to find your way back. Oftentimes, "being lost" makes us feel confused and frustrated. When we begin focusing more on "how we got here", instead of "how we get out", we can become stuck in one place or even more lost.

- **The external war:** There will be times in grief where you feel like fighting. KNOW YOUR ENEMY.

You wrestle not against flesh and blood but against principalities. Go to the root of it, not the fruit of it. Your biggest enemies are the ones you CAN'T see. Fight but fight through prayer. Take up the "weapons" of the spirit, aim and shoot. Your "weapons of warfare" will only be mighty and truly effective when it's through God. That's the only way to "pull down the strong holds," break the captivity, and break free from things that bind.

Fighting your neighbor or your loved ones will never bring you peace. It may cause external silence for a while, but it can cause more damage than good. Use your energy to pray for them and speak peace. You have the ability to shift atmospheres with your words and sound, use it and use it for good.

A time to cry:

If you feel like crying, cry. Sometimes grief requires tears. It is the body and soul's way of release.

In time of extreme grief, it is a myth that strength is not showing emotion or not crying. Especially in cases of death and/or serious loss, we can pretend it's "ok" in front of others to cover the effects of grief, when internally we are falling apart. Strength is not in holding it in. Strength is knowing when to let it out and choosing to let it out.

A time to heal:

Allow for time to heal and time to deal. Don't rush it. Healing is a process. Rushing can cause a wound to be re-opened and even become infected. Some wounds will require intensive care by the Master Physician. God may need to cut away certain things and people that may cause you to become infected. God may need to surgically remove things that may block the heart or cause it to become "attacked." He may need to catch some things that has been trying to reach your brain to keep you paralyzed or stunt your growth. Whatever it may be, allow it time. Allow Him time.

Be aware of where you are in your seasons.

Seasons have a beginning and an end. Don't stay in your winter coats in June. When you have healed, go out from the place of grief and do not return. Moments of sadness may occur when you remember special dates and precious moments and that's ok. We all have those times. We remember and we keep living.

Don't allow grief to become you. The process of grief allows us time and steps to healthily heal from emotional and mental pains, but, like everything else, too much of something can be unhealthy.

When your healing time has ended, it's time to become an "outpatient." You still keep in contact with your "REGULAR PHYSICIAN", but you will then be in position to go and to live. Grief never comes to make us sedentary. It puts us in a position to be healed, not to be dead.

Grief is meant to be a season, not to be a lifetime.

Communication: Addressing the Feelings

Sometimes you have to address the feelings before you can address the matter.

When a person says, *"I feel..."*, it is no longer just about the issue, it now includes their feelings.

For example:

> A man and a woman are talking about how she feels.
>
> The woman says: **"I feel like you hurt my feelings when you yelled at me."**
>
> The man's response is: **"I was yelling because you did _____."**

This example happens a lot with both men and women on both sides of the scenario. Many times, the feelings are missed in the conversation.

If the first response that was made was to address the reason then this does not/will not solve your problem. To solve the problem, you must break it down.

In these cases, it is best to think: First reach the person, then reach the issue.

Prioritize. Obviously, the person means more than the issue, so take that into consideration. Their feelings and how you address it may be the barrier that keeps you from reaching the actual issue AND could create more issues.

In the example, a wiser approach would have been for him to address his part in her feelings. When a person says, *"you hurt my feelings..."* that calls for an apology. Whether the cause for yelling was your fault or not, hurt was caused. To not address this and fix this will cause more damage internally, both emotionally and mentally.

When you do not address a person's feelings, it says two things: 1. ***"This person does not care about me."*** and 2. ***"This is not a safe place to share my heart."***

Remember: Men think left side or right side of the brain, which is either logic OR emotion. Women use both sides of the brain, which is logic AND emotion.

Men:

When thinking logically, it is wise to be conscious of her feelings.

Be careful of how you say things and what you are communicating when thinking logically. Sometimes, guys can come off a little rough and insensitive when they are being direct and to the point. To women, it can often sound like orders, reprimand, or them being crass, even when it may not have been the guy's intent. Just be mindful of how you are saying what you have to say to her.

Again, women do not disconnect from their emotions, they are a packaged deal. When communicating with a woman it is wise to take her emotional side into consideration. Pray for wisdom in listening. Let her share things with you, don't try to TAKE it. This is not a rush, get to the point conversation. However long it takes is however long it takes. If she is sharing, it is up to her to decide how big of a "piece" to share.

Some women will not be forth coming with their emotion if they do not feel that this is a safe place to share it. In these cases, it is best not to become upset when she doesn't want to tell you. Just create an atmosphere that allows her to be comfortable in doing so, and remember that when she opens up, SHE DOES NOT WANT YOU TO FIX IT, she wants you to listen.

Women:

Try understanding both of his sides.

When communicating with HIM, it's is wise to see things from his side. If he is on his logical side understand that he is not thinking emotionally. He is not trying to be callused or short with you, he is trying to get to the point. If he is on the emotional side, don't look at him funny. You are in a perfect position to understand and bring logic to his emotion.

If he is upset and frustrated about things like his work, life, or lack of reaching dreams by a certain age, **don't fuss him out of it.** Listen, support, encourage and pray him out. Pray for wisdom in seeing and God will give you wisdom in doing. Pray for what it is that you see, God will begin to show you what's beneath the surface. Ask God to reveal strategies to build.

Now, many times the building process takes time and construction and it will often call for adjustments. You may have to be the one who adjusts. DON'T COMPLAIN in this process. Pray for wisdom and to see the hand of God in and within this process. It may feel uncomfortable, but keep praying.

When he is down, encourage more. When he wants to talk, listen more and pray for the wisdom in listening.

Women, remember that you are created to be a helpmate. You as an emotional and logical being can bring the balance. You do have the opportunity to see different angles, BUT you cannot see clearly if you always have "tears" in your eyes.

Men and Women:

Saying "I know" is not enough. You have to DO something.

One of the worst things you can do when your spouse is trying to tell you how he/she feels, what hardship your actions have cause him/her, or what needs to change, is saying **"I know but..."**

When a person is telling you how they feel about an issue, or about a particular thing or action, it's important to pay attention. When people are expressing how they feel, it is not about the issue, it's about how they are affected by it.

If it's something they desire to be heard on, then it's something that needs to be acknowledged and addressed.

Never respond to a person sharing how they feel by saying *"Yeah but...", "I know, but...,"* or *"I understand, but..."* If you did truly "understand," you would not dismiss it with a "but...".

The one thing you never want anyone to feel in a relationship is that they don't matter. If someone is trying to tell you something, listen. Hear what they have to say, especially when they are telling you that they are affected by something you are doing/not doing.

One of the biggest killers of marriages is pride. The refusal to see past your point to see them, the need to prove your point because you are right and they are wrong, the *"I'm not saying 'I'm sorry',"* and thoughts, words, and/or expressions of *"They want it done, they can do it themselves."* are just some of the examples of pride.

Pride is all built around self. Self keeps it singular. It does not focus on anyone outside of your point and your feelings.

See the bigger picture:

Whatever hurts them hurts your relationship.

Acknowledge the person's feelings, address the issue and then act. If you really do "know," then your actions should show that you "know". They need to know that they have been heard and that you are putting things in action to protect them from this "issue".

If something you are doing or not doing is hurting them, then there needs to be a change. Don't just sit there, say "ok", and leave it at that. Don't let it just end with the conversation. Let it end with a change of action.

Men:

Be careful with your words and notice when she is uncomfortable.

There may be times when a woman says nothing, in hopes that a man will change what he is doing or stop. One of the biggest times of "quiet" is when she **is being affected by the things he says.**

Whether it's because of something good or something not so good that was said or done, she thinks and she feels.

Always remember that what you say has an effect. When what you say is good, she thinks and she feels. When it is bad, she thinks and she feels. Either way, she thinks, she feels and then she produces. Everything you say, has the potential to speak, shape and create life or death.

When Adam saw Eve, he saw her, identified her, gave her position, and then named her. Men, your voice still does the same and we still listen for it. Wives listen for it. Daughters listen for it and so do other women.

What you say has effect not only on your wife and/or your daughter, but it can also have an effect on other women.

You must be mindful of what you release into a woman's atmosphere. She can create so much with just a seed.

Men: Be AWARE

There are things that women can say to other women that you can't.

Be mindful of your conversation. What could be "innocent" and "a joke" to you, could be sexual innuendos to us.

If you have a close female friend or have a female friend who is close to your family, you cannot joke with her as if she is one of the "bro's." Never forget that she is female. She processes differently than you.

Jokes about body parts are a big "No No."

You may be saying a "joke" about the body part, **but she hears "*he has noticed or is paying attention to (insert body part).*"** This can be bad in many ways.

It can:

1. Cause insecurity,

2. Cause her to feel hurt,

3. Encourage and/or active dormant emotions or struggles,

4. Look like a sexual advancement

5. Cause her to look at you as potential,

6. Cause her to look at you as a threat,

7. Cause her to view you differently (what was a friend, either **moves back in friendship at the thought of it coming between or altering their friendship** OR **move her closer to entertain what "could be" in a relationship or encounter),**

and more.

You need to be careful of what you say!

Married men, all of the above is especially for you.

When you do not watch what you say, you not only allow things to go on inside of the woman, you evoke things to go on in the inside of your wife.

Know it or not, your wife is watching and she processes what she sees and hears. It is NOT good, for her or your marriage, when you are not mindful of or are wise in what you say to other women, friends, a close family friend, church member, co-worker, etc.

No joke or comment is worth your marriage or your position.

Pay attention to your words, they have life. Words have the ability to create/bring things into the lives of others. Just because you think it is innocent, does not mean it won't do damage.

Avoid the sex talk.

Sex talks are NOT wisdom with any woman outside of your wife. Even if it is a joke! Conversation evokes thought. You definitely do not want to have other women 1. Thinking about sex and 2. Thinking about sex with you.

It doesn't matter how "close" you are, it is NOT WISE.

They say, "Sex sells," but you have to keep in mind what exactly is being sold and how much it is actually costing you. Again, it is not wise to have sexual conversation or discuss body parts with women outside of your wife, publicly and privately.

"But I said it in a group setting!"

It does not change what or how a woman thinks just because something is said in a group setting. She could view it as "code" for something else, and either way, it WILL alter her perception of you.

Never forget: Your voice has power.

If you are going to speak, why not impart wisdom? The power of life and death are in the tongue and it is important to remember that. The word helps us not to create "monsters" in conversations and give us principles that could help you save yourself and your marriage.

• **Watch your "jokes" and your conversations.**

> *"Do not let any unwholesome talk come out of your mouths, but only what is helpful for building others up according to their needs, that it may benefit those who listen." Ephesians 4:29*

• **Be known as a beacon of wisdom, not a person of foolishness.**

> How do people "know" you? Is hot and cold coming out of the same faucet?

> You can diminish your place, authority and influence by what you say and by what you cause others to perceive. Let your voice be trustworthy, without foolish or corrupt speaking. It's "ok" to joke sometimes, and sometimes it is not. It depends on the relationship AND the assignment. Hot and cold makes a person look and sound unstable and can confuse boundary lines. YOU MUST BE CAREFUL. You could be inviting things "in" that don't belong and it has the potential to take root and grow "abnormally".

•Private conversations can "shed light" in other rooms.

"What you have said in the dark will be heard in the daylight, and what you have whispered in the ear in the inner rooms will be proclaimed from the roofs." Luke 12:3

The "light" can also represent ideas. When you have "dark" conversations or jokes, it has the potential to light a match or a flame in others. Many times, you can start innocent "fires" that <u>catch on</u> and/or destroy.

•Check yourself.

"A good man brings good things out of the good stored up in his heart, and an evil man brings evil things out of the evil stored up in his heart. For the mouth speaks what the heart is full of." Luke 6:45

Why are you doing what you are doing? Why are you saying what you are saying? Could it be a cry for attention in yourself? What makes you do it?

•Be aware of what you get FROM your jokes and conversations.

"So is my word that goes out from my mouth: It will not return to me empty, but will accomplish what I desire and achieve the purpose for which I sent it." Isaiah 55:11

Words take on assignments when they are released it from our mouths. You must be mindful of your motives and what it **could accomplish.**

•Sometimes, it may be best to be quiet.

> *"If you talk a lot, you are sure to sin; if you are wise, you will keep quiet." Proverbs 10:19*

Proverbs 10 teaches a lot about watching what one says and speaking in wisdom. Sometimes, it's wisest to keep quiet. Not everything requires an answer, and not every thought requires a conversation.

•Whenever you speak, speak with purpose through Christ.

> *"And whatever you do, whether in word or deed, do it all in the name of the Lord Jesus, giving thanks to God the Father through him." Colossians 3:17*

•Remember you are going to have to give an account.

> *"But I tell you that everyone will have to give account on the day of judgment for every empty word they have spoken." Matt 12:36*

Don't let your words and conversations be empty. Make every word count and have meaning and the purpose of building others in destiny and in God.

Never forget that you were created in Gods image and likeness, and your very voice, has the ability to create worlds and speak things into existence. Be aware and be wise with what you say, especially when it comes to women.

Always remember: Married or unmarried, Woman still listens for the voice of Adam to identify her, name her, or call her... No matter the woman, she is always listening. Be careful that your voice isn't calling "her" to things and places she doesn't belong.

Fussing for Change or Just to Be Fussing?

Men and women:

Don't let anger and frustration build up so much that you lash out.

Sometimes people hold in their feelings or thoughts until they can't take anymore and they explode. Explosions are not good and tend to cause damage.

Try talking about things before you fuss about them. If something is happening or not happening that is affecting you, it may be time to have a conversation. Don't hold it in and explode. Put out the little fires by having conversations where you share information.

And, if you must fuss, do it with the purpose of seeing change, not for the purpose of unleashing anger or frustration.

If you are in the practice of fussing for hours about the same thing, stop it!

Opening up emotionally is like opening a faucet. Whether it is anger, hurt or frustration, you have control over how much and what you release. Give the situation what it needs, don't drown it.

If it calls for a cup, pour the cup and turn the faucet off. Don't let your emotions cause you to let that faucet run on full blast, until it overflows, causes damages, or drowns everyone around you.

- **Check to see if what you are fussing about is really what you are fussing about.**

   Don't be moved by frustration for something and then use another issue as a way to vent about it. Don't fuss about the straw that broke the camel's back, when what you are really mad about is that there is even a camel when you wanted a dog.

   If there is an issue, talk to God about it, talk to your spouse about it, deal with it or let it go. Don't go around collecting issues and then look for the smallest opportunity to bring them to light, especially when what you are fussing about has nothing to do with why you are angry.

- **Check the "cup."**

   Many times, that "cup" that you fill to give to others, needs to be handed to GOD first. Let Him taste it to see if what you are serving is table appropriate. Doing this will often keep us from serving "unhealthy," bitter or poisonous drinks to others.

Once you say what you have to say, forgive.

Don't hold on to negativity and carry it with you. It's heavy, and, as long as it's with you, you are not free. Sometimes, the weight of what we carry is so heavy that pieces of it can crush and hurt those who are around you.

Yes, someone may have done/not done, said/didn't say/won't say, been/not been/could have been/ should have been/would have been, BUT what are you going to do and what are you doing about it? Unforgiveness is not something that God smiles upon.

Matthew 6:14-15 ESV "For if you forgive others their trespasses, your heavenly Father will also forgive you, but if you do not forgive others their trespasses, neither will your Father forgive your trespasses."

- **Forgiveness is a necessity.**

    There is nothing that they have done to you that is worse than what our sins have done to Christ. Yet, He loves us and continues to forgive us.

    How many times have we sinned? Disobeyed? Failed Him? He yet loves us and forgives us. How many times have we said words? Thought things? Misrepresented Him and His name? He still loves us and welcomes us into His arms of forgiveness.

    Your marriage is a reflection of Christ and His church. If He can forgive, so should you.

- **Let Christ be the example of forgiveness and sacrifice.**

    Forgive as you have been forgiven. If you say, "I forgive you" then do it! After you forgive, let it go. Ask yourself *"What good is this doing me?"* If the only answer is to lament and wallow in sorrow or pride, let it go and let it go fast.

Acts of Compassion

Men: When you yell, scream and/or threaten her, you break off pieces of her heart and spirit.

She is a valuable yet fragile creature, made up of mind, soul, body and spirit and she was made to function with emotion. The soul is made up of the mind, will, and emotion.

As her spouse or significant other (boyfriend, friend, fiancé), you have been given access to her mind and heart. Tread carefully. Your words and actions matter. Always keep in mind Proverbs 18:21. What you say has an effect. And, with access to her heart, mind and spirit, you must be sure that your words and actions are not killing her.

Women: Your words have life.

Is what you are saying helping your marriage or relationship or are you hurting it?

Watch how he responds when you speak to him. Are your words killing him or his countenance? How can he be strong for you when your words are weakening him?

Whether he is your friend, your boyfriend, your "man", your fiancé, or your husband, it is imperative that you speak what

God says about him, to him and about him. Don't just say what you "see" or don't "see." Say what you have the possibility to see and desire to see. Speak it into being.

If he is low in spirit, you be the one to use your words to encourage him and call him who he is in God and what you know he can become. If you, who has the position, his heart, and his ear, do not speak encouragement and words of affirmation, then who will? You have one of the loudest voices his heart hears; use it wisely.

What are you saying about what GOD has given you?

We as people, both male and female, oftentimes take for granted the relationships that are closest to us. And, in that, our speech sometimes becomes reflective of how we feel at the moment, regardless if it's directed at them or deflected towards them.

Every God given relationship, has a gift of a person IN it. We must never forget that. Whether it's a friend, sibling/family member, significant other, or spouse, our lips should bring life and encouragement and it should happen often.

Friendship, in itself, is a gift and so is the friend. Friendship joins two or more people in unity, a sense of comfortability and camaraderie. What we say, think and do even regarding them is important.

When dating and journeying into the process of marriage, what you say to your significant other, not only builds them up, but you are also, in a sense, investing in your future.

Marriage is ever evolving and requires you to be in tune with God to hear what HE says about the "gift" He gave you. Everything you say is a brick. You can either throw it or use it to build your house. If you throw it, keep in mind, the damage you make, could be damage to your house and/or injure, or even kill, those who live in it.

When you are married, you are one. As you build your spouse, you build yourself, your home, and your union.

Does what you say reflect what you really think?

*Genesis 2:23   "And Adam **said**, this is now bone of my bone and flesh of my flesh; she shall be called Woman, because she was taken out of man."*

The word SAID, in that verse comes from the Hebrew word אָמַר **'âmar,** (aw-mar'); which means to answer, appoint, assign, avouch, bid, boast, call, certify, challenge, charge, command, commune, consider, declare, demand, demonstrates, desire, determine, indeed, intend, mention, name, plainly, promise, publish, report, require, respond, say, speak, specifically say, still say, suppose, talk, tell, term, think, use, and utter.

I gave this definition because I believe we all need to take a closer look. "Said" does not mean something that just comes out of our mouths; it is what we answer, what we decree, what we publish, what we tell, what we call, and it often stems from what we believe.

Not only do we need to be mindful of what we say, **we need to also be mindful of the things we think that lead us to what we say or believe.**

Below are a few questions that may be helpful in looking more closely at areas that may be guiding what you "say" about your spouse, friend, significant other, loved ones, etc.

- What do you "think" regarding him/her?
- What do you "say to yourself" when you see, hear, or are close to this person?
- What do you "publish" or make known to others?
- What do you say TO this person?
- What is your "intention"?
- Do you "boast" about this person?
- Do you "boast" about God because He gave you this person?

- In your MIND, do you "certify" or validate them as the title that you gave them (friend, confidant, boyfriend, girlfriend, fiancé, husband, wife)?

- In your WORDS, do you "certify" or validate them as the title that you gave them (friend, confidant, boyfriend, girlfriend, fiancé, husband, wife)? How? Why?

- In your ACTIONS, do you "certify" or validate them as the title that you gave them (friend, confidant, boyfriend, girlfriend, fiancé, husband, wife)? How? Why? Would they agree?

What you believe is important to what you say. It is also reflected in what you communicate, even without words.

Justification and Defense

There is a difference between justification and a defense. When communicating and/or interacting with others, it's important to know, identify, and understand that justification and defense are not the same thing.

Justification tells the: "Why I did what I did."

Defense says: *"I did not do what you are saying that I did."*

When people are defending themselves, you will hear the statement "I." It is not always because they are self-centered or trying to make it "about them." You will hear "I" because they are representing their client (themselves), and are disputing the accusations or "charges" that are being made against them.

When you approach someone with an accusation, remember that it is you who have brought it up. You introduced your "case" as them committing a "crime" against, involving, or affecting you or based on something YOU saw, heard or experienced. In wisdom, you must allow them to address your accusations and/or state their defense.

Being the judge, jury, and executioner in conversations and relationships, is unwise. Even in a real court it doesn't go like that. Only a fool answers a matter before hears all sides. (*Prov. 18:3*)

When taking up "charges" against someone in relationships and in conversation, there are a few things that we can learn from actual court cases.

1. In a court case, ALL evidence is presented to the judge. A righteous judge never walks in feeling that he has everything figured out and knows all the details without actually hearing all the details. A wise judge knows that ONLY a fool answers a matter without HEARING all sides. They don't "just know", they HEAR and take notes.

2. The prosecution is not the judge AND he is not the only one allowed to present his case.

3. The DEFENSE does get a chance to rebut what is being claimed, even when prosecutor is presenting his/her case. They are allowed to object when false statements are being made against them.

4. When in court, THE TRUTH is important. It's not ok to allow belief to overshadow the verifiable truth.

5. A person's opening statement will declare their stance on your accusation; listen.

Justified, or not guilty by reason of self-defense, insanity or otherwise says: *"Yes. I did it, Your Honor, now let me tell you why."*

Not guilty is a statement of: *"I did not do it, Your Honor."* or *"I believe I am being wrongfully accused."*

Each one is dealt with differently.

An admission of guilt accompanied with the "I", is justification. In conversation, when a person is given you a *"reason why I did/ didn't do _____,"* instead of seeing "what they did," it then **becomes Justification.** Justification is an issue of missing the point that the point is not about them, it's about what the person did and how it affected you or others.

Before you get mad, get information with understanding.

1. **Speculation is not grounds for punishment**. Prove your case. Hear all sides. Judge. Don't go into an argument with punishment already on the table. Wisdom says, "Judge righteously," not judge out of anger or unproven speculation.

2. **When your case is built upon false facts, misunderstandings, and partial truths, you may need to readjust your "charges."** When you come in and say, "You stole my watch!" and later find out that they found it on the ground and did not know it was yours, your case is no longer "you stole it." The case now becomes "Now that we both have an understanding, where do we go from here?" And in this case, justice would be for you to apologize for false accusations and they willingly return your lost property, and then you thank them for finding it.

Oftentimes, when people refuse to "drop the case," after finding out they were incorrect, it is not because they believe they still have a "case," it's because pride won't let them be wrong.

If you are wrong, apologize. We all have built cases with evidence that support our case and then later found that what we thought had happened or how we thought a person was, was not really the case. Don't go on like there is something that the person did wrong just because you don't want to face ego. In those cases, also watch out for making things about others when what really needs to be corrected is you.

Be fair.

If you are going to reach a summation or "issue a ruling," make sure you are being a righteous judge. A righteous judge cannot be biased before a court hearing can even take place. Neither can the jury.

Sometimes it may be wisest to have an impartial person, who speaks and communicates wisdom, to help mediate a dispute. Sometimes, we can be so close to a situation that we cannot see it for what it is, and it may take outside counsel to bring insight.

Just like the lawyers pick through the jury to weed out bias, it may be wise to also do the same when picking wise counsel. When choosing someone to mediate or counsel, be sure to NEVER choose someone just because they are on your side, because the side you are on, may not always be right.

Tips for Guys: *Women May Not Tell You But...*

It is NOT the thought that counts. It is the <u>thought,</u> the <u>action,</u> and the <u>follow through.</u>

Women are not just "ok" with you presenting us with a thought as a gift. Saying to us phrases like *"I thought about doing this for you"*, and then not doing anything with that thought, is not good. It does not get you brownie points. It actually has the potential to injure your position with her mentally, emotionally, and even physically if this behavior is continually practiced.

Don't practice getting someone's hopes up with things, suggestions, and ideas that you have no intention to follow through with.

It is better to say nothing, than to say anything and do nothing.

Intentions are NOT results.

Its ok to change your mind sometimes, but be sure to communicate. If you promised to take her somewhere nice and then an emergency comes up, tell her. Don't have her in the dark on the things you previously chose to shed light on.

There is a difference in an emergency and poor planning.

Every once and a while, something is going to come up unexpectedly that may alter your plans, that's life, and that's ok. It is not ok to poorly plan and consider them emergencies. Whether it's dating, marriage, friendly outings, etc., it's important to have 1. good time management and 2. good money management. Romantically and socially, these are the two areas that quickly cause major problems in relationships.

It's not ok to consistently:

- Invite yourself and or others to places that you know you cannot afford and expect others to just "cover you."
- Make plans with someone and then show up late, not show up or cancel at the last minute.
- Talk about ideas that you have no intention of making realities.
- Have intention but no follow through.
- Throw romantic things together.

"For where your treasure is, there will your heart be also."
Matthew 6:21

Whatever you treasure, you should put your heart in it. If you treasure your friendship, relationship, and/or marriage, then the things that you do with them, for them and the time that you spend with them, should come from the heart. Don't just go there, be there. Give them your presence AND your attention.

Be mindful of how you treat the ones you love. It's important to always be considerate of people's time, their effort, and/or their sacrifices. No one should be taken for granted. No one should be disrespected.

A lack of respect or honor in time, is disrespect.

Time is one thing that you will never get back once it's gone. Time is valuable and it should not be wasted. Don't ask anyone to do things unnecessarily. If you need a favor, then ask. If they can, let them and be sure to appreciate it. If they can't, then they can't. Don't discard or disregard them because of an inability to do something. Even if you think that they could have done it, or had it to spare, always remember you never know what they are going through.

Romantically, you should NEVER just throw things together.

Always remember to think, plan, execute and present. Don't just run to your local pharmacy and grab something, especially for special moments, events, birthdays, and anniversaries. Think about what she likes and/or would like, plan it out in advance, buy it/get it/do it, then present it to her. If it can be wrapped, wrap it. If it can be made into to an experience, then make it into an experience for her. Be creative. Be present. Be considerate. Be patient. Be what she needs and do what she needs to feel valued.

If you don't "have it," say you don't have it and plan accordingly. BUT, if the reason you don't "have it", especially when you are supposed to have it, is because you spent it on videogames, candy, junk food, new rims for your car, etc., then there is a problem.

Prioritize. Sometimes you will need to sacrifice what you like, for what you love. If you love playing videogames, that's ok, but put it in its place. Don't have no time available for her but have time for video games. Don't spend 3 hours on games and 20 minutes with her. Don't set money aside anxiously awaiting a new game, movie, etc. but when it comes to her, she gets a last-minute card and bear for her birthday.

Where ever your heart is, it should be a place where you invest your treasures. Especially when it comes to marriage, it is important that you **set aside funds and your time to value that which is valuable**.

Relationships are where heart and treasures meet. Marriage relationships are where heart and treasure reside. You and your wife are in it together. To esteem her, is to esteem yourself. To focus on her, is to reflect the best parts of yourself. You are two sides to one mirror.

She is your treasure. She belongs in your heart, not just in your house. She needs to know that you are thinking of her and to know and see that she is, and/or her needs, thoughts or desires are, being considered. Even if it's picking up her favorite cookies when you ran to the store for a soda, she needs to know that she is valued. It's not enough to just say it or only say it once or twice. When you have a woman, action is required.

Simple Questions?... Nah

It can be frustrating, yet be a bit funny to women, when a man thinks he "knows" what she is trying to ask, say or explain before she says it. And then again when he gives her answers. Although it can be useful information, it usually doesn't answer the question we are asking at all.

Thinking *"I know you"* is one of the biggest illusions anyone can have. Man, woman, parent, child, pastor, friend, it doesn't change. You may know about someone, but no one but God truly knows a person.

Mankind only has the ability to see what's on the outer appearance. You can only see a person's heart if you are shown it, and, even then, we must remember that we do not "see" all of it.

We know of people. We know certain traits, mannerism or habits but we do not KNOW anyone. Many times, we do not even fully know ourselves. We often get to see things, thoughts and behaviors in/about ourselves in times of trouble, lack and uncomfortability, that we didn't even know existed. This not only applies to life, but it also applies to men and women in conversation.

Sometimes, you will be on the same page and sometimes you will not. It's not intentional, it's just that women think differently and our process is way different than the way men process.

Men:

Never assume that you "know," because there is a big possibility you probably don't.

You may have a general idea, but you will not have the specifics if she does not share or have the opportunity to share them with you.

Guys often **search for the cut and dry** in a question or conversation, and desire that she "gets to the point," or may even think, because it is taking so long for her to reach her point, that she may not have one.

But what he doesn't know is, that **while he searches for "the point,"** many points were being made, questions were formed and that everything she mentioned throughout that whole conversation had a purpose. **The conversation is the point.**

Men tend to search for the one (the point) and women tend to collect the many. Women are gatherers. We collect information about a lot in a little time. Generally, when we ask a question it is for more than receiving an answer.

Just because she asks a question, and in thinking you know why she asked, you preempt her and continue to go on in conversation, doesn't mean you knew where she was going and what she was talking about.

She may choose to continue on your journey through conversation, but that is not always where she intended to go. Either way, her journey or yours, she knowingly and/or unknowingly gathers information. It is the way God designed us so that we may help.

For every one question, a woman searches for answers to many other questions that she hasn't even asked yet. The answers open doors to receive more questions to be answered, whether it's now, later, or within her own mind.

A simple question is not so simple.

"How was your day?" is a question that will receive answers to the questions:

1. *"What happened at work today?"*

2. *"Were you ok?"*

3. *"Are you ok now?"*

4. *"Is there anything I should know?"*

5. *"Has your attitude or demeanor changed?"*

6. *"Did something affect you at work that I should be prepared for at home?"*

7. *"Is there something I need to do to help you?"*

These are just a few of the questions that was asked when she asked, *"how was your day?"* Although she was polite in asking about the day, being polite was not the point. She was gathering information that answered: How was the past? What does he need in the present? and What could I expect in the future?

If he had a bad day, it may be affecting him emotionally, so she may expect or gear up for mood swings, irritability, and/or for him to be a bit withdrawn. With this information, she prepares herself and things around him, to cover him, make his day better, give him space, be there if he needs to talk, and/or pray for him and the situation.

Don't look for her to consolidate, because 9 out of 10 she has consolidated already.

There is a method to the "madness." She never talks just to be talking. Take time to HEAR her, not just listen for the point. Don't assume. Sometimes you will have to ask her questions to get the definition of what she is saying. If it's not clear, ask.

You are never wasting time talking with/listening to her; you are investing.

Listening says *"I value you. You, your concerns, and your words are important and they are safe with me."*

Saying *"Get to the point"* hurts her, and thinking it, hurts you.

Never forget that the conversation is her point, and when you miss the conversation, you miss "it" (the very thing you were looking for). When she shares through conversation, she gives her heart, thoughts, her emotions towards it, and what is valuable in conversation.

Hear Her Out.

Ways in conversation

I'm going to break down a few of the common practices in male/female conversation, what they do, why they are and what we can do to better understand, nurture, or gauge them.

Men:

In conversation, when she interjects, let her. Generally, she is not trying to change the subject, manipulate or navigate the conversation, or come against your point. She is actually trying to keep up and better understand what you are saying.

When she does this, she is trying to be in the PLACE where you are, NOT the position.

Communication is about GIVING AND RECEIVING.

You are giving information and others are receiving it. When communicating with a female, it will take details, and often requires allowances for answering questions to be able get through the "journey" together. If your goal is to reach the destination of received understanding, don't leave her behind.

If she is asking, she is interested.

Never say she is not listening.

9 out of 10 she hears you just fine. She will sometimes question your meaning or interpretation of what you are saying or have said. <u>Interpretation is based on the mindset of the beholder.</u> What you say may not necessarily be what she gets/understands. Many questions bridge the gap of interpretation.

It is unwise to answer without listening.

Occasionally in male to female conversation, a conclusion or remedy is drawn up and given before she even finished what she is saying. Although you are trying to be helpful, you are also being rude and preemptive. Oftentimes, women feel abandoned, unheard, unappreciated, and made to feel unworthy, when they consistently are cut off in mid conversation or mid thought with anecdotes and antidotes.

You may find that we usually need you to hear, not to fix.

Hearing is the most common way to say:

1. *"I support you.,"*

2. *"I value your thoughts.,"*

3. *"Your feelings matter.,"* and

4. *"Your heart is safe with me."*

The bible *says, "Out of the abundance of the HEART the mouth speaks".* When she speaks, she is sharing so much more with you than her words.

Women:

He is not going to be able to explain all the time. Some stuff is time and/or thought sensitive. When he is on a roll in a certain area, it may be best to hear him out THEN ask questions.

When you get a question, lock it away or keep it secondary and his heart primary.

He is not always going to be in a position where he can listen.

Sometimes he is going to be busy, his mind is going to be on other things, and/or he will just plain be tired. Give him a break. Everybody has their time when they are mentally or emotionally unavailable. It's not that he doesn't love you, or that he doesn't have time for you. He just may need a space and time to regroup or get his thoughts together.

The Regrouping Space

Women:

When a man comes in from work or a long day, give him time and an opportunity to gather himself and his thoughts.

Men need to shift "hats." When he comes through the door, it's not time to bombard him. Give him some space. Unless it's an emergency or he is open for it/desires it, give him a kiss and/or hug, say *"hello"* and that you missed him, and give him at least 15 minutes. Preferably 30 minutes. Try not to put things on him before he has had a chance to "take off" what the world, day, and/or work place has put on him already.

He is HERE for you, give him time to regroup.

If he likes the occasional game or a certain show, give him a little time to enjoy it, it's ok. If you are not a fan of it, give him space or give him quiet. Giving him personal space of an hour or two a week won't kill you.

Men:

When she does give you space, do NOT abuse it. This is not an excuse to hide out in your man cave.

Unless it's an OCCASIONAL sports game, give yourself an hour tops. Be sure you are spending time with her, way more than you spend with your TV, games, media, church, or other people.

You reap what you sow. You want to see good fruit in her, you MUST sow seeds of time, love, affection, and undivided attention and keep it watered and nurtured daily or your "fruitful vine" will dry up.

Try inviting her into your personal space sometimes. Let her know that she is more important than the game, show, other people, etc.

Be sure you are not spending more time with your TV, games, friends, people, phone, or social media than with GOD.

You are a product of what you "eat." If your spirit is being feed garbage, then what you do, say think, and become will reflect garbage. Nothing in life is more important than your relationship with God.

Be sure that you are not spending more time watching movies, playing video games, watching TV/games, on social media sites, in the man cave, hanging with the fellas, or with the church, than with your children.

They need you. Your time. Your attention. Your love.

They are your assignment gifts from God, to nurture, to raise, to love. They are a harvest. It is your responsibility to plant what will grow and ensure that it is fed with love daily, watering it with the word.

Guys:

When she comes through the door, it's not time to instantly make your requests known.

It would help her out a whole lot if you helped out. Actually, she needs you to help out. Don't know what to do? Genuinely ask her what you can help her with, and do it.

Please don't sit there all day hungry, waiting on her to fix you something to eat, when you very well could fix it yourself.

A day off for you is NOT necessarily a day off for her, especially if you have kids. Mommy duty is still on, which means cleaning duty is still on, accountant and/or administrative duties are still on, the supporter, homework checker, nurturer, coach, mentor, educator, cook, doctor, lawyer and sometimes police is still on, not to mention she still has you and herself to take care of.

It doesn't help her for you to stay in the bed throughout the day, ordering room service.

There may be time when she can cater to you in that way and then there may be times when she cannot. Work together. You are in this together. Helping one another may mean you will sometimes have to help yourself.

Sometimes she needs a break too.

On your days off, try giving her a day off and try your best to help out sometimes.

Try giving her a break from the kids for an hour. Give her some time to herself. You could even try grabbing her favorite snack or ice cream the night before a day off. It could better help her enjoy the hour or two you give her for herself. If it's in the budget, order out. Give her a break from cooking. If it's not, choose at least one night out of the month to cook, even if it's hotdogs and French fries, you can do it.

Believe me, it makes a difference.

If she occasionally invites you into her personal space, go.

Take in that lifetime movie, eat a couple of Oreo's with her, snuggle up, etc., it's her way of sharing a piece of herself with you. It's not just about "time"; it's about her...

Women: Don't be jealous!

If he occasionally wants to hang out the boys, take in a movie by himself, watch the game, have a few friends over, or have some quiet time alone, let him. Don't allow yourself to be angry or upset. He is not a robot. He needs to have an avenue of release. You are fun to be with, but there are also other things he may like doing too. Let the man relax.

He cannot be with you, or hugged up or talk to you 24hrs a day, 7 days a week, for the rest of his life. That is not living. Even you have stuff you like doing. Let him enjoy peace and quiet for a minute. There are so many things that call for his attention in life, a brief moment of silence or football game is not going to kill him or you.

Don't smother him.

If he needs room to breathe, let him breathe. I'm not saying for you not to be cautious, aware or close, I am saying *"Let him do what he needs to do."*

If he is working, let him work. You can't keep calling him all day, or get upset when he can't stay on the phone or answer as soon as it rings. He is supposed to be working. Many times, that requires focus. It is not that he doesn't love you, or that he doesn't think about you, but, in order to focus on the job, his mind needs to be on the job.

A text here and there saying you love him, encouraging him or giving him certain information is okay, and so is a call every once and a while, to let him know he is loved or thought about. These tend to generally be good. But calling back to back to back to hear him breathe, argue with him, complain, and/or talk about nothing and everything, may not be good for him or in him keeping his job.

Watch the stress

He does not need to be stressed and he doesn't want you to be stressed out either. When you call him, or talk to him, remember: **Not everything is an emergency.**

Don't get yourself into a panic, especially about simple or non-emergency things. Picking up the laundry from the cleaners later today, is not a cause for panic, it's a cause for information.

Many times, we succeed at emotion but lack in information. We tend to give more information than what is needed. It's not a bad thing. It's just that it gets kind of hard to decipher what is important when everything sounds important or as if you are fussing at him.

It is easier for him to understand: *"Honey. Please don't forget to pick up the dry cleaning by 5. You need it for tomorrow and they will be closed."*

Verses

"Oh, my gosh babe! Don't forget the dry cleaning like you did the last time. That was such a mess! I had to call the cleaners and beg them to let you get your suit in time and it was only by God's grace that we got it. That didn't have to happen if you had listened to me. Are you even listening now? Babe. Did you hear me? DON'T- FORGET- THE- DRY- CLEAN-ING. Please do not forget it this time. They close at 5. Please get there by 5. They are not going to be open tomorrow so you better get there before 5. I hope you don't forget...."

Women, this is stressful. He knows he forgot the dry cleaning the last time. He was the one who didn't do it and more than likely got fussed at about it the last time. Now he has to remember to pick up the dry cleaning and regroup from being fussed at. When you call to give information, it does not always have to accompany a fuss, rebuke or panic. Give the necessary information when necessary and leave that other stuff for another time (Or forget it).

Things He May Not Say

"Sometimes I don't understand you."

Ladies sometimes we give them too much information. It is not that our information is bad, it just may be that the information is too much to process at that time, or you are opening so many doors in conversation, and he is having problems following you.

"Sometimes, it would be nice if you took me out and had a special day for me."

Guys want to feel appreciated too. It makes them feel special when you go out of your way to speak their love language that they have been "speaking" to you. They need to know ***"This relationship is not one sided. She sees 'me'."***

"Sometimes, I need a hug too."

Men have their vulnerable moments too. There will be times when he needs you. He may want you just to hold him, just to be with him, and/or just to listen to him. It is not a weakness, it is humanity. When you see or hear it, don't discuss it with others. They do not need to know his vulnerabilities.

"Sometimes I just want to be alone."

Sometimes he needs to gather his thoughts or reboot from life. Sometimes he just needs some time with GOD alone. He loves being with you but sometimes being with you causes him to have to focus on you when he needs to focus on himself. Allow him space and time to talk with God.

"I need your support."

Men need to know that you support them. It needs to be verbal, physical, and through encouragements and recognition. They need to see it, they need to hear it, and they need to feel it. It is very important.

"I need to hear what is good about me."

Words of affirmation help build him from the inside. It's not about ego. It is about having a reminder that *"There is something good about you."* and *"You are not failing and you are not a failure."*

"I need you to pray for me."

Ladies, he is fighting so much and you have no idea about how many mental, emotional, physical and spiritual battles he faces every day. Keep him covered. Pray not only for his strength but for his safety and for his peace.

"I need you to help me dream again."

He has a vision but he also has realities. Sometimes he can be so focused on his reality, or what seems to be a reality, that he loses sight of his dreams and vision. Do what you can to encourage him that his dream is a possibility and that his vision can carry on.

"I need you to tell me you believe in me."

Ladies, you need to say it and say it often. There will be times where he doesn't believe in himself, and he will need you as a reinforcement. Now, it's not for you to badger him with, or say it routinely. When you say it, believe it. He will know the difference in when it is rehearsed and when it is genuine. You know that you believe in him, so let your words say that you know you believe in him.

"I need you to look good."

Women, men are visual creatures. They were created that way, and nothing you do or say is going to change that.

Men like to see their women look nice. Especially when you are married, he needs to see you look nice. **You may have had a hard day, but the bonnet and house coat are not going to fly every day.**

Pick yourself up here and there, and help him visualize you in all your "hotness" and beauty. It's okay to dress up for him. You did it when you were dating. You put on your best when you knew you were going to see him. Try doing that again.

Frequently dress up, for no other reason than him. You may go somewhere or you may not. That is not the point. The point is to allow him to "see".

The bonnet and pajamas are okay, but that should not be all that he sees. If you dress for work, for church, for events, for friends, then you can surely dress for him.

"I need affection."

This is a given. Married women do not withhold yourself from your husbands. They need you. They need your touch and all that you bring to the table. Your body belongs to your husband and his body belongs to you.

When you withdraw yourself from him, it leaves him without and it leaves him open for frustration and temptation. You don't want him entertaining "other options" because you took you of the table. It makes it easy for temptation to present itself. **Don't let the enemy use your refusal and resistance to open the door for temptation** to come in through someone else's willingness and acceptance. Again, pride is a killer of marriages. When you take away his prize (you), you make room to entice his pride.

"I hate having to fight with you to get to you."

Ladies, this goes back to saying and doing things that cover what you really want. Saying "I'm ok", when you know you are not, is not helping him get close to you. He feels like you are hiding from him and/or rejecting him.

Rejection causes rejection. Say what you mean and say what you want. They are not always able to just figure you out. And, it is stressing them, instead of helping them get closer so they can love on you.

If you say you want space, they will try to give you space, not come "look for you". If you are looking for the chase, then do romantic things and positive things that invoke a chase. Negative hints to "chase" say to him *"Leave me alone"*, not *"Come get me"*.

Things She May Not Say

"I want to be held."

Sometimes, when she is sad, crying or fussing, or had a hard day, she just needs you to hug her and/or hold her.

Guys, there is something special about just being in your arms that rejuvenates, revives, and/or rebuilds her. Your arms provide, reassurance and safety. She needs you. Sometimes it is just nice to be held without a reason. Whenever you can, hold her.

"When I run, or walk away, I want you to come for me and assure me that you love me."

Generally, when women walk away, we really want you to come for us. It shows us that you care enough about us to come and get us, and that you don't want to lose us. Although it's a strange thing to do, we do it. And, when we do it, we look for you to come and find us. Like the loss sheep, we expect you to leave what you are doing and find us or bring us back.

"I want to feel like I'm 'worth it'."

We want to feel like we have value and are still considered valuable to you. Where a man's treasure is, there will his heart be also. We want to know that our place is secure in your heart as your treasure.

"I need to know that I am the only one you <u>want</u> and <u>see</u>."

She needs to know that you think about her and fantasize about her and only her. She wants to know that she is the center of your world and your attention. It is not that she is insecure, she just needs to hear it from you. Even in the beginning, Adam spoke to Eve about who she was to him when he called *her "bone of my bone and flesh of my flesh"*.

Men, women need to hear it, see it and know it.

"It hurts me when I have to fight for your attention."

Women, especially wives, do not desire to have to compete for position in your time and/or heart. It is damaging to us and causes seeds of insecurities to be planted.

Establish and maintain a standard and a balance,

1. where she knows that she is your priority and that her position is not one where she has to fight,

AND

2. when you do have to focus on life and the people in it, she knows that it does not impede or impose on the position and time you have reserved for her.

"It hurts me when you look at other girls."

Being the center of your affection, we do not like when you make it seem as if there is a competitor or if there is another applicant for our established position.

We know you look, but it is how and why you look at other women that bothers us.

If you look lustfully, we know that you have a certain interest of lust towards her. If you look at her as a higher or sexier standard, it says to us that we lack something that she has, and that what she has is interesting to you. If you look too long, it's disrespectful to us and it makes us wonder what you could be thinking about that is making you look at her in that way and for so long.

"I don't like it when you hide yourself from me."

As a woman, if I can't see you, then I can't see when I may need to help you.

We need you to be open with us. We want to know your true feelings, and what you are thinking. We want to know you. All of you. Completely. We need to, from the beginning, know that you are being "completely naked", not hiding yourself from us in any way. In Genesis, man was only known to hide when he sinned, and it is the same way with women and how we think.

The human condition says, *"If you hide, then there must be something to hide."* When you do not talk to us or shut us out, we begin to wonder what you could be hiding. It is not always about finding something to accuse you of, or thinking something negative, like you are cheating. It could be that we feel that there is more to the story because of your refusal to tell the story.

If we say, *"how was work?"* and your answer is, *"Work was work.",* you leave us to fill in the blanks of what work was like. That is never really good to do.

She may miss that something is wrong or misinterpret when something went right. **YOU DO NOT WANT US TO FILL IN THE BLANKS.** If she asks a question, it is easier to tell her. It may take extra time, but you may want to chance it.

"I need you to tell me what you like and what you want sometimes."

It gets hard and frustrating sometimes when we have to figure out what you like all the time. It would help us out a lot if you say some of the things that you like so we can put it in our memory banks. When you tell us, it gives us more options to work with.

Now, don't go overboard, or overload us with your likes. Don't make them executive orders. And, don't expect us to do everything at once. We just need information here and there, to help us know how to better care for you and what you need.

Remember, you are **suggesting information,** not placing an order. We need you to tell it, not fuss it.

If you like something and would like for her to add it to the grocery list, say something like *"Babe, you know I could really go for some (you fill in the blank). You know it's my favorite."* and leave it there. Depending on the situation, funds and/or your health, you may be surprised to see it on the menu in the near future.

"I need to feel your touch often."

We are not only emotional beings, but we are also physical as well. We need you to hold us, cuddle and physically show your love.

"I need to hear your vision."

We are following you. Especially as wives, in order for us to know what we are supposed to be doing, we need to know what the plan and vision is. Tell us what God told you. If EVE never knew not to eat of the fruit, she never would have needed the serpent to trick her into eating it. Ignorance would have killed her first.

When we don't know, it is like we are walking blindly. When walking blindly, we can begin to carry out actions to what we think might help or be good but, in turn, might hinder and be bad for you and/or the marriage.

"I need to know when things change and when things need to change."

We are here to help. We cannot help when we do not know. If there is a change, we need to know so that 1. We can do our part and 2. We are not doing things to "help" in vain. We are not being nosey or trying to be controlling, we are trying to follow. Please give us what we need.

"I need to hear that I am doing a good job."

Say it and show it. She has a need to hear it just like you do. Let her know that you see her efforts.

"Sometimes, I need a break, need to cry, and need to release."

Women are emotional creatures and sometimes we need to take time to process our emotions to regain balance. You may see us crying and we may not really be able to tell you fully why that is. If you see her crying, just hug her. Let her know she can be vulnerable and that her vulnerability is safe with you.

Now, I am NOT saying for you to be an enabler to emotional and irrational behavior, but I am saying "if she has a moment where she just needs a hug or a brief time to think, allow her to have it." There is a difference in a consistent emotional imbalance and a moment of vulnerability.

"I need you to listen."

Sometimes when she wants to talk, she just need you to listen. She will oftentimes figure it out on her own, and, periodically, when she needs an answer, she will ask you something like *"What do you think?"*.

Sometimes, the best way for women to process what is going on internally, is to say it out loud.

Her talking to you is her trusting you with her thought and her process. It is a privilege not a punishment. **We do not share who we are with people we cannot trust.** If you are getting her complete thought, then know you have her complete trust in carrying it.

When we tell you thoughts that we are just trying to process, it is not a burden for you to carry.

It may be:

1. Something to hold just for a minute, while we organize it, and put it back in its place,

2. Something we value your view and opinion on, and/or

3. Something for you to take to God.

"I need you to come home."

Work, school, church, and other people, places and things are good, but she needs you to invest in and/or return to your home. She needs to know that you LIVE there, not just sleep there.

She needs to see and experience your physical presence. Coming home from work and going right out with the boys, to an event, etc., on a consistent basis hurts her internally and often succeeds at helping her feel insecure, rejected, and emotionally alone.

It is also not good for her if you are physically there but mentally or emotionally somewhere else. There will be times you may have things on your heart/mind and we understand. There may even be times when you just zone out or need a mental break, but try not to mentally and/or emotionally leave her while she is talking to you or spending time with you. Also, try not to make a habit of choosing to leave mentally when she or the children are around. She needs you to be there holistically, fully aware and fully present.

"I need more time with you"

She needs to be able to spend quality time with you, as much and as often as possible. Quality time with your wife needs to be a part of your schedule. It helps her release the world while she reconnects with you. When you invest in her quality time, you invest quality in your marriage.

Her "Quality Time" 101

Women need to feel that they are your priority.

There are common statements made by many men, when they are asked about their wives, and about making time for her. Here are a few examples and a peek into what it looks like from her side.

"She knows I love her, and I prove that when I go to work and every time I provide for this family."

Yes, you are a provider. You work hard. You want to give her everything she needs. But, guess what? She needs your time.

It's not a little thing to women. Time IS necessary. It's something that brings most of the "water" to your "vine". She needs it and she needs it to be focused.

"But we were together when we watched TV!"

No woman wants to be or feel like time with her is "by the way". "By the way" is a term used to describe her as being an addition to and not the priority. Yes, you may be watching TV with her, but many times your focus can be the television and not her.

Your joy at that moment may be the game, your show, etc. and you are pleased that she is with you. Her joy in watching with you is not the television, it's getting a chance to be with you.

"But, she asks me to watch her shows with her, and I do. I don't even like those types of movies, but I watch it anyway, just for her. Doesn't that count? If it counts, why is she still complaining?! "

Yes, it does count. She sees it, and internally, she is grateful.

When she talks to you about needing quality time, she is not saying that you **"don't do anything"** she is trying to say, **"I need more"** and **"I need more of you."**

Understand, it's never about the shows when she invites you to do something with her. It's always about you and her. Her invitations are to invite you into the areas of her life and likes so that she can share these, and other parts of her life, likes, and desires with you. She invites you "in" (into her heart, her time, desires, likes, dislikes, etc.).

It's ALWAYS deeper than the invitation.

When you accept her invitations, it says to her: *"Your interest matter"*, but, when you plan for her, invite her in, and reserve focused time with just you and her, it says to her, **"YOU matter."** She needs both, to feel that her interests matter and that she matters.

Now, in regards to it counting…

It counts as a loving response to her invitations, but it does not count as 1. being INVITED to come IN and 2. Investments and Deposits.

She may not fully understand that when you invite her to watch the game, or your favorite show with you, that it's your way of including her "in". Please be patient with her. She can become a little jealous that your focus is more on the TV than on her, and may even do things to try to get attention in the middle of what you are watching or doing. Don't worry. It's not malicious. She just wants to be and know that she is the center of your attention.

In cases like these, make a choice.

You can choose to:

1.   Stop watching and focus on her.

Or

2.   Invite her to watch with you.

When you choose to invite her in, it may help to try doing a little extra. Pop some popcorn, bring some beverages, put your arm around her, snuggle her close, put your feet up and relax together. Make it a "together" event.

Split the difference

Watch your show/game/etc. but be sure to take time to give her needed/wanted/desired attention. Try your best to have focused alone time with her. Hold her, talk to her, ask her how her day was, listen to her, do something special for her that is all about her.

Always invest in what really matters. Again, never spend more time watching tv or playing video games than you invest time with her.

Investments and deposits

Deposits need to be more than the withdrawals in order for the "account" to remain active.

Your deposits are things that you put into her. Words of affirmation, quality time, gifts just because, random acts of kindness, breaks from the kids, surprise dinners, vacation from mommy/wife duties, etc. are deposits that allow her to give and to function.

Everyday life requires her to render withdrawals from her "love bank". Whether it is through her time, tasks, and responsibilities or it requires who she is and who she is to you, she is always giving out.

When you pull energy, virtue and the essence of who she is out of her, it is a necessity that you put back into her what she needs so that she will be able to replenish, regenerate, and reproduce.

Investments

Investments are made when there is an overflow and/or consistency of deposits. Intimacy is one way to invest. Intimacy is not just sex. It's when you invest the essence, secrets and vulnerability of you with them and their essence, secrets and vulnerability is invested with you that intimacy is achieved. It is something that only you and they share. Knowing, on both sides, that "who truly I am" is safe with you.

<u>Investments of Time don't happen when you only spend just enough time to fill what is needed to cover the deposits.</u>

Women see investments as being something that goes above and beyond the necessary.

In times, and in cases like illness or pressing times, where there can be no deposits, she will often reach back to refuel off of what had been previously invested.

"My wife and I have sex, and she still complains that we are not intimate."

Sex can be a part of intimacy but intimacy is NOT sex.

Intimacy includes time and is made up of various parts. Her definition of intimacy may include various ways of allowing you to see, know, and experience places, thoughts, and the essence of who she is.

Quality time is one way she is allowed space to show you more of herself, and for her to receive more of you. Your investment of quality time is one key that can unlock many doors. And, it may even unlock doors that she, herself, does not even know exists.

Repeat after me, *"The journey requires time."*

"I took her to see wrestling, the game, and the car show and she still says that she needs for us to go out."

Even though we love to be included, and are often glad that you wanted to share this experience with us, we would like our desires to be considered sometimes. It's ok to ask her *"what would you like to do?"*, and then make plans and do it.

Even if it's taking her out for her favorite ice cream, it shows that you took some time with her in mind. It shows her that you thought about her, studied her, planned for her, and took action and it was all for her. That speaks VOLUMES.

"I know she wants to take a vacation somewhere, but I have got to work."

The key word in vacation is VACATE.

You need a vacation and you need a vacation together. You need time away from everyday life and its surroundings. You do not work every day of the year, and if you do, something needs to change.

If you have a tight schedule, there are still things you can do. Trying using an off day to go somewhere and spend the night. Then, when you do get vacation time, take it and go somewhere together.

Long trips

Plan to be away. Take time to plan your trip and save towards it. Whether it's a road trip of romance, or a trip to Tahiti, whatever you do, be sure to plan it. It's never fun to travel to a different place just to be locked up inside the room with nothing to do, nothing to eat and no place to go.

When you plan, take into consideration what you would want to do, eat, and experience while you are there. If you are going to rest, then plan to rest. Be sure your meals are there if you want to cook and restaurants are around if you want to rest from cooking. Familiarize yourself with an idea of what kind of foods you may want to try and financially plan for it.

"I want to go away, but we are trying to save our money."

You also need to save your marriage. Do what you can. Invest in time away with each other.

"But we don't have the money for that!"

Quality time does not necessarily have to be expensive.

Plan a picnic, and if it's too cold, plan an indoor picnic. Get a blanket, make some sandwiches or buy some dinner get some beverages. Sit, talk, and enjoy each other.

Get a sitter and make her dinner. Husbands, make it a romantic night for two. Run her a warm bath, get a glass, and fill it with sparkling grape juice or raspberry ginger ale if you need to, light some candles and let her relax while you serve her.

Go out for the occasional meal. Can't afford a luxury dinner right now? Take her to breakfast. Go to lunch together and just sit and talk and enjoy the time you spend together.

Make time for hand holding. Enjoy "talk walks." Hold hands as you walk in the park, at the museum, to the ice cream shop, etc.

Make it an "us movie night." Go to the movies, sit next to each other, cuddle if you can. Rent a movie, pop popcorn and cuddle. The local public library should have movies you can rent for free. At home or in the theater, make it about just the two of you.

These are just a few examples of what to do when times are hard financially. Be creative. Be aware. Be focused. You will be surprised with what you can come up with when you think of her and ways to show her you love her.

Women:

Acknowledge what he does when he is trying to do something for you that says. "I love you" or "I was thinking of you".

Encourage him, and say "thank you." Even if it's something small, it's still something he didn't have to do. He did it because he loves you. Be sure to appreciate and verbally acknowledge it.

<u>A little can go a long way, if you nurture it, instead of kill it.</u> Becoming upset, or disregarding his effort, is not a good way to encourage him. He is doing something right, build from there.

"Does he even hear me?!"

Yes, he hears you, but he may not fully understand you. Many times, we speak out of frustration, and frustration may be what you are communicating.

Communication is KEY. Talk with him, don't assume he knows. He wants to provide what you need, but he won't know what you need until you tell him.

Be sure that you:

- **Say it clearly.**

  Explain, don't complain. Talk, don't nag. Say what it is that you want, need and desire. Nobody wants to hear you fussing all the time. It doesn't help, it hurts.

  Mean words cannot only hurt him, but it can also hurt your relationship. His ear and heart is open to you because he wants to hear you, your heart and your needs/concerns. Don't fill it with nagging, complaining, and with words that hurt. He is yours, value him.

- **DON'T DO IT PUBLICLY!**

Your purpose of talking to him **is talking to him.** Don't include others. It is very disrespectful, it puts him on the spot, and it can even embarrass him when you make private conversations public domain.

Discussions like these need to happen when you both are alone and are able to be free about how you are feeling.

- **Don't be mad you can't cruise this year because the money just isn't there.**

  Plan, save, and do what you can. If you all are unable to afford it, then you are not able to afford it. Don't go racking up credits card bills. Use wisdom and do what you can.

- **Don't be aggressive.**

  Aggression is not your friend in dealing with or talking to your husband.

- **Say so he can understand, not like he is a kid.**

  Talk to him like a man. One who you respect, value and want to reach understanding with. **Say it respectfully.**

  No man wants to be treated like he is nothing, or that he is being demanded to do something.

  He is not your servant, nor is he your enemy, nor is he your child, just keep that in mind. Respect and honor.

When you request something of him, you expect him to honor your request out of his love for you and respect for the position you hold in his life. It is only right that you take the same principles regarding his position in your life.

Remember: Disrespect never helps; it damages.

"He did what it took to get me, now needs to do what takes to keep me."

Ladies, please give him a little credit. You have to admit that he has way more responsibilities now than when you guys were just dating.

You ARE his responsibility now. He is husband, provider, confidant, etc., and in life, he may have to become more focused on one or two things more than the other so he can provide for his household.

It may not be that he has forgotten about you or is willingly taking advantage of you, it could just be that his focus is on maintaining stability.

Refocus with wisdom.

Communication is key but patience, compassion and understanding unlocks the door.

There is a term that says, *"the squeaky wheel gets the oil,"* and we often take this approach when trying to convey our needs and displeasures.

The problem is that we choose to "squeak" instead of communicate.

Sometimes we "squeak for oil" when what we need is air. Many times, it not really about what we are saying or thinking that it's about. Some frustration may come from lack of quality time with him and many times It's from lack of quality time with HIM.

How much time do you spend with God, learning you, and allowing Him to grow you?

"We never do anything!"

Don't say that. It's not what you mean. What you really mean is "*I would like/need some quality and focused time with you outside of the house. I would like you to plan something special, just for you and me, and for us go and do it.*" And that is what you need to say wisely.

When you tell a man he never does anything, it devalues him and his efforts.

"All you do is work! You don't do anything for me!"

Him going to work and providing is a major thing for him and for you. He is not just working for himself, he is working to provide for you.

Being the provider is his way of saying **_"Baby I love you and I got you."_** Appreciate it, and appreciate it verbally. Randomly acknowledge the hard work that he puts in. Many days, when he wants to quit or stay home, he doesn't, because he knows he needs to care for you. So, to say he does _"nothing"_ is a bad statement to make.

Ladies, you must communicate.

The goal is for him to hear your concerns, thoughts, heart, etc., not your disgust and frustration. You can accomplish more by talking than by fussing. Again, he doesn't "just know", you have to tell him and tell him clearly.

If you would like to go out, say something like: **_"I would like to go to (fill in the blank) on Friday (or whatever day) just me and you. I need this."_**

Whatever you tell him, say it clearly, lovingly and respectfully.

Tell him what you need. Don't expect him to know or interpret what you mean.

Basically, men want to feel respected and for us to communicate clearly what it is that we need. A loving husband naturally wants to provide for his wife's needs, but he can be blocked by her in doing it **when she isn't clear or comes to him combatant.**

"Until I get more attention, he is not getting any 'attention'."

Again wives, don't withhold yourself from him sexually as a tool to manipulate him into doing what you want. You are his and he is yours. Don't deny him access to you. Denying him you can backfire on you. You never want to put him in a place emotionally, mentally and/or physically to believe that receiving your love is an ultimatum nor do you want him get accustom to being without you.

Ultimatums usually result more in fight or flight, than in positive results.

Your body is not a tool to get what you want, it is an instrument to maintain, feed and restore what you both need, and it is connected to you.

Don't devalue yourself by detaching that part of you and holding it for ransom.

Remember, he loved you as a whole person so much that he married you. He paid the price, and has been paying every day since for the whole you, the good and the bad. When you take away his benefit of the prize that is you, you may be opening the door for him to seek a job with better benefits.

Not all men will cheat or see cheating as an option, but lack of sex can cause big and unnecessary problems. Many become frustrated, agitated, distant, feel alienated, and begin to spend more time away, whether it be work, being out, or going to the "man cave".

Wives, remember that sex is a place where you connect. Never allow anger, frustration, and/or dissatisfaction to keep you from each other.

"But he doesn't _____ ... And he won't _____..."

Many times, you will find that the reason some guys won't do something is 1. They don't know how, 2. They are not fully aware of what is needed to be done or how quickly it's needed, or 3. They were not appreciated, feel undervalued, was rejected on previous attempts or their efforts were ignored.

Besides communicating instruction, be sure that you don't complain more than you validate, congratulate, and appreciate.

One way to encourage him to "do" is by acknowledging what he does and has done.

Identify the good and speak on it. Tell him *"thank you"* for the little things. What may be little to you may be something big for him. Acknowledge it, cherish it, and say *"thank you."* Even if it's a candy bar, say *"thank you"* and take time to enjoy it. He didn't have to do it, and he did it because he thought of you, so, what he did was his act of love from his thoughts of you. Appreciate it.

He has a lot on him as the head of the house, tell him the specific ways he has positively impacted your life, the lives of your children (if applicable), the home, the community/church/others, and tell him what a great job he is doing.

Send him a text or write him a letter saying how much you appreciate what he does for you. If he dresses up and looks handsome, tell him. Wherever there is a positive, tell him. You are investing in him and feeding/watering his seeds of love and his tree of leadership, his branches of growth, connections and service and his leaves of covering. Your words and actions can help him grow.

Appreciation and encouragement, many times, can help motivate him in becoming or working towards doing or being the things that you requested. Promote and encourage what you need and desire to see. If you desire that he cooks more often, then it may be best to praise, appreciate and enjoy what he cooks already. He will not be motivated to do more if the little that he does do is not received or appreciated. If you "be faithful" over the few, you may start to see more.

"I Am Not Happy. I Want to Leave."

"I'm not happy."

This is the number one statement heard in Christian counseling from married, covenanted couples.

When asked why they are unhappy, many times the "unhappy spouse" projected their reasoning for being unhappy on their spouses. But, the sense that happiness could come from people, places and things is unrealistic. Happiness is a state of "be"-ing. It's where you, the person on the inside, lives and breathes, and it can only be obtained by choice.

Why are you not happy?

Sometimes, the journey to "happiness" starts with choosing to look up, instead of looking around.

Never forget that every single day you have power, and every single day you have choices. Opportunities are everywhere and many times it boils down to choice.

Will you:

- Choose to be grateful for what you have, instead of becoming upset with what you don't?

- Choose that *"today will be a good day"* and speak life into it, even when all around seems like it's going haywire?
- Choose to forgive?
- Choose to love?
- Choose to help others?
- Choose to be an inspiration and encouragement to others?
- Choose to spend time with God?
- Choose to confess the best and stop allowing negativity be released from your mouth?
- Choose to chase your God given vision and leave mediocrity, complacency and fear alone?
- Choose to follow the way of peace?
- Choose to let go of negative words and thoughts?
- Choose to pray instead of complain?
- Choose to live and not die? Even in your relationships?

Remember that life is made of happy and sad.

Life can be full of joyful, fun and enjoyable moments. Cherish the moments, but understand that you live in the world, not just in the moment. Things happen every day. There are going to be good things and then there will be things that hurt us, anger us, frustrate us, and can even make us cry. Remember, these are "moments" too, don't live there. Mourn if you must, but don't live there. If you are angry, hurt, frustrated, take time to heal and then release it.

Ask yourself, ***"Will I allow 'how I feel' to consume me?"***

Emotions are seeds, the heart is good ground, and your mind waters it. Whatever you plant, will grow into something completely different and bigger than you can imagine.

Understand this: No ONE person can make you happy.

If you are looking at what others appear to have and comparing it to your life, stop it. When looking to others, you have to keep in mind that you don't know what they did to get it, and you don't know what they have to do to keep it. Not everything is as good as it seems.

Husbands:

"My wife just doesn't make me happy anymore"

Ask yourself,

- What does make you happy?
- Have you shared it with her?
- Why does it make you happy?
- Are you sure it's happiness or are you just wishing to live in a moment or event that you enjoy?
- Have you opened up to others about what you feel? Why or why not?
- Do you usually share your thoughts with your spouse? Could it be better?

Identify how you feel first, and then understand why you feel, so you can deal with what you feel. She doesn't just know what's in your head. You need to tell her, and when you do, don't do it from a place of frustration, do it in love and with compassion. Help her "see" you, and your point, through understanding.

Are you looking at the lives of other men and comparing it to the life you have?

Many men tend to look at the lives of other men around them and/or men they "think" have the life or lifestyle that they want or have desired.

Many times, that "grass on the other side" is turf. It's not real. And the funny thing is that many of the men that are being watched are secretly desiring the life, love, family, etc. that the guys watching them have.

Take into account what you have at home. It may not be perfect but it's yours and it has the possibility to be workable if you are willing to put in the work.

Again, counseling may be necessary and a wise choice before deciding to take off and leave. It may give you a place to share your heart, how you feel, and help her better understand what you need, want and/or desire. Sometimes it may take someone on the outside to speak your heart to your wife in her "language."

Wives:

"My husband doesn't do romantic things and I'm tired of talking. "I'm tired of this. It's like he doesn't get it, and I'm just not happy anymore."

Many times, he may not "get it" because of how it's communicated to him and/or how he is trying to communicate it to you.

There could be many reasons he is "missing in action." Maybe you are not speaking his language. Maybe you have not spoken to his needs, and it is affecting his ability to emotionally tap in or connect with you. Maybe he feels like what he is doing romantically is bad because of your response.

He may be trying in his own way to do something for you romantically.

Many times, it's subtle and tiny to us but, to many men they were "truly making an effort to be more intentional" in their own way. It may not be large or really noticeable, but any change for you, whether large or small, is a change made <u>for</u> you.

Maybe he does not understand your language, the full meaning of what you are saying, or he does not understand the importance of what you are asking.

This is where wisdom and strategies meet conversation. Outside of counseling, you may also have to change how you say what you say and alter your normal way of doing things. But whatever you do, do it IN LOVE not out of frustration.

If he is not doing it right, teach him, but be sure to show him in love. Don't be motivated by your frustration. God has been patient with you all your life, you could show a little more patience, grace and forgiveness in this moment.

If he doesn't get it, try saying it "differently."

Remember: If he is trying then he is making a step in the right direction. He is not going to get everything right every single time, but when he does do something acknowledge it. Say thank you. Encourage with kindness.

Never compare him to you and/or other people.

It's unfair and wrong to line him up next to a standard set in your own mind. Let go of the image that you placed in your head, and ask God to show you the blueprint so you can build. You didn't make your husband and he didn't make you. He is not going to just "know."

Plus, both men and women are finicky creatures, who honestly do not know what we want. We just know what we don't want, and generally, we don't know that we don't want it until it's being done.

It may be time for you to take the initiative.

He may not know what you like or he might be thinking that he is doing a good or "ok" job in his own way. Try planning some things for you guys to do and invite him to schedule some time so you can do it together. Establish a romantic mood or initiate the type of physical contact he likes and let it lead into the contact that you like.

Speak to his mind before you try speaking to his body. Maybe he is not responding because of your response and past responses with him. Again, rejection does not say "welcome" to the person being rejected. Love is not a game of search and rescue or a tug of war; it is something to be enjoyed and a tool to build a better, united life.

It may be what you are NOT SAYING, that he doesn't understand.

If you desire something, be clear. Speak to him respectfully and clearly. Invite him to try new things and the things that you desire. You define what you desire in your quality time. If he is making the effort, then give him the tools that he needs. Don't be angry and want to put him off when it's you who refuses to give him the tools he is looking for.

For example, if he asks you what you want to do, tell him what you want to do. If its dancing, say it. If it is going to a certain restaurant, say it. If it is getting a room for just you and him, away from the kids, work, church, school etc., say it. If you want a foot rub and a hot bath, tell him. Don't tell him "anything" or "it doesn't matter" when you know that there is something that you want and it does matter. Give yourself a break and don't be afraid to say it.

It is confusing to him when you say you need quality time, and then when he tries to give it, you become mad at him for something he did or didn't do.

You can't hit him and then expect for him to smile.

Sometimes his actions or lack of action is a direct result of our actions, behavior and/or words. You may be training him to run from you with the things that you are putting in place for him to run to you.

If he feels abused by you it is not going to be easy for him to keep running to you. You may be your own worst enemy. If one second you are all "lovey dovey," then the next second you are snappy, then the following second you want to hug and cuddle, and then the next second you are angry want him to *"get out!"*. HE IS GOING TO STEP BACK. He doesn't know who or what he is going to get. Many times, he steps back to see if you are ok, if he is going to be ok with you, or if he is not seeing what it is you need from him.

***This same principle applies to husbands with their wives.**

Men and Women:

When you are angry or frustrated, take time to ask yourself: "Is this issue bigger than God, worth my marriage and/or more important to me than my husband/wife?"

If not, deal with it or drop it and love each other. Nobody knows how long they have on this earth. Don't allow little things to cause big problems. You don't know how long they are going to be around. Treat them with the love they need, and hold them close while you can. Don't allow pride and refusing to forgive be the thing that separates you.

If you are a person who holds on to drama, confusion and past hurts, please let it go. Many people lose life, love and happiness because the refuse drop what they are holding over their husband's or wife's head.

Husbands, wives and those looking to marry:

Gods mercy is new every morning, and yours should be too. Today is a new day, don't carry over anything into today that doesn't belong in today. Leave the hurts of yesterday in the forgiveness of yesterday.

Repeat after me: "I WON'T DO LEFTOVERS."

Every day is a "new" day.

Each day should be filled with new, new love, new compassion, new passion for God, life and your spouse. If YOU are not happy, take some time to go before God and find out why you are not happy. It is not always about what someone else did or didn't do. Oftentimes, we can play the blame game, when most of the blame is often with us. In many instances, it's not really about being "happy"; it's about not feeling fulfilled.

There is a joy that accompanies fulfillment and, many times, that is what is missing. The job of making or keeping you fulfilled is never another person's responsibility. That is between you and God.

Take time to examine yourself:

- How is your relationship with God? Do you spend quality time or do you say "hi" here and there and let HIM know what you need? Are you doing the same thing with your spouse?
- What is your purpose? Are you walking in it?
- Do you know the difference in your purpose, your gifts, and your tolerance?
- Who have you been sharing your dreams/goals/vision with?
- Are you Joseph? -shared dreams with people who want to kill it and you.
- Are you Mary? - surrounded with Elizabeth's who 1. understands your process 2. See God's purpose in you and 3. their baby/promise leaps when you are around.
- Who do you spend the most time talking to? God? Your spouse? Or someone outside your union?
- Are you complaining more than you appreciate?

Look deeper. There is a lot more "good."

Go Deeper. - God is good and His mercy endures forever. When you can't find the good in them, find the good in God. When was the last time you lost yourself in His presence? When was the last time you and your spouse, both, went together?

Be deeper. Create more "good." Be what you want to see.

Watch what you say. (even when it never comes out of your mouth)

The prayer is never: "Lord, change my spouse."

The prayer SHOULD be:

"Lord work on me. Help me to love as You love, unconditionally. Help me to see how You would want me to see. Help me to speak how You would want me to speak. Open up my compassion, understanding, and my capacity. Fill me with You. Help me to reflect Your heart towards my spouse. Open my ears so that I may hear You clearly and hear the heart of my husband/wife. Please give me wisdom with what I hear, see, and speak, both inwardly and outwardly. Show me ways to reach my spouse, deal with, relate to, and build him/her. God, I need Your divine wisdom and strategies to build me, my spouse and my marriage. Please help me. Amen"

Many times, God wants to deal with us first. The door to our own hearts may be the first door God desires to open, enter, and reside.

"Lord, help me..." is a prayer that can be done daily. Prayers like this and the one above are also helpful in watching what you say when you are mad, frustrated, unsettled and feel like walking away.

Praying *"Lord help me..."* is a way to refocus our eyes from the person/issue back to God. When we are able to refocus on God, many times, we begin to see 1. Things from a different perspective, 2. Things we never saw before or may have missed, and 3. Things about ourselves that we may not have even known or noticed.

Focused prayer oftentimes helps us to also see what we need to say in it and about it. As stated many times in this book, what you say, inside and out, is important. Things are not always what they seem or how they seem.

Understand that the fight is so much bigger than you know.

The enemy comes to steal, kill and destroy and he will do all he can to break your marriage up. Cover your husband/wife in prayer daily, no matter how you feel. The enemy fights them, their thoughts, and their emotions. They are carrying weights that they may not be telling you or want to burden you with. They need you.

Cover your marriage in prayer. Temptation is all around. Focus requires determination and sacrifice. Things may not be going exactly how you would want them, but it's yours. Be determined to fight the real enemy, with weapons of warfare, through prayer.

Cover your family in prayer. Children need to be covered as well. They see, hear and experience things that you may never know. Remember that the enemy will search for any area where he can get in. When a family is broken, it affects everyone involved, including children.

Marriage requires sacrifice. Marriage is work. Marriage will require doing things that you don't want to do, you will never get around that.

Always remember: *"There are 2 people in this relationship, neither one is perfect."*

You may have to deal with him/her, but remember he/she has to deal with you.

You are not always easy to get along with. You are not always right. You do not always do the right thing or say the right thing. You have your days when you feel frustrated, angry, hurt, etc. You have your good and your "not so good" moments, and God still loves you.

If you have someone who loves you, treat them with compassion. They may not think like you, or talk like you, or deal with things as you would, but that doesn't make them less than you or undeserving of you; it's makes them human.

Everyone is different and it's selfish and unfair of you to grade your spouse in comparison to yourself, especially when you are more focused on your good and his/her bad.

Fight the Urge to Run and Hide

Sometimes we are faced with fight or flight situations. Sometimes, our minds come up with things that prove to cause more damage than good, and it ends up being a hindrance instead of help.

We face challenges and our minds come up with solutions that say, ***"Things are tough, let me leave."*** or ***"Things are tough. I'm going to release and/or get out my feelings and frustrations."*** Either way, the purpose is to be relieved of stress.

Fight the urge to run and hide in conversation

"Ask and it shall be given unto you..." Matt.7:7

Even GOD requires that you say something. Nobody is in your head with you. No one will automatically know every time what you want or how you want it. Don't mention a topic, and then, get mad that he/she did not fill out the blanks. You want something: Ask

It can be frustrating not getting what you want, BUT it is not anyone's fault but your own IF you haven't stated/refuse to state what you want. If you need something, say something.

Men:

Again,

1.She will not just "get it." You have to tell her in detail what you want.

We need details! Mentioning topics IS NOT ENOUGH. Saying things like, ***"I need a shirt,"*** is not sufficient.

> **When do you need it?** -Is this something that requires immediate attention or is this something you will need within the week?
>
> **How do you need it?**
>
> **What kind of shirt?** -Work? Leisure? Church? Black? White? T-shirt?
>
> **Do you have it or do we need to buy it?**

All of these questions are questions that NEED to be answered. Help us help you. If you do not share details, we may not know exactly what it is you expect or need. If the shirt was for a specific occasion or event, let us know. If it needs to be a specific color, let us know. We need you to tell us what you want.

2.Ask her. Never demand.

No one wants to be made to feel "less than" or disrespected. When you demand, it makes us feel disrespected. How you talk to us is important. We are here to help you. It is our pleasure to serve you, especially when you are a pleasure to serve.

Always remember that you command respect; never demand it.

3.Say "please" and "thank you" as much as you can.

It's not just polite; she needs to hear it. Show her that she and her efforts are appreciated. Appreciation is a form of respect. She may be a help to you, but she is not a slave.

Women:

Once again...

1. He will NEVER just "know" or "get it." You need to tell him.

2. Don't give too many details all at once. Ask for what you need and allow him to do it.

3. Say it calmly, respectfully and in its simplest form. Sometimes we make things too complex and difficult when the matter itself is simple.

If the car needs to be washed say *"honey, please can you take the car to the car wash today? I really need it."*

instead of

"(Insert name here), the car is dirty and I was driving it all over town. You knew I had to go to work. Why didn't you wash it? I was embarrassed to be seen in it. Who wants to ride around in a dirty car? Didn't you see that it was dirty? I can't

believe you would let me drive around in it and you tell me that you loved me. Your car doesn't look like that...."

When you approach him like this, it is NOT a motivator for positive change.

4. State what you want, ask respectfully and with love, and say "please" and "thank you,"

5. Show your appreciation.

One of the biggest complaints that men say that they have is that they do not feel appreciated. It is also a big reason why many men say they choose to walk or step away.

Don't assume he knows how you feel about him. Don't just tell him; show him you appreciate him. Even if you get him a card or write him a letter, do something that says, *"I appreciate you and all you do."* It goes a long way. You may even find that he may begin to do more for you, and could possibly become considerably more willing and joyful in giving and doing, when he feels appreciated.

Many men may also choose to "walk" when they feel disrespected, unnoticed, and unheard. Disrespect is NEVER good for your husband or your relationship. Ignoring him is not good either.

Men are natural born leaders. It damages them when those who they lead refuse to hear their voice and/or instruction, and also when their position is challenged or dismissed.

Fight the urge to run away.

Every marriage has its ups and downs, but you have to fight for your marriage.

"For we wrestle not against flesh and blood but against principalities..." Eph. 6:12

The fight that you have is not with each other. It is ALWAYS against the things that come to attack your marriage, household, and family unit. Principalities use strategies to overtake, control and command.

Whatever comes in, comes to steal, kill and destroy. It comes to steal joy and steal focus from what you have and from what you have the potential to build together.

If the enemy can get you to focus on each other as the problem, you will be so focused on fighting each other, that you will not join together to fight him.

This gives the enemy access to your household, your children and your legacy.

Once a seed is planted and allowed to grow, it becomes a tree that produces more fruit.

There is a parable in the bible about an enemy that snuck in while a man was sleeping. That enemy sowed tares in with the wheat of the sleeping man's field. Tares, also known as darnel, were toxic/poisonous.

The enemy still does this principle today.

While we are "sleeping" or are unaware, the enemy comes in and plants things in our minds, in our conversations, in our children, etc. They are toxic to our relationships and poisonous to us, and they can kill us, little by little and quickly. We all must be aware of who, what and why we fight, because, sometimes, **the fight that we face is just there to keep us unaware**.

The fight often develops with the things on the inside. Unchecked, it can become inwardly acceptable, outwardly visible, and/or harm the person and others he/she is around.

Examples of these are:

- Pride
- Unforgiveness
- Stubbornness and unwillingness
- Focus and drive
- Determination and wanting to give up
- Anger
- Lust
- Lack of desire- (frustration could also be a cause of this)
- Lack of trust
- Lack of communication

All of these are things that can and will affect any relationship, especially a marriage. All of these areas can be used as weapons/tools of the enemy to destroy and many times, they are placed in our own hands.

A refusal to deal, is a refusal to heal.

When we allow things like pride to keep us from each other, we are damaging what we have and the strength of unity. It's like tearing down your own roof. You still would have a house, but now you are exposed and vulnerable to the "outside elements."

Don't leave your spouse and your home vulnerable. Don't allow pride to displace and replace you or him/her. Again, pride is killer of relationships. You have got to watch it.

Be careful of the fight in your mind.

The battle of the mind can become the issues of the heart. The unaddressed and/or unsolved issues of the heart can cause "attacks" to the marriage. Cast down imagination.

Don't let your thoughts cause you to see things are not there and miss the things that are.

Beware of Snakes

"Now the serpent was more subtil (crafty) than any of the wild animals the Lord God had made. He said to the woman, "Did God really say, 'You must not eat from any tree in the garden'?" The woman said to the serpent, "We may eat fruit from the trees in the garden, but God did say, 'You must not eat fruit from the tree that is in the middle of the garden, and you must not touch it, or you will die.' " "You will not certainly die," the serpent said to the woman. "For God knows that when you eat from it your eyes will be opened, and you will be like God, knowing good and evil." When the woman saw that the fruit of the tree was good for food and pleasing to the eye, and also desirable for gaining wisdom, she took some and ate it. She also gave some to her husband, who was with her, and he ate it." Genesis 3:1-6

Watch out for the serpent.

"Now the serpent was more subtil than any beast of the field which the Lord God made..."

The serpent is not as big as everything else. The serpent is not as loud as everything else. The serpent is often hidden in the grass.

Be careful of the little things. It's the smallest things that are the most underestimated. In every relationship, there are going to be some things that will arise that you will have to deal with. Deal with it. Don't sweep it under the rug; get rid of it altogether.

People are going to do things that anger, upset, and frustrate us, but oftentimes, they won't even know that they have done it and/or the effect that it has on us.

Sometimes, the things that bother us the most are caused by misunderstandings.

Determine if it's something worth discussing. If not, forgive and let it go. If yes, discuss it (don't fuss it), and then come to an understanding, forgive and let it go.

Be careful of "grass covered agendas".

Hidden agendas are also things that can infiltrate a marriage. Be watchful of yourself and your surroundings. Not everyone who says, "I come in peace," really comes in to bring peace. Pray for wisdom in how to identify and handle those who come to deceive.

Couples also need to watch for their own hidden agendas. They should continually ask themselves why they are really doing what they are doing, or saying what they are saying. Sometimes, we tend to tell ourselves or others one thing, when deep down it is really something else.

Identify what you are doing and why. If it hurts or has the potential to hurt your marriage, you spouse, your family, and/or yourself in any way, don't do it, say it, or pretend it.

Beware of people, conversations, and thoughts that casually introduce and/or feed negativity, seek vengeance and sow discord.

It was the serpent that presented the ideas that caused separation between God and mankind. It was mankind who chose to listen and obey.

Be mindful of who and what you allow to influence you. Be careful of what you entertain.

Anything that comes to separate you from the presence of God, the promised of God, and the word of God, get rid of it.

In these situations, it may be wise to ask questions like:

> *Is she/he causing me to doubt my spouse?*
>
> *Since he/she has come around me, have I been doubting the love, honor, and attention of my mate?*
>
> *Since he/ she has come around me, have I been doubting the love and patience I have for my spouse?*

Also, be careful of conversations that promote and/or harvest doubt. If you find that any of the answers to the above questions is "yes," then you need to evaluate and/or eliminate anything and/or anyone that responds contrary to what GOD said, and/or goes against positive growth or confidence in your marriage.

Be mindful of those who tell you "yes," when God says "no".

Promise accompanies obedience. If God says "No," don't let anything and anybody tell you it's a "yes." That is a sure way to miss out on receiving obedience's blessing.

The consequences are ALWAYS more than what you think.

The serpent told Eve that she would be as God and would know good and evil. **She looked at the serpents offer of the knowledge as being good thing, not as the knowledge becoming a part of life.** When she took of the fruit, she introduced EVIL to the good that she already had access to.

You must be careful of what you allow yourself to believe and consume. You could be digesting things from others that could separate you from your spouse and from God.

You must reject those who want to 1. Help you see yourself as GOD and 2. Introduce evil to good.

The position of God is never the position you want to take. Beware of those who continually advise you to take matters in your own hands and eliminate God. Only God knows everything. If only a fool answers a matter without hearing the sides, then, when you choose to become god instead of seeking God, you will continue to answer foolishly.

Beware of people who always have something negative to say about your marriage or your spouse and those who try to "introduce evil to good." Again, everyone comes in with a seed and every seed has the potential to grow when it is planted. You must be careful of the seed and ideas that you allow to be planted in you and/or your spouse regarding your marriage.

Don't be like Eve, who jumped at the opportunity to get something that she did not possess, at the risk of losing what she already had.

You should be careful of seeking for and desiring "the knowledge of good" when you already have it. When you look at what you think you lack, instead of what it is that you have, you can forget that what you already possess is good.

It may not be perfect, but it has the potential to be better.

Eve already had access to good but she **still** went looking for it.

Beware of those who try to change your view from seeing "good."

One of my father's quotes he often uses is *"One's perception is often one's reality"* and I believe that quote could be applied here.

What you allow yourself to "see" will be what you begin to see. The first thing the enemy went for was her belief, when he said to the woman, *"Did God really say...?"*

Many times, the seed of disbelief is still being sown with a question. ***"Did God really say...?"*** In a marriage, it often sounds like *"Does He/She really love me?" "Am I beautiful?" "Is what we have or who I am good enough?"* and *"What if...?"*

Often, those seeds that are planted become planted during conversations 1.) with ourselves and 2.) with others. There is a reason the bible tells us to "Cast down imagination" and that we should "think on these 'things'."

The enemy drops seeds of doubt by asking a single question, and when we entertain it, we begin to define the question and answer it. Our answers then become our perception. If I perceive a thing as bad, then I begin to eventually see and treat it as such. Keep in mind that emotion will follow whatever decision you make. Like it or not, you were designed that way.

The mind, based on what you feed it, thinks and then makes a decision. It then tells the heart, and, if the heart chooses to believe it, then the mind creates a way in or a way out.

Throughout the creative process of God in Genesis, whenever God created, he saw that it was good. You must ensure that your "view" of your marriage remains as it was when you joined together and created it. You saw good possibilities. You meant good for each other. You had good conversation. You had good fun. You planned to have a good life with each other. You saw the good that could come in the future. Never lose focus of the good. Let that be your vision and your continued goal.

Go back, and see it from "the beginning..."

Be careful. If the serpent was "more subtil", then there were things that were less subtil.

The enemy has many devices in all different shapes and forms. The tactics might be different but the goal is still the same: **Approach.- Reposition sight.- Cause separation.**

The best way to lose sight of God is when the enemy can **get you to look at you.**

Pride is the number one killer of relationships. Pride is the reason we don't speak, we don't apologize, we harvest anger, we feed hatred, we lie, we cover our sins and indiscretions, we stand our ground even if it's not right, we refuse to forgive, and we seek personal vengeance.

When Pride says *"Me!"* it stops listening to *"we"* in relationships. In every relationship, we must be careful of the enemy of pride. Parents to children, children to parent, husband to wife, wife to husband, friend to friend, boss to worker, co-worker to co-worker, family member to family member, leadership to leadership, believer to believer, believer to non-believer, etc., every person, in every area, needs to be watchful of pride.

Pride closes doors that should be open and opens doors that should be closed. It makes us feel *"I should be here"* and for others *"you should not,"* which is not always the case. Look at anger. It's not a sin to get angry but it is harmful to you and everyone around you, when you allow it to join pride and get into your heart. *"As a man thinks in his heart, so is he."*

When anger reaches the heart, it becomes rage, bitterness, and/or unforgiveness. You begin to act out what's on the inside. Tempers, adult tantrums, separating oneself from others, harsh words, nasty attitudes and dispositions are all fruit that come from seeds of anger and pride that has reached the heart.

Beware of the seeds that you allow to be planted. Guard your mind. Guard your heart. Guard your marriage.

Again, watch what you say AND what you allow to be said over you or regarding you, your marriage and your spouse.

I know sometimes you want to vent but be careful not to release "venom." Venom is anything toxic that can harm, taint and/or kill. Don't forget that from the beginning the enemy came in as a "serpent."

Spouses, be aware...

Genesis 3:6 NIV *"When the woman saw that the fruit of the tree was good for food and pleasing to the eye, and also desirable for gaining wisdom, she took some and ate it. She also gave some to her husband, who was with her, and he ate it."*

Let's focus on the part that said *"...She also gave some to her husband, who was with her, and he ate it."*

1. **Eve was the one who gave forbidden fruit to her husband.**

   It wasn't the serpent. It was his own wife, bone of his bone and flesh of his flesh, who gave it to him. You must be careful of what you feed your spouse. Sometimes you could knowingly and unknowingly be feeding them "forbidden fruits" like fear, distrust and insecurity. These are also things that, when consumed, can separate them from you, separate them from purpose, and cause them to cover up and hide.

2. **Adam knew what God said, yet he noticed the enticing fruit, not the state of the enticed wife.**

It is important not to ignore the things that affect and infect your spouse. Be present. Be attentive. Again, pray and ask for wisdom to see and to uproot the seeds of the enemy that you see growing or being planted.

Sometimes it is going to take for you to speak up. It is going to require that you not only stand beside them, but that you walk in your authority and come against things that come to displace your marriage and/or your spouse, by remind them of and standing on what God said.

3. **Adam ate it.**

Don't just allow things to happen and don't participate in things you know is wrong.

When you do not keep the standard, you lower the standard, and many times it becomes either something that you continue or you continue to lower. Life is like an ice tray. Whatever you allow in one area, has the potential to spill over into other areas.

Are You Building Insecurity?

Husbands:

Accountability supports

Trust is the foundation for trust. If she sees that she can trust you, then she will feel that she can trust you. If your actions look suspicious, then you look suspicious. It doesn't matter if you *"weren't doing anything untrustworthy."*

If you can, avoid negative appearances. Take the verse *"Don't let your good be evil spoken of"* and apply it to your marriage. If anything you are doing or saying can appear "evil" to your spouse, don't do it.

Unless it's a surprise for her for a birthday, anniversary, special moment, etc., why is there a need to hide it?

"And the eyes of them both were opened, and they knew that they were naked; and they sewed fig leaves together, and made themselves aprons. And they heard the voice of the Lord God walking in the garden in the cool of the day: and Adam and his wife hid themselves from the presence of the Lord God amongst the trees of the garden. And the Lord God called unto Adam, and said unto him, Where art thou?" Genesis 3:7-9 KJV

From the beginning of the fall of mankind, we have been covering our nakedness and hiding.

What are your fig leaves?

What are you using to "cover" yourself? Is it adequate? Are you protecting what you consider private but still leaving yourself uncovered in relationship?

Sometimes we cover up the things that we feel are personal, but in a marriage relationship, that could be the very thing that is damaging the relationship. Be it a friend of the opposite sex, division of the assets, hidden agendas, secret desires, secret conversation or whispers on the phone, etc., it has the potential to be a "cover up" or appear as a "cover up."

When should you cover?

Cover in counseling.

Protect yourself. If someone wants to meet, have private counseling, whether it's ministry or secular, make it a team effort! Don't leave yourself naked with other people and covered with your spouse. That is a very dangerous thing.

I often see men and women, men especially, swept away by conversation that pertain to counseling or calls for them to comfort.

For men, the "need of a savior" creates a platform for you to rescue or invest in a woman's way of escape. BE CAREFUL!!!!

This is often a tactic used to bring distention and cause separation. When a woman says, *"I need you"* through conversation, the man in you stands up. You must be aware.

Not all women who say they need help is really looking for your help. Many are looking for your concentration, your emotion, and some are even seeking the rights and positions that belong to your wife.

Don't be fooled by tears and soft, heartfelt words, or by being drawn in by your own need to help or be a "hero." Many times, that "hero" becomes a victim, when he is not aware.

Cover yourself with wisdom. If a woman that is not your wife needs something, point her in the direction of God and your wife. ALWAYS make three your minimum. The conversation may require more people to be involved than you, your wife, and God, but it will never ever be less.

Never take on the role of *"I got this".*

You may be a preacher, teacher, counselor, wise man, tribal elder, a senior citizen, pastor, apostle, protective brother figure, friend, neighbor, altar worker, minister or concerned citizen, but you do not have all of the answers. You will never see all the angles unless God shows you, and you will NEVER see all that your wife sees.

Men know men and women know women. Yes, each individual person is different, but the nature is not. As a man, you can often identify the nature of man. As a woman, she often identifies the nature of a woman.

As much as you see, even prophetically, it is about as much as you don't see because you don't know what to "look" for. There are certain things that woman can identify, even from just a "hello."

God created Eve as a help mate. If God gave you a spouse to help, let her.

Cover yourself from other women.

Again, there will be many times when that "damsel or sister in distress" could be just a woman looking for attention.

It's not always malicious, but beware: **Conversation feeds a void in intimacy.**

When a woman speaks, she is sharing pieces of herself with you. When offering counsel, it's best that she knows she is sharing with "us" and not "me." She doesn't get just YOU, there is a unified package deal that will not and cannot be separated.

If she needs to "talk," direct her to a wise woman with a prayer life. Let your words be few and fueled with prayer and wisdom. Even through text, it's best to use wisdom.

If she "wants a man's opinion," be sure she knows it's coming from a MARRIED MAN. The question and the answer she receives should be presented to and by the package deal.

She should NEVER have you alone, even if it's through text.

You don't need:

1. anything that separates you from your spouse, even conversation

AND

2. anything to be misconstrued.

Women have ways that they themselves do not notice, have not identified and do not understand. Even the sincerest of heart can develop feeling and/or behaviors and not even realize it.

Cover your wife. Cover yourself. Cover your relationship.

- If there is anything that she has to say to you that she cannot say in front of your wife, she should not be saying it.

- If there is anything that you say and/or do that cannot be shared with your wife, you shouldn't be saying it or doing it.

- Don't try to cover emotional infidelity with spiritual reasoning. God is not the author of confusion. If you are confused emotionally regarding your wife and/or relationship because of time spent with this person, cut it off.

- You don't "got this" and you will never have it. Stop trying to handle things by yourself. Proverbs says that only a fool answers a matter without hearing all sides. It's time to stop answering matters without having information and instructions that God has. It's time to start hearing the heart of your mate that wants to fulfill her God given purpose to help and cover you. It's time to stop going alone and start proceeding "as one."

- When you proceed alone, you enter situations as a fool, unarmed and unprepared. Operating in the "Lone Ranger" mentality can seriously damage your spouse as well as your relationship. Sadly, you may not even notice the effects of your decision to walk alone until after you and your spouse are naked to the world and emotionally, mentally, and spiritually hidden from each other.

As a husband, you cover your wife and your household. Your job is to protect her, your family, and your relationship, and that often means leaving the rest of the world "uncovered." Nothing hidden, nothing covered, from God and from her.

Always keep in mind that women were created to be helpmates.

Women SEE where men need help, and just like with the ways we can see areas to help you, <u>we can also see the areas that 1. are lacking, 2. are access points, and 3. can hurt, damage, or weaken you.</u>

Not every woman uses the knowledge she sees/ has about you for your good.

Wives:

Any man outside of your marriage is not your "savior"; God is.

I don't care how good of a listener he is, stop making self-deposit into other men's "bank accounts." Every conversation you have includes pieces of you, whether you know it or not. We not only think logic and emotion, but we also SPEAK our thoughts "IN" logic and emotion. Each conversation includes deposits and glimpses of our soul.

Again, the soul is defined as "the mind, will and emotion". The three go hand in hand. The good and not so good thing is that the mind will take emotion by the hand and lead it or emotion may take the mind by the hand and run with it. The WILL will always be a follower.

Many times, the mind will become active with sight. Sight, being the things that we see naturally AND what/how we see things mentally. We must be careful because "sight" can cause us to think, create scenarios, and to come up with plans of action.

We are emotional creatures and everything we do has emotion in it.

As stated previously, conversation is a part of intimacy for us. When we, as women, speak, we are using our words as an expression of our mind and heart. And, with each opening, we not only "give out", but we take in.

When the heart opens to let things out, we then fill the spaces by taking things in. When we complain that *"he is not taking enough time for me,"* we fill it with people that do. When we say things like *"I don't trust him,"* we begin to gather someone who we do trust. If he doesn't listen, we hold on to someone who does. Again, we tend to fill the voids...

When you, conversationally and emotionally, replace and/or fill the voids with men and even women outside of God and your husband, you begin to psychologically, emotionally, and in some cases physically, replace and fill the voids with them and not your husband.

Beware and be wise.

- If you are spending time talking to any man outside of your husband, and you are not talking to your own husband and God, STOP IT!
- If you are spending MORE time talking to him than you do your own husband, stop it!
- If you are talking to him about your husband privately, stop it!

Don't give the enemy access to your heart and the door of your home by giving another man knowledge of the "hidden keys". When you speak, you give out details and pieces of yourself and you don't even realize it.

If you can't wait to get on the phone with your guy friend and not your husband, then something is wrong and it's time to evaluate and separate yourself from the guy friend.

Take time to ask yourself,

1. Why are you excited to talk to him?

and

2. Could your husband be included in EVERY conversation? If not, why continue it?

    If so, why isn't he included?

EVERY conversation and interaction that you have with men outside of your relationship should be something that honors 3.

God, your husband and yourself. If a conversation or interaction dishonors God or your husband, then you shouldn't be having it.

Cover yourself. Cover your spouse. Cover your marriage.

You may be the voice of reason, a wise and virtuous woman, a spokeswoman, counselor, pastor, preacher, minister, apostle, doctor, best friend, God sister, sister figure, like a cousin, grew up with the family, friend of the family, but you personally cannot do anything for him.

You DO NOT have all the answers and you will NEVER see all of the picture. Only God can. You will NEVER have all of the details. Only God does. Don't think otherwise.

Don't be fooled by common traps of intimacy through conversation.

- **You are NOT *"the only one he can trust."*** If he can't trust God, then how can he trust you? You and your husband are one; if he can trust you, then he should be able to trust your husband.

- **No matter what he's going through, he doesn't "_need you._"** He needs God, so point him in that direction.

- **Don't fall by the wayside by allowing men to enter the intimate parts of you, even in conversation.** Conversation leaves you naked. If you are naked, then you are vulnerable. If you are vulnerable, then your husband's treasures are exposed. When you are exposed, you leave room for attack.

Allow your husband to "see" you, and cover you from the rest of the world.

Be wise. Your husband is a protector and there are predators in the world that you will need protection from.

Not every man that seems to be sent by God or seems to be friendly is going is actually sent by God or friendly. Some may be sent as a trick of the enemy and could successfully destroy the union, faith, and hope in your marriage and even in yourself. Be aware and be wise.

Husbands and wives:

Continually cover yourselves from the world but be naked and unashamed with God and each other. Watch the tactics of the enemy. Remember, the enemy comes to steal, kill and destroy.

If any conversation or interaction, male or female, comes to steal time, joy, or peace from your relationship, kill joy, passion, or trust from and in your relationship, and/or is destroying your relationship, cut it off.

God will NEVER send you someone to tear up your marriage. HE says, *"the two shall be come one."*

It's the enemy that wants the "one" to become two.

Accountability

Husbands: When you don't have accountability, you plant or water seeds of insecurity in her.

She does not ask you where you are going and what you are doing just to be nosey or act like your mother. She is genuinely concerned.

When you say things out loud or to yourself like *"You/she ain't my momma."* Or *"I'm grown. I can do what I want when I want and I don't have to tell you anything,"* you not only cause her to worry unnecessarily, but you also plant and water seeds of insecurity.

When you become married, you become one flesh. When you cause her insecurities, it is like ordering a big helping of distrust for yourself. When she suffers, you suffer.

Not being open about what you are doing can cause her to imagine it. Lack of information can, and most times will become imagination; a simple trip to the grocery store can quickly turn into a kidnapping.

Wisdom says, "Be open. Be honest. Be Considerate. Be one."

You are one. Why not share? You have nothing to hide so why cause problems unnecessarily? A simple conversation, phone call or text could keep peace in the home and in her heart. Why not do it?

"Blessed are the peacemakers: for they shall be called the children of God." Matthew 5:9

Children of God answer problems, not willingly create them. As a husband and a son of God, and as a representation of Christ with His church, your goal should be to lead in wisdom and uphold peace. One major way is accountability.

Your children are/will be watching. A hiding father teaches his children to hide, and his wife and daughter to know and/or grow in insecurity.

You are the first man your daughter will ever trust. You may not know it, but she sees or will see how you function, and is developing/will develop feelings and beliefs that can, and sometimes will, be carried with her throughout life.

- **For a daughter, she learns the standard of leadership from you and what to look for.**

   If you have a problem with truth, seeds of distrust become planted, and your daughter may grow up looking for and expecting "the lie."

Your standard of practice becomes either **a standard,** or becomes **a charge/responsibility** for her to dig in certain areas, to be able to clearly hear or find truth, even when she already receives it. Learning from her father, she may develop a **distrust in areas where she should be trusting** and a **trust in the distrust** of others.

If you are a man who, in love, stands on integrity, honesty, openness and unadulterated truths and you establish your house on it, she will grow up looking for and expecting to receive the truth, and, when she knowingly hears lies, she could run from it.

- **For a son**, **he learns behavior and outcomes.**

  You are the leadership standard that he has that teaches him how to create the standards in which he will lead.

  If you have a problem with honesty, he will learn to adapt to a world of dishonesty. He will either grow from it, grow with it, grow away from it, or grow tired of it.

If you are a man who stands on honesty, openness and unadulterated truths and establish your house on it, he will grow up looking for and expecting to be a standard of truth, and when he knowingly hears truth, he will build with it.

The Parent Dynamic

Moms, you shape your daughters into what she shall be.

Dads, you seal, validate, and protect it.

Raising Daughters

Moms:

As a woman, your journey is to build a woman, full of God, full of virtue and knowledge, wisdom, peace, and other things that are required for her to be the woman God has called her to be in destiny.

You know what it is like to be girl, teenage girl, woman and all the things that accompany being a female, both negative and positive.

You are able to see what dad is not able to see in her, because you are a woman, and you can identify the traits that hurt and that grow. Your voice is necessary, but it can be often ignored.

Because you have the ability to "see" her, you may get resistance when she cannot hide behind a soft voice and a smile.

Not only can you "identify" her, she can "identify" you. Just like you can "see" her, she can "see" you. Do not allow her to be disrespectful with familiarity. Do not allow her to manipulate with what she "sees."

Being a help-mate, we have the ability to see what is needed and what is lacking, in not only men but in our own children and the people around us. We also have the ability to use it for bad or good.

Do not allow your daughter to practice control and/or manipulation in any form. Once practiced, it will develop and eventually be used on others knowingly and unknowingly. **Don't forget that the things we practice, become a part of us.**

Dads:

You speak to and into who she is, and in your authority, you shape, smooth and refine 1. who she is 2. who she will be and 3. who she will look to be with.

Daughters tend to run to their fathers for protection, direction and validation; the key components in leadership. Based on how you lead, she determines how she wants to be led by a husband in the future.

Your voice is the strongest voice she will ever hear. Use it wisely.

You must be careful with her heart, and you must be careful with yours.

Her heart is open to you, use wisdom and love when handling her. Don't dismiss her when she wants to talk to you. Remember that she is female. When she shares her words, she is sharing that which she holds valuable. She needs her father to acknowledge its value and acknowledge her as valued.

As a father it is also wise to listen in wisdom. Because your heart opens to her, you have the potential to be manipulated.

Because you are the protector, you may valiantly leap into *"I got this"* mode and it could be a set up to 1. get what she wants, 2. Test your loyalty or 3. Keep you from seeing/knowing/noticing what is being done, not being done, or what she does or doesn't want to do.

Sometimes fathers dismiss it as her being "spoiled" by him or him "being wrapped around her little finger." Now, I am NOT saying, "Do not be good to her" or "Don't give her your best." I am saying, "Use wisdom. Operate in love. And do what is best and what is needed."

Raising Sons

Dads:

You pave the way and teach to pave the way. As a man, you see, know and impart what it takes to be a man. You know the struggles of man, how a boy and man processes, and the discipline that it will take to carry him from boy into manhood. You are a leader raising a future leader, who will one day know what it takes to lead and cover his home. You are the prototype that teaches how to be and create prototypes. The things you impart, only you can impart them.

As they grow into adulthood, you may begin to see what looks as defiance and/or a challenge towards your leadership and position. It is them coming into their own sense of becoming a leader. Don't kill it. Use it, teach it and reposition it.

Your sons were made to be leaders, but it will take you to teach them how and when to lead. Every leader is a follower and every follower has the potential to lead. Train them. Let them know that you are the leader of your household while teaching them that youth is a season of preparation for the homes they will lead in the future.

Moms:

You are the nurturer who brings about a balance. You teach how to balance emotion with logic. Your role shows that there is a need for support. Your attention to detail (when they are sick, not eating well, etc.) is something that they need and learn from you. You help their holistic development, mentally, emotionally, physically, and socially.

From childhood to adulthood, "mom" is the parent that boys tend to run to when they need compassion, belonging, nourishment, a shoulder to cry on, etc. Based on how you nurture and support, he may determine what he wants and looks for as a support in a woman/wife and the nurturing he expects to be given to his offspring.

Your voice is often necessary and they are more open to receive what you say than ignore it. You are viewed more as "helpful", than as a challenge. Use it wisely. Your position is not to manipulate nor control. Be careful not to use your position in his heart to keep him under your thumb or away from others.

Be careful that you DO NOT ALLOW your son to practice disobedience, disrespect, or not accomplishing goals and assignments.

Be careful as you "help" that you do not hinder growth, and that you do not do for him what he needs to do for himself.

Don't be an enabler. Don't worry about him being upset. He knows you care, but may not be able to see it until he is older and can see how you loved him enough to teach him discipline.

Be a confidant, but still be a parent. Do not allow familiarity to lessen your authority and/or your voice.

Parents:

Do not be guided by social stigma. Stigmas will always change and they will often surround and be geared by self-focus and not the fulfillment of God's Purposes, God's way.

Your purpose is:

- **To guard**
- **To guide**
- **To teach**
- **To love**
- **To multiply**
- **To disciple**

Fathers, you are the priest of your home. Which means you:

1. Go to God on their behalf.

2. Live by the principles of God.

3. Introduce them to the principles God.

4. Teach them the word of God.

5. Teach them the ways of God.

6. Lead them to the throne of God.

7. Show them the love of God.

8. Love them and show love to them.

9. Show them how you love, honor and cherish your spouse.

10. Show them how to love others.

11. Correct and Discipline.

12. Make disciples that will go out and do the same.

Mothers, you are the supporter, nurturer, and encourager of your home.

You:

1. Go to God on their behalf and/ or (if applicable) Support, encourage, and join alongside their father/your husband in going to God on their behalf.

2. Support, nurture, teach and encourage them in and to live by the principles of God.

3. Teach and encourage them in and with the word of God.

4. Lead them to the throne of God.

5. Show them how you love, honor and cherish your spouse.

6. Show them the love of God and encourage them to show love to others.

7. Correct and discipline.

8. Teach, nurture and encourage your "disciples" to go out and do the same.

Parents, when you teach, teach with purpose. Be intentional with your children and do it from the beginning to the end. Don't wait until they are a teenager to start or stop teaching them.

Be Mindful of Your Voice.

It is important that we purposefully be mindful of the things that we say to, over, and about our children. Matthew 3 shows us a perfect example and foundation of what to say to and regarding our children.

God with Jesus

When Jesus started his ministry, He had not only the assignment of God, but also the approval and the verbal endorsement of HIS FATHER.

Matt 3:17 KJV says, *"And lo a voice from heaven, saying, 'This is my beloved Son, in whom I am well pleased'."*

Let's see how this act of God establishes a foundation for what should become acts of parenting. The NIV helps break it down a bit further:

"And a voice from heaven said, "This is my Son, whom I love; with him I am well pleased."

"A voice from heaven"-

- **God didn't allow his position to keep Him from speaking.** Children need to hear your voice and they need to hear it from your position.

- **God is God but He yet found it necessary to speak to the world about HIS son.**

- **Your position of authority holds more weight than you think it does.** Your voice makes a difference, in your child as well as in the earth.

- **What you say is as important as when you say it.** Beginnings matter to your children, their seasons, their confidence, and the strength of their platform and it should be important to you. As your child grows and learns, show your support, verbally, physically, psychologically, all the "ally's", let them know you are there.

- **Jesus was at the start of His ministry and the first thing that was heard was from HIS FATHER.** Your children are going to hear negativity and face oppositions in life. Allow your voice to be the first and the "loudest" voice that they hear.

"son..."

- Up until this point, the people, as a whole, had known God's voice in judgement and/or instruction. Parenting authority requires balance. Correction is not the only thing that needs to be heard.

Validation -*"This is my son"*

- ***"This is"***- identify and call out

- ***"My son"***-Remind them of where they came from and what they are made of.

Affirmation-*"whom I love"*

- Verbally confirm your love to them and allow them to see that you are not ashamed to tell it to the world.

Reaffirmation- *"...in whom I am well pleased"*

- They need to know they are doing a good job.
- They need to know when they are doing things that are pleasing to you.

Are Your Children Afraid of "You?"

As a parent, it is your job to teach and train up your children in the way they SHOULD go. And what they learn, they use it to become and teach others. Sometimes they learn from what we say, but mostly, they learn from who we are and how we function.

How we knowingly and unknowingly deal with them and talk to them, are tools that teach them how they should be dealt with and how to deal with others. We must be careful that we are not teaching fear.

There are 3 ways that fear can be taught by parents.

1. They learn fear from us.
2. They learn fear in us.
3. They learn to fear us.

Learning the fear from us.

Whether it be to protect them or train them to be aware, we often teach children to be afraid of what we consider to be "monsters." Eventually children grow up associating "monsters" with fear and avoid them. This is not always a bad thing, but it needs to be a balanced thing.

Growing up, "monsters" were scary things or things that could hurt you. They hide under the bed, in the closet and in dark places. Now, as adults, we see that the "monsters", AKA dangers of the world, are real and if we do not watch out, they could hurt us and the ones we love.

When we teach children to fear the "monster," they do not know that they are the ones with the power to wisely avoid, resist, fight or conquer the "monsters." Many of them grow up believing that the "monster" is bigger or stronger than they are and/or can be.

Children process fears that are taught by their parents differently.

- Some children will grow up hiding from the monsters, and teach their children to hide too.

- Some children will grow up and forget or stop believing that there are "monsters."

- Some children will grow up and see the "monsters" and avoid them.

- Some children will grow up and try to prove that they can "fight" and beat the "monsters" their parents warned them about, just because they feel that monsters are not going to rule them or that they CAN handle it.

You never know how a child is going to react to fear. Teach them wisdom instead.

Learning the fear in us.

When our fears become us, we show it and teach it to our children. If we are living a life that is too afraid to try, we can teach them to be too afraid to branch out of their own comfort zone.

Children are always watching and learning, and the biggest thing they learn from us, is who we are. Oftentimes, we reflect what we believe on the outside, even when it is something that we are trying to hide from the world.

Fear, anxiety, and how we deal with life is being seen, processed, and often duplicated or replicated by our kids. One of the biggest fears is the fear of the unknown. We could, unknowingly, be teaching children not to go for the goal because of fear of failure, or teach them not to expect success, because they might fail.

When you teach fear, you teach them to expect or accept failure. Instead, teach confidence, wisdom, and to go for victory. The bible tells us that Christ gives us strength to do all things and they need to know that.

Teach your children what they CAN be, CAN do, and CAN produce. Teach them how and when to walk and to run. Teach them that if they run and fall, they can get back up and try again, they don't have to stay there. Teach them that when they walk, run, stand or get a chance to sit before others, to have integrity, speak and move in wisdom, and when and how to help others in their journey.

Learning to fear us.

Children do what they are taught. If you have a bully's mentality or behavior, the children will either 1. become or 2. run. They will either take on the essence of who you are, or become the victim and survivor of the essence of who you are.

Take for instance, a parent is verbally abusive. The child sees it, learns the behavior, and adjusts to it. Their "adjustments" are ever evolving, ever learning, and a self-preservation mechanism. Based on what they see and/or experience, they DEVELOP. You may begin to see signs of them being verbally abusive to others, exhibiting signs of avoidance, nervousness, reclusiveness, developing bully like speech, tactics and/or mannerisms at home or school, issues with anger, etc. These are some of the same signs that they might exhibit if they are being bullied at school or work.

Children are resilient and can adapt to their surroundings through learning. Learning what works and what doesn't, children begin to form character based on what they see consistently.

The goal is teaching respect. There is a difference between leading with fear and leading with respect.

Here are some questions, answer openly and honestly. This is between you and God. Feel free to take as much time as you need to think on the question, then think on the answer. There is no wrong answer, it just might be an answer that shows you where you are and may need to change.

In your personal notebook, use as much space to write as you want. Remember, this is between you and God. If perhaps you start see yourself less than what/where you would have wanted to be in these questions, allow God to open your heart, mind, and life and let today be a new start on the path to better.

- Are you communicating love enough? How? When? Where?

- Do you "bark" orders? Why?

- Does your child "bark" orders? If so, why? And where did they get that from?

- Does your child cringe when you speak?

- Does your child run to you or away from you when you enter the room or area where they are?

- How often do you embrace/ hug them? Could it be better?

- How often do you say, "*I love you?*" Should it be better?

- Do you exhibit signs of frustration consistently?

- When you are angry, how do you deal with them? Could it be better?

- When you are angry how do you deal with your spouse? Why? How could you be better?

- How do you speak when you are angry? Is it damaging to the person? Is it damaging to the relationship? Is it damaging to all those who are around you?

- Why?

- How can it be better?

379

Remember, each question is a tool to help you assess where you are. It's okay to remind yourself of the questions. Again, there are no wrong answers, there may just be areas that you may want to work on.

"Life Support" Doesn't Stop At 18.

If you are a parent that is praying, *"Lord, just let me get them to 18."*, stop it.

Your children are going to need your support and guidance well after 18 years old. The worst thing you can do is say, *"you are grown now, so go be grown,"* especially when they are just being introduced to adulthood. Your children are your children, pray for them.

They don't know what being an adult really is, or the responsibilities it will take. Whether they choose to go to college, the military or work after high school, they will still need you. They need to hear your voice that says *"I trust you. You can do this! Mom/Dad is here, and I am praying with and for you."*

Don't just leave them to the wolves.

There will be some choices they will have to make on their own, and honestly, some of those decisions are not going to be wise ones. But you are going to need to trust God and continue to pray.

Never give up! There will be some areas that you will have to trust that you have trained them well. Some areas, you may have to undergird and remind. Some areas, you are just going to have to pray and pray hard that God helps them to see, understand, avoid, and/or overcome.

The beginning of the journey of adulthood can be tough for both the child and the parent.

Children were not born with a handbook. They all have their own individual personalities, likes, dislikes, strengths, weaknesses, influences, and leadership qualities, and it can be difficult to gauge what life (good, bad, and all that comes with both), will look like. But, you are not in this alone.

The bible says, *"In all they ways acknowledge HIM and HE shall direct thy paths."* This includes parenting. From birth to adulthood, you must seek GOD for direction, protection, and guidance. Nothing is too small or too big to God. He cares for us so much, that He allows us to come to HIM about anything, large or small, little or much. He knew your children even before the womb, and He has a plan. ***"For I know the plans I have for you, declares the Lord, plans to prosper you and not to harm you, plans to give you hope and a future."*** *Jeremiah 29:11*

Before your children were born, God had a plan and a purpose for their lives and for your life in the role as their parent. In order to know that purpose and plan, you have to seek God. As parents, your job is **to train up your child in the way __THEY__ should go.** The only way to know, is to acknowledge God and listen for instructions.

Parenting requires patience at any age.

The older they become, the more their needs will change. Babies require more attention to detail and the older they become, the more there will be details that will require attention.

The older children become, the more they grow into who they are going to be. They are going to learn responsibility and things about the world and themselves that they never knew. There will be some "details" that you can help with and there will be many that they will have to handle themselves. Keep praying for wisdom, direction, for their protection and for knowledge on how to deal, teach and impart.

Don't be alarmed or panic. There will be times when you can be there physically, and then there will be times when you cannot, either way prayer is in order.

There will even be times when you will need to be there financially, even into adulthood, and then, there may be times when you are not able to, or you may have to withhold as a teachable moment. It may be hard to see your child hurt and/or be uncomfortable but if it is necessary for them to establish and see growth, then you must do what you have to do for their sake.

Teach your children that, although you love them and have their backs, God is their source.

Teach them to be financially wise, even at young ages. Teach them responsibility. Teach them blessings from obedience. Teach them consequences for disobedience, bad behaviors, and negative or bad actions. Teach them discipline. Teach them forgiveness. Teach them second chances. Teach them the value of what they have and what it took to get it. Teach them the value of who they are and what it takes to keep it. You are the parent, it is your job to teach.

Never be afraid of doing what is right because of how you think it will make them feel. **Love promotes discipline. Discipline reflects love.**

The Potential "Step-Parent"

Keep your ears and your eyes open.

When dating, or considering marriage, listen to your children. When your children tell you that they are or feel uncomfortable with or around that person, pay attention and hear them.

You never know what a child sees or has experienced when it comes to the other person, listen to what they have to say. Use wisdom. Don't just dismiss what is being said to you.

Sometimes children can feel uncomfortable because they are uncomfortable with change. And then, there are times when children are uncomfortable because they were given reason to be.

Discern if this a cry for help, or if it is being said because feelings of abandonment, feelings of displacement, and lack of attention.

Listen to your children.

If they say anything that would raise a red flag, write it down or make a mental note of it.

If you know your child to be honest, investigate in wisdom. Let your child know that you hear them and that they need to let you know of anything else that is going on, or if anything else happens. Based on what you receive from your in-depth investigation, deal with it.

If you know them not to be honest, take what they are saying and quietly investigate, in wisdom, to see if there is any truth to what they are saying. Don't go around kicking down doors or knocking people across the head, but don't choose to discard or discount what the child has to say either. They may actually be telling the truth. In all things pray. Pray for clarity, wisdom, and for "how" to deal with it.

Don't turn a blind eye to abuse and misuse.

Don't let your desire for another person keep you from protecting your children. A man or woman who loves you, should also love your children. Their attitude, speech, and behavior should reflect the love in which they say that they have.

Verbal, mental and physical abuse is unacceptable.

No one should be allowed to talk down to, or curse, your children. Words have power. Make sure that the power is giving life to them, not tearing them down.

Be aware of those who use little opportunities to take their anger and frustrations out on your children. Sometimes people have misplaced anger and can focus on children as targets or avenues of release. Be watchful and prayerful.

If a person mistreats your children in the dating process, it is a big chance they will more than likely escalate/increase in the mistreatment the more they become familiar to the parent and the child.

If you notice any signs of abuse, do what is necessary. Not everyone may know or understand that their actions negatively affect the child/children. In those cases, it may be best to address in wisdom. Talk to them about what you see, share the effects of their actions, and allow them to answer. Use wisdom in listening. Depending on the nature of the negative actions, and the reasoning or thinking behind it, you may want to re-evaluate the relationship or even end it.

In cases where it is evident or proven that the intent is malicious, cut it off immediately. No relationship is worth the safety of your children.

Never worry that you will remain alone because of making the right choice.

What God has for you is always better than what you can get for yourself. If you had to choose to let go for the safety of your children, then you made the right decision.

God will never send you someone that will put you or your children in danger. The bible says, *"the blessings of the Lord makes rich and adds no sorrow."* Sexual, physical and mental abuse is sorrow and is not your or your children's portion.

The Step-Parent: Adolescent children

Children are impressionable. Watch what you allow to be said.

Never let ANY ONE speak down about your spouse to your children. It's rude. It's hurtful. And, it has the potential to destroy the step-parent and child relationship, as well as the husband and wife relationship. When you don't put a stop to it, you leave the child and the step-parent in the place of vulnerability.

Children will begin to take on and believe that which is taught to them, and if they hear things like, *"You don't have to listen to him. He is not your father."* or *"She can't tell you what to do,"* it can get into the child and become the attitude. What children are taught, they begin to practice, and what they practice, eventually becomes them.

It is not something small, a joke or a just a "minor issue." It is something major that can kill the connection, damage the people, and sever the relationship.

Sowing discord breaks up unity when it is allowed to 1. be planted and 2. to grow.

As a parent, it's not only your job to stop it, it's also your job to uproot it so that it cannot grow.

It may take returning to the source, or the "spot," where it was planted by telling your children, ***"This is your parent. You will respect them as such, and anyone who tells you otherwise is not speaking truth."***, and by teaching them what a father/mother is, and how the father/mother should be treated. This is a moment of training them up in the way they SHOULD go. **Re-direct them back to 1. Respect 2. Position and 3. Responsibility.**

Respect is a must.

Teach them to honor the Step-Parent's place as a leader and/or a provider in the home. Remind them that the love that the Step-Parent gives them, comes from a willing heart. They are paying a price that they willingly pay to love you and the children, and although they don't always do things perfectly; **they are doing what they think is right, and they are trying.**

The wedge:

Disrespect causes division. Beware of practices and mindsets that invite disrespect. Whether it's Parent VS Parent, Parent VS Step-Parent, Child VS Parent or Child VS Step-Parent, respect has to be a key component in your conversations, dealings and relationships.

Parent VS Parent.

Fighting each other does not help things become better. Do what you can, even when you don't particularly like each other, to work together as best you can. You are/will be a family. Like it or not, you are in this together.

If you are concerned about how the parent or step-parent treats or raises the children when you are not around, it would be wise to be in a position where your words are seen as helpful and not harmful.

You can know more and bring about a positive change by working with the parent instead of working against them. When you work as a team, you have a team to work with. You understand that all of you are working together for the good of the children and that family unit. No one is doing it alone.

Parents and Step-Parents: You may not care for the estranged parent, but it is important that speak respectfully regarding them, especially in front of their children. Children need to know that the step-parent came into their family unit to love, not to cause confusion or be a threat.

No matter how wrong the other parent may be, the children will generally side with their parent, because it is their parent. Parents, many times, are who they know and who they love and who they will protect.

Slighting the parent in front of the children, is to slight the children. Not only do you disrespect the parent, but you also disrespected the children. And you, in turn, invited them to lose respect for you and/or disrespect you.

Parents: Do not allow your children to be disrespectful to or regarding your potential mate, yourself or your "Ex."

Do not allow a standard to be made that cannot continue. **Do not allow yourself to justify a child being disrespectful to anyone in the role of leadership.** Let them know that if they have a problem, there is a right and respectful way of doing it. As a parent, you should remind them that you have their backs and support them, but they must do what is right and what is honorable.

The wedge can sneak in any place where there is tension, strife, disrespect and where we allow things, practices and behaviors that are contrary to unity be or continue.

Step-Parents and Parents:

Be sure to:

- **Watch how you treat the child when the parent is causing trouble or stress.**

  Whether it's the parent or the estranged parent causing the stress, remember who it is that upset you. The children are not the stressful parent. They are not the ones causing the harm or tension. Subconsciously, we can begin to lump the parent and everything that is connected to them as a problem.

  Be intentional. Try seeing them as individuals and not extensions of the problem. Be mindful of your frustration and anger that it does not include or transfer over to the children or others.

- **Share the love.**

  Be sure that you don't put your spouse on the pedestal of being "more important" than your adolescent children. Children need to know that they matter as well. Parents, they also need to know that they need to respect the step-parent and your relationship with them.

  Sometimes single parents are forced to choose between their significant other OR their children. It is a PACKAGED DEAL. You/He/She came with kids, so if you/they want a relationship with a parent, then that person must want and love the kids.

  If there are no plans on stepping into the father figure/mother figure role and all the responsibilities that go with it, then the person should not be pursuing the father/mother.

- **Do not allow the "Ex" to dictate the NEXT.**

  This is a large issue that frequently comes up in relationships that involve step-parents or potential step-parents.

  There may be an "Ex" who has a problem with someone other than them raising their children, someone other than them being around their children, and/or the fact that the other parent has moved on.

If there is a problem, do what you can to face it and deal with it. Again, do not allow disrespect to happen in any form, from anyone.

You, your Ex, and your mate/potential mate have a responsibility to find a system that works for your children and your family unit.

- **Be appreciative.**

  Help your children to acknowledge the Step-Parent's contribution to them, and to their lives, and verbally thank them.

  Having and taking care of children that are not yours, can be difficult. If you have someone who goes to work inside and/or outside of the home to provide for them and protect them, the least they and you can do is say *"Thank you."* Let the Step-Parent know that you see their effort and you appreciate it. A card with words from the heart or a gift to just say *"You are appreciated"* can go a long way.

  Step-Parents, let the children know you appreciate them too. It is not always easy for them either. They need to know that you see them, and that you appreciate what they do for you, your spouse, and around the house. **They need to know that you appreciate them being a part of your family.**

Togetherness is important.

You do not want the Step-Parent nor the children to feel like outsiders.

Each person needs to feel, see, and know that they are a part of the family unit. Adding a Step-Parent is **an addition of a person to a growing family, not a subtraction of a position, person, or the amount of love given.**

The Step-Parent and children may need to be reminded that, with this union, comes perks, not demotions. Each person now has an extra person to love and support them, and will now have more people for them to love and support as well.

Being the "Step-Parent" to Adolescent Kids

Express your concerns.

Communicate. The children may not know what to do, how to do everything, or what they did/are doing wrong, and your spouse may not know or understand how you feel or what makes you feel that way. They are your family. Talk to them.

Discipline and instruct together.

You and our spouse are one, a unit, and it is important that you move like one. Children need to know that you are a United Front and they cannot play one against the other. If you say something, it should be as if the parent said it too. And if the parent says something to the children, it should be as if you said it as well. You are a team and your decisions are made, established, and corrected together.

**This is not an advantage to always get your way, inflict pain, or get vengeance. You are an adult, so your reasoning should be of an adult who is making decisions and requests that HELP the children, not hurt the children.

Sometimes they need your words to teach them, instead of your hand of discipline.

Discipline is not only punishment, but it is also education. Teaching requires patience, compassion, information, instruction, guidance, understanding and wisdom. All of these are needed in raising a child.

Not everything requires a punishment, but everything requires love, wisdom, and understanding. There will be times where discipline and firm punishment is necessary. And then there will be times you will need to redirect knowledge and embrace opportunities to impart and to teach. In all things, be wise and use love.

You are a watcher for their soul.

Pray for, protect, and cover them as if they were your own children. You stand in the gap for them when needed. Be "responsible." Respond-See-Enable. Do what you can do when things need to be done on their behalf.

Do not withdraw yourself or your love from them when you are angry or frustrated.

Children feel it when you emotionally, physically, and/or relationally step away, and, it often sets up seeds of rejection that tend to grow.

If you become angry, frustrated or upset with or because of the children, be sure to be careful of what you allow them to see or hear from you.

Sometimes it's the things that we don't say that cause a lot of problems. If it is the children who have caused your anger or frustration, let them know that you dislike what they said or did, but that you still love them.

Be sure to reiterate your love for them as much as possible.

They need to hear you say, *"I love you"* and *"I'm proud of you."* Don't let them only hear your voice when you are fussing at them or correcting them. Words of love and affirmation need to be heard more than words of correction.

Sometimes kids don't know how to communicate how they feel.

From tantrums, to attitudes, to crying, to being goofy, they all are ways of communicating how one feels. Many times, it can be translated into *"I need more of your time and attention."* or *"I could use a hug and a shoulder right now."*

Kids don't always say what they feel because they don't always know how, or if, it will be accepted. Sometimes, they act out to get a response.

Ever hear the term *"bad press is good press?"* It's not just children that do it; adults do it too. When people, young and old, seek attention, they will, many times, use action to speak instead of words. *"I'm angry, so I fold my arms, roll my eyes and become agitated, so that you will see me and know that I am mad."* Sound familiar?

What you feed will grow.

There may be times when the children may become distant, especially in their pre-teen and teen years. This is the time for you to create a supportively safe environment for them. Life is changing for them, and they are trying to process it in their own way. Remind them that you love them, you are there for them, and you are here if they ever want to talk.

There will be times it will get frustrating, but stay the course. They may not see it now, but they will appreciate it later.

With life changes, the perimeters of support will alter as well. The things that used to work when they were little kids, may not work when they hit their teens. It's ok. Move with the flow. Feed the positives. If they are doing well in school or at home, reward them. Do something special, just for them, that they like.

Remember: Home is not built in a single day.

Be patient. Be compassionate. Be prayerful. It's also going to take Devine Strategy to help children reach their full potential and destiny. No one "just knows" what to do. It's ok. Take a deep breath and keep giving your best. Things aren't always as bad as they seem.

The Step-Parent: Teens and Adults

Step-parenting can be a journey, and, it can be an even rougher journey, when you are dealing with step-children who have established ways, minds, and personalities. Whether the other parent is alive or deceased, you may have to deal with how the step-children feel about you joining the family unit.

You may have to compete with Memory and Emotion.

The other parent still holds a position in their minds, heart and family. Your job is not to try to remove him/her, or his/her memory. Your job is to let them know that you come to add in love, not to take away or replace what they have or had.

<u>If the parent is deceased</u>, it is important that you honor their memory and the legacy he/she left in the hearts of his/her children.

This may require that you be a little more patient with them as they deal with how they feel.

Birthdays, anniversaries and/or dates that recall special life events are sacred things to the children. Allow them to grieve, celebrate or remember when those times come. There may be little things that you can to do to support them and how they feel that could help bring you closer together.

If the parent is alive, you may have to deal with the memory and emotion that comes along with the position the estranged parent once had. Children tend to see their family as "whole," even when it is broken. Even when the parents have not been together in 20 years, you may still find that some of the children are hurt that a person, outside of the estranged parent, is going to be marrying into the family.

In each case, you are going to have to be reassuring that you come as addition, not as a replacement, and that your love covers all that is attached to the person you are marrying/have married.

In all things, be patient, be kind, be loving, be understanding and move with compassion. It will take work but it is worth it. Talk with your spouse and work together to find ways that work for your family unit. Show your children/step-children that you are together in all that you do, including loving them.

You may have to love and show love "in spite of."

Let your love be evident, even when their love isn't. Love is an action, not just a response.

Teach. Support. Invest.

It can be beneficial and speak to how much you value them, when you share part of who you are and what you do with them, especially when it comes to teenagers and young adults.

Take time to teach them what your passions are and how you use it to prosper. Share with them. If you know how to create, then teach them how you create and how they can apply it to benefit them or others. If you are good in finance, then teach them finance and good financial principles. If you play or create music, teach them what you know. Be patient.

Support them and their passions. Help them create ways to expand or strengthen their talents. Help them create ideas that build finance around their passions and/or talents. Support them. Introduce them to people who are in their desired field or know about their desired field.

Rome wasn't built in a day, but it was built, brick by brick, day by day. It will take time. It will take energy. It will take patience.

Start by building and supporting the things that they love and are interested in. Invest time, money and yourself in THEIR passions. If it's rap, basketball, football, soccer, dance, gymnastics, music, poetry, etc., support it, and support them.

Don't run away when they show you the beginnings of potential. Encourage it. If they invite you to it, or mention it to you, support it and encourage them that they can accomplish it.

Remember individuals and things will vary, case by case. You are dealing with developed thoughts and emotion. One thing that applies to most cases is respect, and it is something that is important.

Respect Feelings

Everyone has their feelings, and to them it's real. There is a quote from my dad that says, *"Feelings are real but they are not always right."* When dealing with the way that people feel, it's important to **identify what they feel** before you can address the "why."

Don't forget: First you address the person, then you address the issue. Sometimes they will not know how to express themselves or deal with their emotions. They sometime just know that they "feel."

Respect Them.

They are not just your husband's/wife's children; they are now yours. It's important they know that you love and care for them, as if they came out of you. They should know that they have your love and support and that you would fight for them.

Respect the memory of the dead.

Don't try to erase, replace, or ignore the memory of a deceased parent. Be respectful. Be kind. Be patient. Be yourself. The pain that they feel, and the feelings that they have, are very real. Allow them to grieve if need be, and you comfort, support and be there if they need to talk. Pray for them. If they don't want to talk, then it's ok. Some want to remember, and some don't, so allow them and their process.

Respect their space.

In the case of teenagers, they may need a little more leniency, support and space when they are coming into their own. They are going to be dealing with who they were, who they are, and who they are going to be. Many times, the teenage years are when they are going to start exhibiting certain characteristics and qualities that they, themselves, do not understand. Pray for wisdom. Pray for wisdom in teaching, correcting and loving as they grow and go through their process.

In cases of adult children who may not want a close relationship with you- Relationships are give and receive. Some people will come close, to love and be loved. Some will stand back and observe to see if the love is genuine. Some will step away.

If someone does not desire to be close right now, it's ok. You can love them and still be at a distance. Let them know that you care for them, and that your friendship and love is here, if and when they are ready.

You don't have to fight with them, but you may have to fight FOR them. Still pray for them. Love them. Encourage them and show you care for them.

Don't try to buy love.

Gifts are nice, but don't use them as payment for love, attention, or bribery. Let them come to you freely, in their own time, in their own way. If you are going to give gifts, let them be genuine and from the heart.

Birthdays, special occasions, *"thinking of you"* and *"just because"* gifts are good.

But, *"Here is some money so you can behave."* = Not good.

Let your life and conversations command respect, not demand it.

When Parenting/Step-Parenting a teenager or adult, it may be wiser to live a life that commands respect, rather than just verbally demanding it, especially without giving it. Granted, there may be times when you may have to tell them that their words or behavior hurt you, or makes you feel disrespected, but, **don't come to blows, come to an understanding.**

Many times, things are led by emotion and need logic to bring back balance. Don't follow or combat negative emotion with negative conversation that is led by negative emotion.

Remember that the goal is understanding so that it can bring peace or resolve. Logic is necessary. Without logic, you and the children will remain in an emotional state, oftentimes not reaching a resolve.

Have a balance. Use emotion to identify the "what" and logic to identify the "why." Use wisdom in hearing and responding.

Frequently, people fuss and complain about things when there is a deeper issue of something else.

Listen to what they say, and for what they don't say. Sometimes their "resistance" is because, in some way, they feel rejected. Sometimes them "puffing out their chest," is a lack of validation. Feed the positive.

Sometimes, the cure for "abandonment" is added support, accompanied by verbal encouragements and affirmations.

Always, remember: You are a part of a family and your role in your family unit is important.

Never allow the title or position of "Step-Parent" to have you feeling or expecting to be the outsider. The enemy would have you believe that you are not important but I want to encourage you that, although it may not seem like it, you have power in your position. You have the ability to speak into the atmospheres of your spouse, your home, and all those who are connected to it. It may require subtle gestures accompanied with strategic prayers, but it is worth it.

Acknowledgements

First, I would like to give honor to God, for without HIM, nothing would be possible.

To my cheerleaders: My parents. Thank you for being living examples of Christ and His Church, loving one another holistically and unconditionally. Thanks for always being there to support me and stand in gap for me. I could not have done it without you and what you both instilled in me. You introduced me to Jesus and now I introduce others. Keep up the GOD work.

I am so grateful to my brothers. I love you guys. Thank you so much for being there for me and for praying me through this process. Get ready for the next one.

A, very special, thanks goes out to Colonel David and Mrs. Kim Rabb for EVERYTHING! You guys are awesome. Words cannot express the impact you have made and I pray that God blesses you for being a blessing to me.

Maria Edward, what can I say? I just love you and your spirit. Thank you so much for all of your help. You are a blessing.

To my Cousin "Meeks", I love you girl and thank you so very much.

To my publishing team, you guys rock! Thank you for believing in me and for working with me. I am so grateful, honored, and humbled to be working with you. I absolutely love each and every one of you and I look forward to the future.

To my grandparents, thank you so much for being the example of love. Thank you for the talks and your imparted wisdom. Thank you for teaching the generations that, although love is responsibility, it is worth it. Thank you for sticking together in love, faith and prayer for each other, for us, and for the generations to come. Thank you for your examples that marriage can work in spite of life challenges.

All of my friends and family that supported me and prayed for me, I thank you. For every call and every text, thank you. For every laugh and every joke, thank you. For just being you, thank you. Life is so much better with you in it.

I am so grateful for every church, organization, leader, and brother/sister in Christ that prayed for me and encouraged me to go on. Thank you so much for your support.

And last, but by no means least, to everyone who bought, read, or has been encouraged by this book, I appreciate you. I pray that God reveals Himself to you more and more. I speak peace to every home in Jesus' name, and I speak blessings. May God give you grace, strategies, and joy in your home.